Charlottesville and the Death of Free Speech

Jason Kessler

CHARLOTTESVILLE AND THE DEATH OF FREE SPEECH

Jason Kessler

First edition

Copyright © 2024 Dissident Press
All rights reserved

ISBN 9781948323239 (softcover)

dissident.press

*The drone photos on pages 218 & 219 (~ 11:13 AM &11:40 AM) are copyright © 2024 by James Moore. Used by custom license agreement.

Reproduction Policy: Portions of this book may be reproduced without prior permission in critical reviews and other papers if credit is given to author, full book title is listed, and full contact information is given for publisher. No other reproduction of any portion of this book is allowed without permission.

Printed in the United States of America

TABLE OF CONTENTS

Acknowledgements	1
Prologue	2
Timeline	6
Why I've Written this Book	9
Woke Iconoclasm and the Soul of Nations	11
Shall Make No Law . . .	21
The Powder Keg Blows	26
It Had to Happen to Someone . . .	28
Wes Bellamy	44
The New Jacobins	60
The Battle of Berkeley	68
Meeting Richard Spencer and the DeploraBall	74
The Alt-Right's Syrian Missile Strikes Protest	78
Richard Spencer Speaks at Auburn University	83
The Nationalist Demonstration in Pikeville, Kentucky	85
The Battle of New Orleans	87
The Alt-Right Comes to Charlottesville	91
Mob Violence in Lee Park and a Wrongful Arrest	101
Unite The Right is Conceived	107
"Freedom Of Speech Rally" at Lincoln Memorial in Washington, D.C.	123
The Ku Klux Klan Rally in Jackson Park	126
Press Conference with the Warlocks Motorcycle Club	131
The Secret Closed-Door Meeting	137
A Rush of Meetings and the Permit is Revoked	141
Enter the ACLU	159
The Mutiny from Within	163

Violence	172
August 10: The ACLU Hearing	183
August 11	188
Antifa's Nasty Surprise	205
August 12, 2017: Unite the Right	220
The Unified Command Center	227
Staging "The Resistance"	231
The Antifa Assault on Unite the Right	238
My Entrance into Lee Park	245
James Fields, Heather Heyer, & the Crash that Changed Everything	257
The Press Conference Assault	272
Chief Thomas Lies to the National Press	275
Trump's Charlottesville Press Conference	278
Aftermath	281
The Mock Execution of the Lee Monument	290
Torch March Prosecutions . . . Six Years Later	296
Skokie to Charlottesville: Historical Analysis	301
Epilogue	311
QR Codes	315
About the Author	339

Acknowledgements

This book would not be possible without the contributions of the indefatigable bibliophile Dave Gahary, Peter Brimelow at VDARE for publishing my writing on Charlottesville over the years, Daniel McMahon, aka Antifa Hunter "Jack Corbin" for his invaluable research, to my mother for her love and support, the generosity of several important contributors who must remain anonymous due to the threat of political persecution, and the brave men and women who attended the Charlottesville rally in 2017.

Prologue

Who controls the past controls the future: who controls the present controls the past.
—George Orwell

Whoever would overthrow the liberty of a nation, must begin by subduing the freeness of speech.
—as popularized by Benjamin Franklin

Murder is forbidden in both form and in fact; free speech is granted in form but forbidden in fact.
—Mark Twain

The air was thick with the stench of tear gas and sweat. Lee Park had become a holding pen with hundreds of protesters crammed shoulder to shoulder like cattle. I'd been assured by City of Charlottesville Police Chief Al Thomas that we would have use of the full park but now we were being corralled into two small barricaded squares occupying less than half the park.

I couldn't even enter the speakers' area. "I'm the permit holder!" I exhorted the police.

"We can't let you in there," a Virginia State Police (VSP) officer responded.

"Who can?"

"City of Charlottesville Police."

But they were nowhere to be seen.

Projectiles were flying overhead like artillery shells: balloons filled with urine and feces, rocks, bricks, paint and whatever other detritus the anarchist mob surrounding the park could weaponize.[1] Outside the park, a Black supremacist was screaming racial abuse. We were nothing but "fucking animals" and "inbred pieces of shit," according to the shouts of the hate-filled Black man with veins protruding from his neck.[2]

Ahead of me a tall, lanky man stumbled wounded through a small opening in the barricades at the entrance to the park. He had a gas mask pulled back to reveal horrible purple bruises across his face and his right eye swollen shut.

To my left, alternative right (alt-right) self-appointed leader Richard Spencer was doubled over in agony from being pepper sprayed in the face. A small group of his friends was trying to offer medical assistance by pouring a bottle of water into his burning eyes.

Something had gone horribly wrong. I'd been fighting for weeks with the Charlottesville government over my permit for the event and with the help of the American Civil Liberties Union (ACLU) we'd prevailed in federal court just the night before.

We all came expecting the assistance of the police to separate the protesters from the counter-protesters. My faith in the system had led everyone, myself included, into a deadly trap.

The Charlottesville Police finally marched into the park in a single-file line clad in helmets, body armor, and carrying riot shields. We thought they had finally come to bring order. A cop at the front of the line raised an electric megaphone to his lips: "This has been declared an unlawful assembly! You are ordered to disperse."

Our "public servants" lined up their shields in a row and began to expel the protesters from the venue into the waiting arms of the violent anarchist mob in the street below. Many were clubbed over the head or lathered with caustic chemical irritants. A masked, Black man identified as Corey Long turned an aerosol spray can and a cigarette lighter into an improvised flamethrower, shooting a billowing

---

[1] bitchute.com/video/RqrUtKFr6vlj
[2] bitchute.com/video/LiL1ltKnsinE

stream of fire out towards the crowd as they were bottle-necked through the tiny exit space between the barricades at the top of the stairs.

Shortly after the rally-goers were pushed into the crowd of Antifa, sparking a surge in violence, Hawk Newsome, president of Black Lives Matter (BLM) New York, was asked about his experience. "It needs to be talked about that I've been protesting in this movement for six years and the police always form barricades between hostile groups," he said. "Today was the first time I didn't see that happen and that's a fact . . . They wanted us to fight each other."[3]

Later that day, after we had all left from the park, a Dodge Challenger driven by a protester named James Alex Fields drove into a mob of armed counter-protesters, killing one and injuring dozens more. The police had done nothing to prevent an armed mob of leftists from marching through the streets during a state of emergency. Nor had they maintained the barricades that should have prevented the car from entering the crowded street, where it was surrounding by armed militants. A police helicopter would fall from the skies overhead, killing an additional two police officers. None of these events were within my control, yet I have been blamed for them along with hundreds of other non-violent protesters who attended the permitted event.

It was as though the gates of Hell had opened that afternoon in the summer of 2017, and spilled out into the streets of my hometown in a raging inferno.

My name will perhaps live in infamy after I am gone because I was the permit holder for the Unite the Right (UTR) rally. I have dreaded writing this memoir. I had been running from my past since the rally, until this book, afraid to be trapped in the memories of my life's greatest failure, that old scar that refuses to heal.

Our protest was the victim of an unprecedented totalitarian assault on American rights of free speech and assembly. According to the rule of law, the police should have had to protect our event

---

[3] bitchute.com/video/owsMC6xk9ufw

and prevent it from descending into violent chaos. How were we to know the American system could change its speech rules on a dime to screw us over? UTR had the singular misfortune of being just this much on the wrong side of the Free Speech Movement's[4] "high-water mark—that place where the wave finally broke and rolled back."[5]

The time has come to make this sacrifice for the sake of posterity. The world needs to know the truth about what happened in Charlottesville and I am the only one who can give them the full truth.

---

[4] I see the ACLU free speech victory in Charlottesville as the final victory and high-water mark of the Free Speech Movement that began in Berkeley, California in the 1960s and continued with a string of legal victories until the devastating rebuke of those values at the Charlottesville rally itself.

[5] *Fear and Loathing in Las Vegas*, Hunter S. Thompson

Timeline

May 21, 1924: Lee monument unveiled in Charlottesville's Lee Park
March 22, 2012: City Councilor Szakos calls for removal of Lee statue
March 19, 2016: Zyahna Bryant creates petition to remove Lee statue
November 8, 2016: Election of Donald Trump
November 19, 2016: Richard Spencer's "Heilgate"
November 24, 2016: Wes Bellamy tweet expose published
January 19, 2017: DeploraBall; I meet Richard Spencer
January 20, 2017: Trump Inauguration; Antifa riot in D.C.
January 31, 2017: Signer's "capital of the resistance" press conference
February 1, 2017: Milo Yiannopolous UC Berkeley speech riot
April 9, 2017: Syrian missile strikes protest
April 15, 2017: First Battle of Berkeley
April 18, 2017: Richard Spencer speaks at Auburn University
April 27, 2017: I travel to Berkeley for Ann Coulter speech
April 29, 2017: Nationalist rally in Pikeville, Kentucky
May 7, 2017: Battle of New Orleans
May 13, 2017: Torch demonstration in Lee Park; Airbnb after party with Roman salutes
May 14, 2017: I am assaulted and arrested trying to rescue Emerson Stern aka Meme Alert
May 20, 2017: Antifa stalks us from TapHouse on Downtown Mall; Veronica Fitzhugh attack
May 30, 2017: Application for protest permit
June 13, 2017: UTR permit granted
June 25, 2017: "Freedom of Speech Rally" at Lincoln Memorial in D.C.
July 8, 2017: KKK rally in Jackson Park

July 11, 2017: Press conference with Warlocks Motorcycle Club
July 28-30, 2017: American Renaissance conference in Montgomery Bell State Park
August 7, 2017: Meeting with Charlottesville officials Maurice Jones, Wendy Lewis, and Michelle Christian; Permit denial letter received; Second meeting of the day with Charlottesville officials Wendy Lewis, Victor Mitchell, and Al Thomas
August 10, 2017: ACLU complaint filed in federal court
August 11, 2017: ACLU court ruling; Torchlit demonstration
August 12, 2017: Unite the Right rally
August 13, 2017: Attacked during press conference
August 15, 2017: President Trump press conference in Trump Towers
August 12, 2018: UTR 2

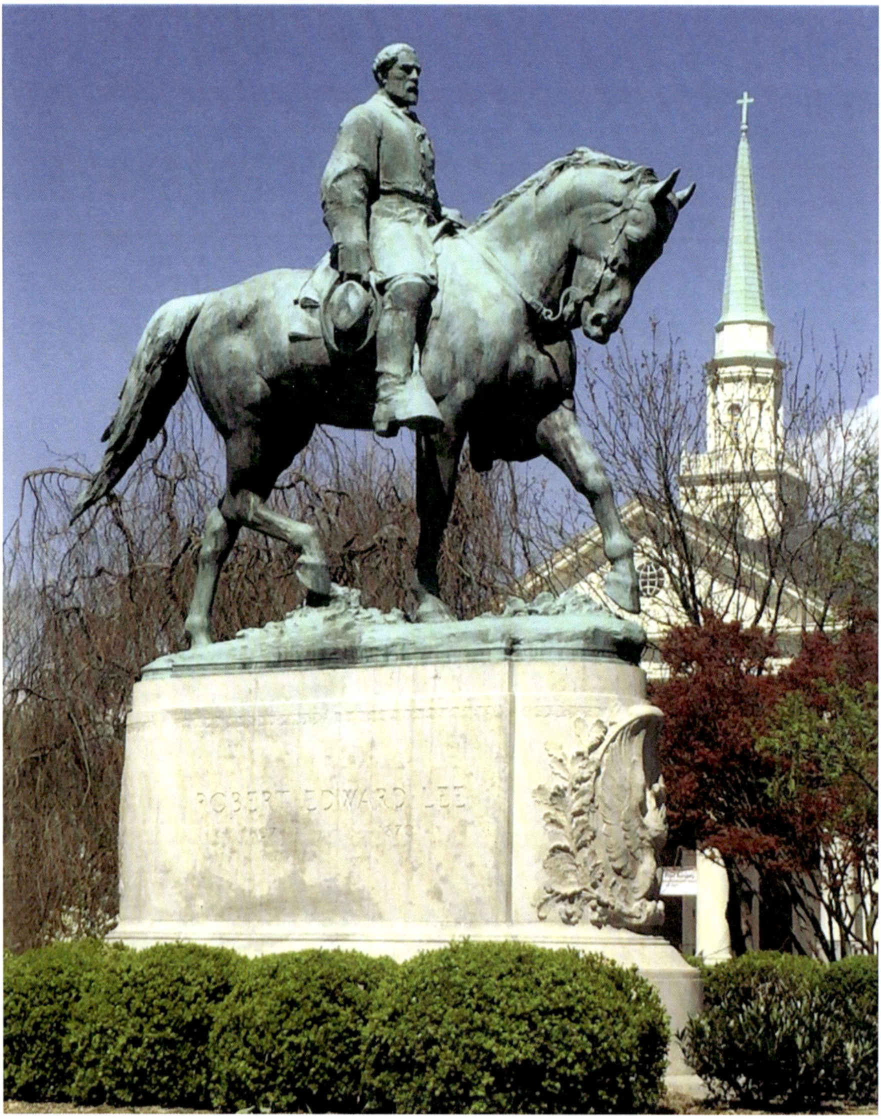
ROBERT EDWARD LEE

WHY I'VE WRITTEN THIS BOOK

As of this publication, there have been various books written about Charlottesville, mostly from the mainstream press perspective, which are fraught with errors and omissions that do not support their hyperbolic narrative about the event.

Two books have been published from the protester side: *Charlottesville Untold* by Anne Wilson Smith and *A Walk in the Park: My Charlottesville Story* by Padraig Martin. Both of these books are excellent in their own way, and highly recommended by this author. *Charlottesville Untold* is a journalistic account of the events as witnessed by a third-party and *A Walk in the Park* is a memoir of a U.S. Army veteran and conservative who attended the protest.

My primary goal in writing this book is to provide new context, firsthand accounts, and personally collected evidentiary details which only I have access to and which would be lost to history without this publication.

Much of my perspective on events, collected in social media posts and articles on various websites were victims of a horrible wave of repressive Silicon Valley censorship of the Internet after Charlottesville. I have tried to recover the past using Wayback Machine archives of banned content from the period. I am also utilizing a trove of documents, images, and videos that I have saved over years of investigation.

There was a civil trial brought against the organizers of the rally, called *Sines v. Kessler*, which I thought would be the great opportunity for me to tell my side of the story in full and on the record. For reasons which remain incomprehensible to me, I was gagged by both the plaintiffs and my own defense attorney when I got on the stand. I have never been given the opportunity to offer a full-throated defense of my actions with regard to UTR.

Not only that but much of the evidence documented in this book was never considered in court because my attorney did not submit it to plaintiffs in time for it to be admissible at trial. This is the first time anyone will be able to receive my side of the events in full.

I do not expect to have mainstream, widespread publication. I am realistic about the fact that millions of dollars have been spent by the most powerful politicians, oligarchs, and news outlets in the world to portray a one-dimensional and inaccurate account of what happened at UTR. No matter how well this book is written, or how high the public interest, my account is dissent from the pseudo-religious beliefs about Charlottesville that the American gatekeepers and publishing houses want you to have access to.

Just holding this copy and reading its forbidden knowledge is an act of rebellion in a time of conformity and dissent in a time of growing totalitarianism.

What I want to do is leave the bread crumbs so that revisionist historians of the future have access to a high-quality document from the organizer himself with all the *samizdat*, or forbidden knowledge, that was hidden from the public when the event spent its time in the white-hot heat of public scrutiny.

There is sacred value in knowing the truth.

Finally, the ambition of this project is not merely to provide previously unreleased material to the public. UTR was the living embodiment of the death of America's inviolable "free speech" commitment. The vital, pumping blood of the project is as a meditation on free speech and a wake for its demise.

Hopefully, at the very least, it can clear the record on my motivations and make the argument to regard the UTR protesters appropriately as martyrs for a noble cause.

First, we need to understand why thousands of people on both sides of UTR cared so much about a damn statue.

WOKE ICONOCLASM AND THE SOUL OF NATIONS

The original purpose of UTR was to protest the proposed removal of a historic monument honoring Confederate General Robert E. Lee (as well as a nearby monument to Thomas "Stonewall" Jackson). Some critics of the rally have made slanderous statements about how the monument was not actually important to the protesters and that it was just an excuse to be racist in public.

As the organizer of the event, I can assure you that for me personally, nothing could be further from the truth. But it is true that I saw the Lee monument as more than a sculpture made of bronze. I saw something symbolic of the soul of my people: their accomplishments, history, and legacy.

It's important to understand why hundreds of people cared enough about a monument to travel from all over the United States and even a few foreign countries to participate in the rally.

The destruction of monuments to White heroes is not a mere trivial or symbolic act. Like a Russian doll, it has inner layer upon inner layer of deep psychological, strategic, and spiritual consequences.

On the very surface level, we perceive simple sloganeering about "racial justice," "change," and "white supremacy" utilized by the most mindless, emotional, and hypnotized masses who tear them down. But beneath the surface platitudes there are primitive cultural and ethnic hatreds which are so ancient that they extend into the primordial soul of humanity. Understanding these phenomena help us to understand the full significance of the Woke movement's racial and political revolution.

For instance, during the racially charged 2020 George Floyd riots, the convulsive demonstrations seemed to focus on unfinished grievances with UTR and its defense of Confederate monuments. But it wasn't just Confederate monuments that were torn down. As many others, including myself and Donald Trump had prophesied, they also came after American Founders like Thomas Jefferson and George Washington.[6]

But it went even further than that. Monuments of kings like Leopold II in Antwerp, Belgium,[7] explorers such as Christopher Columbus in Boston,[8] Captain James Cook in Victoria, Canada,[9] and authors like Thomas Carlyle in Glasgow, Britain[10] were toppled or vandalized throughout Europe, Australia, and the entire Western world. Even monuments of abolitionists, liberals, and anti-racists were torn down. The only common variable was that they were monuments to White men, which speaks to the defining primordial element of the statue toppling.[11] Destruction of cultural heritage "becomes a logical target in the context of ethno-nationalist wars, symbolizing the culture to be eliminated."[12]

As the Western world is violently transformed demographically and politically by the effects of mass non-White immigration into traditional, and even indigenous White nations, the balance of political power has shifted away from the historic populations to a Rainbow Coalition with revolutionary ambitions on their White host nations. As the Black filmmaker and activist Dr. Karsonya "Kaye" Wise Whitehead expressed it, "Dear Racist White People, Your Time is Up."[13]

---

[6] washingtonpost.com/history/2021/11/23/thomas-jefferson-statue-removed-nyc-slaveowner
[7] aljazeera.com/news/2020/6/9/who-was-leopold-ii-why-did-belgiums-antwerp-remove-his-statue
[8] smithsonianmag.com/smart-news/christopher-columbus-statues-beheaded-torn-down-180975079
[9] cbc.ca/news/canada/british-columbia/victoria-captain-cook-statue-vandalized-1.6088828
[10] glasgowtimes.co.uk/news/18503324.kelvingrove-statue-thomas-carlyle-vandalised-anti-police-graffiti
[11] globalnews.ca/news/7101452/madison-wisconsin-hans-christian-heg
[12] researchgate.net/publication/307824971
[13] afro.com/dear-racist-white-people-your-time-is-up

Statues are usually toppled after revolutions or changing of the guard from one set of rulers to another. The formal term for such destruction is "iconoclasm." The roots of iconoclasm can be traced to the ancient Roman concept of *damnatio memoriae,* Latin for "condemnation of memory." After the death of an emperor, the senate would decide whether to grant the deceased leader apotheosis as a transcendent, revered god or banish their memory from public life. *Damnatio Memoriae* involved the destruction of all likenesses of the fallen emperor, from monuments to coins. This was especially useful during transition to politically adversarial regimes, following murders and revolutions.

Since then, iconoclasm has occurred throughout history, sometimes in the context of liberation from tyranny such as toppling of monuments to Stalin and Lenin after the fall of the Soviet Union, or the toppling of monuments to dictator Saddam Hussein after the American invasion of Iraq. On the other hand, iconoclasm often takes on sinister connotations when used by totalitarian ideologies to suppress and censor icons of a persecuted population, be they cultural, political, or ethnic. In these cases, the destruction of monuments is typically meant to demoralize rivals who are also being subjugated or murdered in the flesh.

According to historian Jean-Francois Manicom of the International Slavery Museum in Liverpool, "toppling statues is also undeniably a violent act, an assault on a realistic and symbolic replica of a person. In ancient Egypt, sculptors were called 'the guardians of life,' because the role of the statue in a tomb was to keep the dead alive by serving as a spiritual avatar of their mortal remains."[14]

On the secular plane it is about the dictatorial control of information accessible to the masses. They must forget that there was ever an alternative to the new regime, and certainly any positive depictions which could inspire dissent must be obliterated. Think *1984*'s Ministry of Truth.

---

[14] politico.eu/article/why-we-topple-statues-bristol-edward-colston-antwerp-leopold-ii-black-lives-matter

A prototypical example was the iconoclasm of extreme left revolutionary groups like the fanatical Jacobin during the French Revolution of 1789 and ensuing Reign of Terror (in French: *la Terreur*). The Jacobin not only revolted against the monarchy of Louis XVI in favor of then-radical democratic republicanism; inspired by high minded liberal notions of The Enlightenment, they were in revolution against what they saw as the entirety of bourgeoisie French society.

Like the 21st century Woke movement spearheading Confederate statue removal, the Jacobin embarked on a "Year Zero" project in which the very foundations of society were uprooted and replaced to instill values of the new regime. For instance, an equestrian statue of Louis XV standing in the Place Louis XV was destroyed by Revolutionary decree in 1793. The revolutionaries replaced it with a statue of *Liberty* by Francois Frederic Lemot and renamed the square itself to Place de la Revolution, now called Place de la Concorde.[15] Louis XVI and his

Destruction of the statue of Louis XIV, Place Vendôme (August 1792)

---

[15] arthistory.columbia.edu/sites/default/files/content/faculty/pdfs/baumgartner/iconoclasts.pdf

queen, Marie Antoinette, were guillotined there. Monument destruction was rampant in Revolutionary France and peaked during the years of The Terror throughout which approximately 17,000 people had been officially executed (often by guillotine), and as many as 10,000 had died in prison or without trial.

The Year Zero project also included renaming the months of the year and replacing the traditional Christian faith of the French with Maximilien Robespierre's Cult of the Supreme Being. At the Basilica of St. Denis, the revolutionaries even disinterred the long-dead royals, desecrated their remains, and destroyed their tombs. Compare the destruction of icons during the French Revolution to the Woke Revolution of 21st century America. In October 2023, Charlottesville's Robert E. Lee monument was melted down so that an Afrocentric Marxist group called Swords into Plowshares could refashion the metal into an icon of Black supremacy valued by the City's new ruling elites. Like Place Louis XV, Charlottesville's Lee Park was changed to Emancipation Park, a name with significance for the Afrocentric narrative of American history.[16]

Wokeism has made revolutionary changes to the sacred symbols and founding myths of America. The multicolored "Pride Flag" has replaced the Stars and Stripes in many homes, businesses, and government office buildings in cities dominated by Woke revolutionary values. *The New York Times*' 1619 Project by Black author Nikole Hannah-Jones, proposes the arrival of African slaves to the Virginia colony in 1619 as an alternative to the historically recognized origin of the United States in 1776 with the signing of the Declaration of Independence.[17]

Although we have not yet seen organized mass slaughter from the Woke Revolution in America on par with The Terror, it has succeeded in making Whites the most despised racial group[18] and also the most frequent victims of interracial homicides.[19]

---

[16] In 2017, shortly before the UTR rally, Charlottesville City Council voted to change the names of Lee and Jackson Parks to Emancipation and Justice, respectively.
[17] nytimes.com/2021/11/09/magazine/1619-project-us-history.html
[18] ljzigerell.com/?p=9002
[19] bjs.ojp.gov/content/pub/pdf/cv18.pdf

How racial groups rate each other

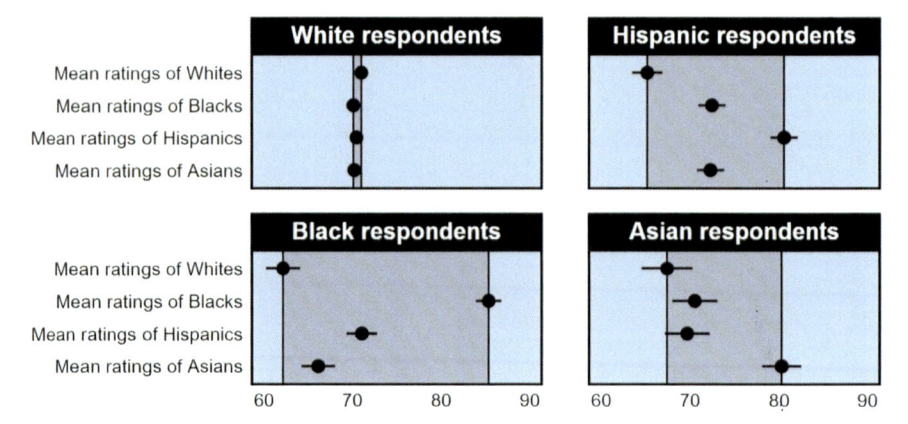

White respondents
- Mean ratings of Whites
- Mean ratings of Blacks
- Mean ratings of Hispanics
- Mean ratings of Asians

Hispanic respondents
- Mean ratings of Whites
- Mean ratings of Blacks
- Mean ratings of Hispanics
- Mean ratings of Asians

Black respondents
- Mean ratings of Whites
- Mean ratings of Blacks
- Mean ratings of Hispanics
- Mean ratings of Asians

Asian respondents
- Mean ratings of Whites
- Mean ratings of Blacks
- Mean ratings of Hispanics
- Mean ratings of Asians

Error bars are 83.4% confidence intervals
Data source: American National Election Studies. 2021. ANES 2020 Time Series Study Preliminary Release: Combined Pre-Election and Post-Election Data [dataset and documentation]. March 24, 2021 version. www.electionstudies.org.

INTERRACIAL VIOLENT CRIME INCIDENTS 2018

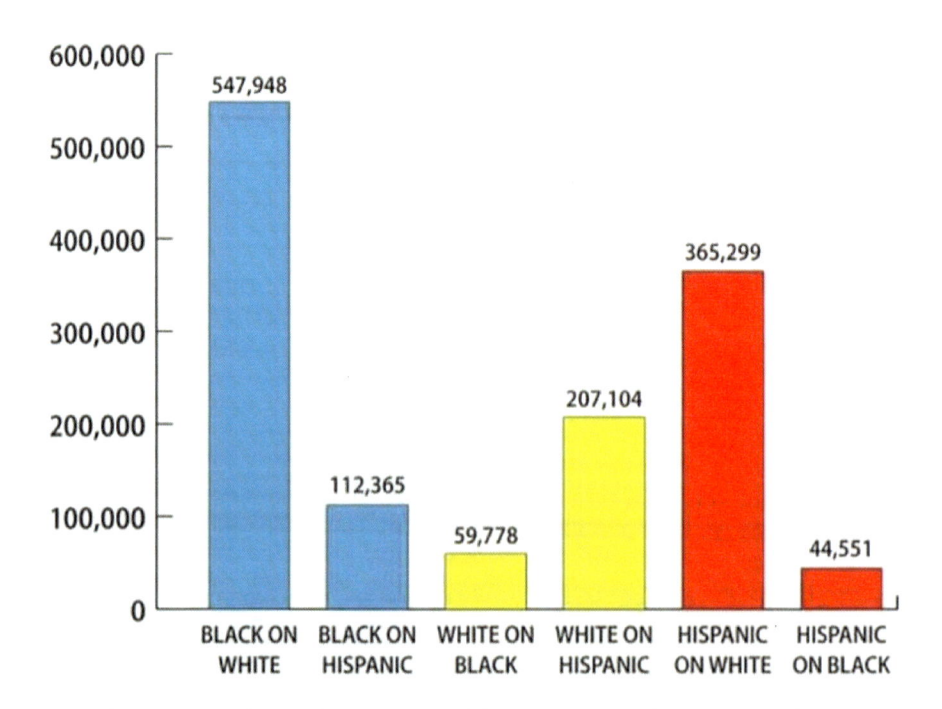

Category	Incidents
BLACK ON WHITE	547,948
BLACK ON HISPANIC	112,365
WHITE ON BLACK	59,778
WHITE ON HISPANIC	207,104
HISPANIC ON WHITE	365,299
HISPANIC ON BLACK	44,551

Source: Bureau of Justice Statistics, National Crime Victimization Survey, 2018 (Table 14)

We can also point to at least 25 victims murdered during the 2020 Floyd riots and how the politics of the so-called "racial reckoning" resulted in the greatest one-year murder rate increase in U.S. history, an increase of 4,901 homicides, or 30% from 2019 to 2020.[20]

Destruction of monuments to White Western leaders cannot be fully understood without comparing it to the destruction of cultural heritage in ethno-religious wars. Throughout the Middle East, the Islamic State in Iraq and Syria (ISIS) has famously destroyed priceless historical artifacts such as Sufi, Shi'a, and Sunni shrines, St. Elijah's Monastery, the Triumphal Arch, and human-headed winged bull statues from the gates of Nineveh (8th century B.C.). Additionally, the militants have ravaged UNESCO World Heritage sites like the ancient cities of Palmyra and Nimrud.[21]

ISIS claims that monuments and heritage sites are destroyed because they are heretical to their Wahhabi Islamic faith, but they also gain media attention with enormous propaganda value from distributing videos of shooting and bulldozing artifacts.[22]

ISIS destruction of statues from 100 B.C. to A.D. 100 in Iraq's Mosul Museum (February 26, 2015)

---

[20] pewresearch.org/short-reads/2021/10/27/what-we-know-about-the-increase-in-u-s-murders-in-2020
[21] nationalgeographic.com/culture/article/150227-islamic-militants-destroy-statues-mosul-iraq-video-archaeology
[22] nytimes.com/interactive/2015/06/29/world/middleeast/isis-historic-sites-control.html

Militant destroys a human-headed winged bull statue from the gates of Nineveh (8th century B.C.)

International Affairs includes an absolutely indispensable 2017 analysis of ISIS' iconoclasm as a military strategy representing "a logical and instrumental means of employing violence to achieve political ends:"

> Accordingly, three linked variables must be present for the manifestation of iconoclasm as a strategic logic: first, the degradation and delegitimization of the existing societal fabric; second, the removal of all reference to the previous society; and finally, the reconstruction of society in keeping with a new ideology or political religion. Although not necessarily appearing in a sequential process, all must be present in some form if a coherent strategy of iconoclasm is to be identified.[23]

It must be understood that the destruction of monuments by Woke zealots is, like with ISIS, not merely the result of a spontaneous

---

[23] chathamhouse.org/sites/default/files/publications/ia/INTA93_5_10_Clapperton%20et%20al_0.pdf

outburst of emotion, but part of a purposeful strategy masterminded by an ideological cadre utilizing iconoclasm as part of its violent, totalitarian political agenda.

First, it cannot seriously be refuted that Wokeism and its Rainbow Coalition are not attempting to delegitimize the cultural fabric of the United States and Europe which they refer to derisively as one of "white supremacy." Wokeism seeks the supremacy of its own ethnos (non-Whites), its own founding myth (1619), and even its own flag (Pride).

The eradication of cultural monuments is just one revolutionary tactic, however. Others include renaming streets, buildings, and even birds.[24] Woke translations of historical events and culture often replace White figures with mythical non-Whites[25] to hide Americans' past, disguise Americans' ethnic cleansing in the present, and in the end, cow Americans to accept dispossession out of sheer self-hatred. Like the French revolutionaries, their Woke American ideological descendants are even disinterring Confederate dead.[26]

The final element of strategic iconoclasm, the totalitarian agenda of Wokeism, is widely acknowledged through the infliction of "cancel culture" to isolate and destroy anyone who challenges the tenets of its *new values*. There can be no rivals to "racial justice." Any dissent is "white supremacist" terrorism that must be confronted and suppressed by multinational corporations and the state.

Removing monuments of White men constitutes an attack on their identity. It's a destruction of their collective memory aimed at preventing their reconstitution as a community and a people. The United States, and indeed the South, was once a predominantly homogeneous White population. Destruction of Lee, Jefferson, Columbus, and all the rest is an attack on the legitimacy of that identity, as the community is being replaced through mass immigration policies.

The same can be said of Europe, as it is absolutely flooded by

---

[24] usatoday.com/story/news/nation/2023/11/01/birds-renaming-inclusive-racist-genocidal-histories/71394771007

[25] indy100.com/tv/doctor-who-isaac-newton-actor

[26] vdare.com/posts/ritualistic-humiliation-black-run-city-of-richmond-virginia-digs-up-remains-of-confederate-general-a-p-hill-after-tearing-down-his-statue

replacement-level immigration from Africa and the Middle East. As U.S. Vice President Joseph R. Biden stated in 2015, an "unrelenting stream of immigration" will make Whites "an absolute minority" in their own communities "and that is a good thing."[27]

When the conquest is achieved, the new rulers of America obviously want statues honoring their own people rather than the Whites whom they've vanquished.

---

[27] x.com/justice_just4/status/1625182357904060416

Shall Make No Law ...

In 1791, the First Amendment to the United States Constitution would enshrine into law the most robust free speech protections in human history. Drafted by future U.S. President James Madison, whose plantation home Montpelier is a mere 12 miles from Thomas Jefferson's Monticello in Charlottesville, it reads: "Congress shall make no law respecting an establishment of religion, or prohibiting the free exercise thereof; or abridging the freedom of speech, or of the press; or the right of the people peaceably to assemble, and to petition the Government for a redress of grievances."

The new law was the culmination of millennia of Western ideas about democracy, the role of vigorous debate in a vibrant polity, and the rights protecting individual citizens from their government. The beginning was in ancient Athens, home of the world's first democracy. The Athenian democracy allowed for open discussion and debate in the public assembly, where citizens could voice their opinions and concerns. Yet it was not without its martyrs. The philosopher Socrates (469-399 B.C.) articulated his belief in the open exchange of ideas thusly: "I cannot teach anybody anything; I can only make them think." Socrates was convicted of impiety by Athenian courts and forced to commit suicide by ingesting poisonous hemlock.

Although there were no legal protections for speech in the ancient Roman Republic, vigorous debate among the aristocratic senators and magistrates was considered vital to the health of the nation. However, writers, politicians, and artists could face severe repression, and even death, for criticism of the emperor and state. This was to be a theme throughout Western history until the American Revolution.

The Death of Socrates by Jacques-Louis David (1787)

The imperial strong-man form of government continued into the European Middle Ages where laws were predominantly derived from kings, often claiming divine mandates and absolute authority. Dissent against the crown was strictly prohibited. A significant crack in this monolith occurred with the passage of the Magna Carta in 1215, signed by King John of England, establishing that the king is also subject to the law and not above it, thus paving the way for individual citizens' rights and liberties.

A landmark in the philosophical rationale for free speech protections was the publication of John Milton's *Areopagitica* in 1644. He argued first that free speech was essential in the quest for truth. It is crucial for a variety of opinions to be expressed through open discussion and debate so the public can arrive at the truth through the exercise of critical thinking. "Give me the liberty to know, to utter, and to argue freely according to conscience, above all liberties."

Second, he postulated the inherent value of intellectual freedom for both personal growth and the development of a well-informed citizenry. "Where there is much desire to learn, there of necessity will be much arguing, much writing, many opinions; for opinion in good men is but knowledge in the making."

Third, that censorship was ultimately ineffective, dangerous, and immoral. Censorship would stifle cultural and intellectual progress, creating a climate where truth was withheld for fear of punishment. And that ultimately ideas cannot be fully contained through censorship and will find a way to spread, even if only through surreptitious conversation.

> . . . books are not absolutely dead things, but do contain a potency of life in them to be as active as that soul was whose progeny they are; nay, they do preserve as in a vial the purest efficacy and extraction of that living intellect that bred them. I know they are as lively, and as vigorously productive, as those fabulous dragon's teeth: and being sown up and down, may chance to spring up armed men. And yet, on the other hand, unless wariness be used, as good almost kill a man as kill a good book: who kills a man kills a reasonable creature, God's image; **but he who destroys a good book, kills reason itself**, kills the image of God, as it were, in the eye. [Emphasis added]

Finally, individuals should be granted the personal responsibility to determine the course of their own moral and intellectual development. He trusted in humanity to determine these values for themselves rather than to have what George Orwell later termed "Big Brother," deciding it paternalistically on their behalf.

The full flowering of the promise of democracy and intellectual freedom seeded throughout Western history came to fruition in the ideals of the 18th century Enlightenment, that movement of scientific reason and individual liberty which birthed the French and American Revolutions, both for better and worse, and transformed European society forever. The English instituted freedom for debate in Parliament with the 1689 Bill of Rights and then Sweden became the first country in world history to enshrine legal protections for free speech with its Freedom of the Press Act of 1766. Censorship of academic and theological texts was prohibited by law. Yet it would not be as powerful as the American First Amendment, since prohibitions on criticisms of the king and state were left in effect.

The period of the Enlightenment saw the most robust ideological defenses of the value of free expression from figures ranging from John Locke, Thomas Hobbes, Baron de Montesquieu, and John Jacques Rousseau. This was the fanatical spirit of devotion to liberty which animated Thomas Jefferson when he wrote: "to preserve the freedom of the human mind then & freedom of the press, every spirit should be ready to devote itself to martyrdom; for as long as we may think as we will, & speak as we think, the condition of man will proceed in improvement."[28]

Perhaps my favorite articulation of the justifications for free speech were given by the philosopher John Stuart Mill in his seminal work *On Liberty*:

> He who knows only his own side of the case knows little of that. His reasons may be good, and no one may have been able to refute them. But if he is equally unable to refute the reasons on the opposite side, if he does not so much as know what they are, he has no ground for preferring either opinion . . . Nor is it enough that he should hear the opinions of adversaries from his own teachers, presented as they state them, and accompanied by what they offer as refutations. He must be able to hear them from persons who actually believe them . . . he must know them in their most plausible and persuasive form.

As can be seen, Jewish demands for censorship of criticism (aka "antisemitism") and legal prohibition of dissenting views on the so-called Holocaust are antithetical to Western civilization, free speech, and an open society. These are the central issues which come to the

---

[28] Letter from Thomas Jefferson to William G. Munford (June 18, 1799)

fore in the story of Unite the Right, Charlottesville, and the death of free speech.

Here is the issue which really goes to the heart of the modern Left's betrayal of the First Amendment: Did what happened in Nazi Germany debunk Western arguments for free speech and assembly? Does it mean you can subvert democracy with violent riots so long as you compare an elected leader like Trump to Adolf Hitler? Antifa, Jews, and the Woke Left believe it did. I do not.

The Powder Keg Blows

On August 11-12, 2017, an event occurred which led to White House resignations, three deaths, numerous injuries, and a massive wave of censorship which saw thousands of social media accounts and websites banned. Hundreds of historical monuments were torn down throughout the United States, Europe, Australia, and the entire Western world: monuments to Confederate soldiers, explorers, American presidents, and European kings.[29] This event effectively shifted policy at the ACLU away from defending controversial speech cases on the political right. Biden cited this event as his impetus for launching his 2020 U.S. presidential campaign.

In the era where identity politics is king and there are protests for "gay rights," BLM, La Raza, #StopAsianHate, and every other group under the sun, this was one of the very few protests advocating in support of White people, the largest racial group in the United States. It was certainly the most important event to the nascent White cause of the early 21st century.

Despite its importance as a historical touchstone, the public has only been allowed to receive a very one-sided, omission-ridden, and biased account of the event. A major impediment has been the intense prejudice of the largely left-wing and Zionist American media, because of their ideological animus for speech they label "racist" or "antisemitic," and the career-ending ramifications of providing details which could be used to defend the protesters.

---

[29] archive.ph/C0r3F

So-called "anti-hate" groups and activists like the Southern Poverty Law Center (SPLC), Anti-Defamation League (ADL), and Integrity First for America (IFA), have used this disinformation to raise millions, if not billions, of dollars. They exploited a vacuum of information to excite the public with salacious stories of "hate speech" and violence to reap the resulting donations and sympathy for their ideological cause.

And yet very little is known about what actually happened at this event, and the truth has become shrouded in disinformation, conspiracy theory, and propaganda. Some know this event as "Unite the Right," "UTR," or just "Charlottesville."

A 220-page report—Charlottesville Independent Review, colloquially, Heaphy Report—of the events by former federal prosecutor Tim Heaphy found that law enforcement and the City of Charlottesville were culpable for violence that broke out between protesters and counter-protesters before the planned speeches could even take place:

> "Rather than engage the crowd and prevent fights, the CPD [Charlottesville Police Department] plan was to declare the event unlawful and disperse the crowd."
>
> As a result:
>
> "the City of Charlottesville protected neither free expression nor public safety on August 12. The City was unable to protect the right of free expression and facilitate the permit holder's offensive speech."[30]

Despite this, a multi-million-dollar smear campaign has attempted to shift the impetus for blame onto the protesters whose rights were violated.

That is why my story has to be told.

I was the organizer of the Unite the Right rally, and for me, Charlottesville was my home.

---

[30] policinginstitute.org/wp-content/uploads/2017/12/Charlottesville-Critical-Incident-Review-2017.pdf

IT HAD TO HAPPEN TO SOMEONE...

I was born Jason Eric Kessler on September 22, 1983 in Charlottesville, Virginia, at the now-defunct Martha Jefferson Hospital, named for the wife of the third U.S. president, Thomas Jefferson, a seminal figure in the town's history. Jefferson was the founder of Charlottesville's University of Virginia (UVA), a consistently top-ranked "public ivy" university from which many American politicians, judges, journalists, and upper-crust elites have graduated over the years. It was Jefferson's storied legacy as the father of the Bill of Rights and his Enlightenment thinking on human liberty that led to the university, at one time, being considered a vital touchstone of "free speech" and intellectual freedom.

Charlottesville is also the home of Thomas Jefferson's storied home Monticello, an updated example of ancient Greek and Roman inspired architecture, set on a sprawling plantation where Jefferson entertained many foreign and domestic luminaries. The significance of Monticello has made it a destination for centuries of national and international heads of state.

I was born into what might be called a conservative Christian household. Both my father, George Eric Kessler, and my mother, Carol Arlene Cutright, were Charlottesville natives. Both worked for UVA when they were first married. At one point my uncle was an orderly at the UVA Hospital.

Grandma Kessler worked in the UVA Bursar's Office and Grandma Cutright was a secretary in UVA's Primary Care Radiology Department.

IT HAD TO HAPPEN TO SOMEONE . . .

Young Jason Kessler with grandmother Winnie Norvelle Kessler (Christmas 1987)

Grandaddy Kessler was an artist with the National Radio Astronomy Observatory, a federal program which "provides state-of-the-art radio telescope facilities for use by the international scientific community," located on UVA campus, and it was a part of his identity.

Like most proud Charlottesvillians, my family loved UVA and fervently followed university sports.

Many of my earliest memories involved the family seated together around the TV or radio enjoying a UVA basketball game, or going to the football stadium decked in the blue and orange hometown colors and singing "The Cavalier Song" (the UVA anthem set to the tune of "Auld Lang Syne"). A line from the UVA anthem goes: "We come from old Virginia, where all is bright and gay." For as long as I could remember, a sizeable chunk of the crowd, maybe 30%, would mischievously yell "Not gay" during this part of the song. It was a pretty funny joke in those times when humor wasn't politically correct and Charlottesville was clearly more conservative. In 2001, campus leftists began to protest this practice until it stopped, a sign of UVA's woke awakening and new values.

Riding a tractor with Buddy Cutright, my maternal grandfather (Spring 1986)

But it wasn't just Charlottesville that changed. I did, too. As a boy I would watch Rush Limbaugh with my parents, although I was too young to understand. My earliest recollection of any concern for current events was following the O.J. Simpson trial with members of my family. I don't recall the racial elements being particularly emphasized by my parents, despite it being one of the most racially charged events of the 1990s.

Although my parents had an interest in politics, it wasn't strong enough to offer any dissent from the basic U.S. government-approved public education curriculum. Their only concern was that I receive a Christian upbringing, thus much of my early education was spent in private religious schools. They felt God shouldn't have been taken out of schools, but didn't offer any kind of alternate view, on say, the American Founding Fathers, Adolf Hitler, or Martin Luther King Jr.

So, I grew up with the understanding the Nazis were the worst villains in human history and Martin Luther King Jr. and his civil rights movement were as American as apple pie. The Founding Fathers were an unimpeachable pantheon of virtuous geniuses whose wisdom birthed the greatest nation in the history of mankind.

I had a diverse group of friends as far back I could remember. When my family relocated to Las Cruces, New Mexico, I attended Mesilla Valley Christian School, and my schoolyard friends were White, Asian, Indian, and Hispanic. There weren't many Black people there.

As I grew older, I would have Black friends, but there was also a racial consciousness about understanding there was a greater propensity for bullying, aggression, and violence among this group. I understood there were racial differences between people, but I didn't see them as that important. As was fashionable with most people, for many years I espoused the creed, "I don't see race," as my governing philosophy on that issue.

My family lived in New Mexico from 1987 until 1993 when my parents got divorced. During those years, the only times I would see Charlottesville were when we returned to visit family for Christmas.

This meant many of my childhood memories of Charlottesville were as "Christmasland": a magical place of gifts, church, nativity scenes, big family dinners, and movies with loved ones. Fantastic lights covered the streets from the city to the surrounding countryside, and our family would drive around Charlottesville and the surrounding sleepy rural towns looking at them all. On occasion there would even be snow.

There's not much to say about my teenage years. I was rebellious and unfocused. I was into underage drinking and drug use. But my grades never suffered much. I remained studious and graduated a semester early even while working part-time jobs.

I began college in the film department of Virginia Commonwealth University (VCU) in Richmond, Virginia. As a shy young man, I spent a lot of time alone in my room watching tons of movies, so my earliest career ambitions were to make films like the ones I loved: *The Road Warrior*, starring Mel Gibson, or *Star Wars*, *Raiders of the Lost Ark*, *Pulp Fiction*, *Tales from the Crypt*, and many film standards.

It was at VCU that I had my first political awakening. It was around 2002. All of my friends were basically hippies: pot heads, rockers, writers, and filmmakers. Everyone I knew watched *The Daily Show with Jon Stewart* and were fervently against President George W. Bush's invasion of Iraq. There was a huge anti-war march outside my campus dormitory in downtown Richmond. I remember joining in. My anger came from how the president had invaded a country that didn't even attack us, lied about WMDs (Weapons of Mass Destruction), and was trampling civil liberties in his "War on Terror."

My parents were not paying for college and had never paid for anything substantial. If I wanted a Nintendo, I had to cut grass in the neighborhood to earn money. So that I could own my own car and pay insurance, I'd been doing crap jobs ever since the very day I turned 15. I got my mom's permission slip so I could begin work as a dishwasher at a small local restaurant in nearby Lake Monticello. Then I flipped hamburgers and worked as a telemarketer. When I lived in Richmond, I was a pizza delivery driver. These experiences working miserable shit-kicking jobs made me feel blue-collar and sympathize with the plight of the working class.

Race, religion, gender, and identity politics—which are everything to today's left—were completely off my radar. I had no passionate views in that domain, although I was a militant atheist with a chip on my shoulder for religion generally. I got most of my news from NPR for years and felt they were a highly trustworthy source of information. I did vote for Obama, but unlike most Democrats, I would suspect, I did not vote for him because he was Black. He was simply the candidate that aligned with my values at the time, especially regarding the paramount opposition to the Iraq War. In retrospect this vote was regrettable and highly embarrassing.

It was during the Obama administration that there seemed to be a radical shift in the culture war, and I didn't like it. It seemed like the country suddenly hated men and I didn't like that because I am a man. And they hated White people and I didn't like that because I'm White.

I was still anti-war and anti-corporate, but I couldn't go along with these new voices on the left blaming people who looked like me for historical grievances which happened long before I was even born. I didn't cotton to pushing race hatred towards Whites and misandry towards men.

The long journey that led me to realize there was a war on Whites and to organize UTR began when I graduated from UVA and had trouble finding work because of my race and gender. I was led to believe a college diploma from a prestigious university like UVA was my path to a stable career and the middle class. After all, why else would I get tens of thousands of dollars in student loans and waste the best years of my life attaining a diploma? But in reality, the careers associated with a bachelor's degree in psychology did not pay well (annually around $30,000 in 2009) and I couldn't obtain one in the first place because they were all government jobs in counseling and social work that discriminated against White male applicants. I remember the culmination of years of fruitless applications to my local community services board was to finally enter the running for one of two positions at a facility that helped individuals dealing with drug and alcohol problems. But there was a full-time position with benefits and a much lesser position which was merely as-needed, filling in for the winner of the main position.

I did not realize this position was without benefits or any guarantee of a minimum number of hours until I attended a training session where I discovered the other positions went to women and minorities without the same college degree I had or any relevant job experience. I had both. I walked out in frustration and resigned myself to a life in the gig economy, where White male college graduates go to waste away while all the big employers rush to staff their businesses with "diverse" populations of women and minorities. This wasn't the country of merit-based opportunity I was raised in.

Second, I knew Whites were a fundamentally decent people. My family and community were always giving: to one another, but also to families and communities of other races. And yet all I heard throughout the 2010s were complaints about how terrible Whites supposedly were. As a child I recalled the Blacks always being the bullies and the ones to get into violent altercations at the drop of a hat. They were the ones whose music glorified gang-banging, drug-pushing, gun-running, and increasingly, objectification of our White women as hoes, strippers, and sluts. Whites were the good ones who believed in love, honor, and compassion, to a fault. It disgusted me when my friends who I grew up with started listening to rap music and adopted the coarse, greedy, and violent trappings of Black culture over that of their own kind.

Growing up I was taught to have enormous pride in my heritage as an American, particularly one from the State of Virginia, home to so many of the Founding Fathers like George Washington, Thomas Jefferson, and James Monroe. The ones who settled this great country and formed our nation were White like me. It was the Europeans who civilized the wilderness, created the trains and planes and cities. We created modern medicine and the great works of philosophy and art. The heroes in the movies were based on us and our fundamental decency. Sure, there were things I was taught in public school that we had done wrong, like slavery and our treatment of Native Americans, but ultimately, we tried our best to make amends, and all peoples of the planet were better off for the contributions of White men and women.

But yet lately I was hearing a different story. Apparently, all Whites had ever done was spread disease, genocide Natives, enslave Blacks, and Holocaust Jews. No one was grateful for anything we'd accomplished anymore and, in fact, our "sins" were so great all Whites would have to pay for things we hadn't done that occurred before we were born, like slavery. But only we had to pay the collective price for our ancestors. None of the Africans who enslaved other Africans were responsible for their deeds, nor the Jews who operated the transatlantic slave trade, nor the Chinese who enslaved men to build the Great Wall, nor the Muslims who enslaved Africans and Europeans, nor the Natives who used slave labor to build their great temples where they sacrificed countless numbers of their own people. It went on and on. All races of men committed war crimes and rape and enslaved people, but yet through the increasingly popular conspiracy theory of "white supremacy," only White people were to blame for these sins of the past. And our debt could never be paid in full. Our oppression in the present in the form of affirmative action hiring discrimination, government funding for non-White interests only, discrimination in university admissions, and constant shaming and blaming of our race was the price we must pay, enshrined in laws like the 1964 Civil Rights Act, so that we'd pay in perpetuity for eternity, or till the end of the United States, whichever came first.

I started to see more and more White women around town being preyed on by Black drug dealers, predators, and even serial killers. Black drug pushers would hang around the UVA campus and Charlottesville Downtown Mall looking to become the "hook-up" for marijuana or something worse like cocaine. Usually when you saw one of them alone with a White woman it was because the women had been hooked into the drug culture, which then led to their sexual exploitation, glorified in the music and entertainment industry. For years a serial rapist had been operating in the Charlottesville area preying on White women walking alone. Then, a young Virginia Tech student, Morgan Harrington, disappeared outside a Metallica concert at John Paul Jones arena on October 17, 2009. Five years later, on September 12, 2014, a young, White UVA student, Hannah Graham, disappeared after drinking on the Downtown Mall. Like Harrington, her body was found raped and murdered. Surveillance footage from downtown businesses later revealed Graham leaving a bar with her killer, a lumbering, dreadlocked Black man named Jesse Leroy "LJ" Matthew Jr., former hospital orderly and cab driver.[31] After he was connected to the string of unsolved rapes and murders, people came forward about Matthew groping young White women on the Downtown Mall. Unfortunately, this kind of thing was just commonplace behavior for Black men in Charlottesville, and none of the "nice" White liberals had the courage to stop them from exploiting and harassing local women. They were all emasculated fools afraid to be called "racist." What the hell had happened to the world and my community?

Local non-governmental organizations (NGOs) like the International Rescue Community were starting to flood more Muslims into the community from Third World countries. Hispanics who'd illegally immigrated into the country were taking many of the blue-collar jobs and driving down wages. This was all that was left to me since the white-collar positions were going to women, Blacks, and the upper-class Whites who always used their privilege to exempt themselves from the discriminatory practices applied to middle- and working-class Whites. In totality, the effect was that my community, and my country, were becoming less White, and it felt like we were under invasion and under siege.

After dropping out of VCU to travel, I returned to college in 2005, first acquiring my associate's degree at Piedmont Virginia Community College in Charlottesville and then my bachelor's degree in psychology from UVA in 2009.

The world I graduated into did not resemble the world I had been led to believe in. The United States was in the middle of a historic recession, and the jobs I was seeking in social work and counseling were government positions clearly being earmarked for

---

[31] wtvr.com/2016/03/03/the-disturbing-timeline-of-jesse-matthews-sexual-violence-and-murder

women and minority affirmative action. So, after all the money and years spent acquiring a worthless degree, I was either doing odd jobs as a handyman in the gig economy or spending my free time lifting weights and watching Baltimore Orioles baseball games.

When the burgeoning racial crisis really hit home for me was after the death of Freddie Gray, a Black career criminal, who died in police custody. Half of the officers implicated in the supposed mistreatment were Black, as was the chief of police and the mayor.

On April 24, 2015, a race riot broke out across Baltimore and in front of the Camden Yards baseball stadium. Blacks were stomping on the windshields of cars and hurling trash cans into the air.[32]

A bunch of nice, demure White people were standing in line trying to make it into Camden Yards to see the baseball game. A Black person approached a White couple and began hurling racial abuse at them. The White man tried to reassure the Black that he supported his cause, but this did nothing to stop the abuse and aggression. He didn't care which political side he was on. The White man's skin color was his team.

The news outlets I listened to like NPR began hyping a narrative they framed as "innocent Black men" being killed by "racists," often White (even if they weren't White, they were still tagged as "white supremacists") police officers. An early example of this angle was in the conflict that occurred between George Zimmerman, a Hispanic man, and Trayvon Martin, a young Black man, which resulted in the shooting death of Martin. NPR, *The Huffington Post*, and other liberal media outlets did not buy Zimmerman's claims he was attacked by Martin and, at the time, I was willing to believe them.

But as time went on and racially charged incidents of alleged racism were portrayed as ubiquitous, I became more skeptical. What I knew from being a man of the street did not correspond with the left-wing media narratives about how Black men are always the innocent parties. Anyone with common sense knows there tends to be more aggression and criminal activity among that population.

---

[32] cbsnews.com/news/thousands-march-in-baltimore-to-protest-police-custody-death

To *The Huffington Post* and NPR, nothing like the Camden Yards riot was happening. When I saw with my own eyes they were covering up reality that contradicted their narrative, my trust in liberal journalism was shattered. Perhaps if I had lost my faith in all liberal enterprises, including the vaunted civil liberties defense of the ACLU, I never would have been cornered into the tragic trap that Charlottesville ended up being.

My disillusion with the political left dovetailed fortuitously with the political ascendancy of Donald Trump. After all Trump was, like me, a former Democrat stringently opposed to the Iraq War with anti-war views generally.

Trump's swagger and demeanor were identifiable by blue collar folks everywhere, including me. He might not have been speaking out explicitly for the aggrieved White majority, but he seemed defiantly unwilling to apologize to their growing enemies either.

I have always tried to remain an independent thinker and was not tied one way or another on issues that other people felt strongly about like abortion or gun rights. Over time I have gradually become more favorable to certain Republican positions, like those on gun rights. Beyond Trump, I was also looking out for a movement that explicitly spoke for voiceless and powerless White people like myself.

With all the free time from not having a post-college career, I followed politics online. My first brush with what could be termed the "dissident right" or "online right" was with the Gamergate movement.

Gamergate was a movement by video gamers to take back their hobby from the encroachment of feminists and social justice warriors (SJWs) being hired by the left-wing gaming corporations and inserting left-wing propaganda into the games hated by the vast majority of the gaming community. I liked a lot of the Gamergate humor and social criticism, but I wasn't an activist for their cause.

While Gamergate often touched on important men's rights considerations, I was frustrated it never addressed the growing racial bias towards Whites, and longed for a civil rights movement to come along for that purpose. Then, out of the blue, this White rights movement I had been hoping for seemed to suddenly materialize.

IT HAD TO HAPPEN TO SOMEONE . . .

I don't remember the first time I heard the term "alt-right." It wasn't a particular person who drew my attention to it. The alt-right appeared to me to be an organic, online groundswell of populist resentment about declining free speech, increasing censorship, anti-White and anti-male hostility, and the out-of-control homosexual agenda.

At that time, a lot of the terms we now use to describe the new left coalition like "woke," "cancel culture," and "Antifa," weren't in wide use, although some people were already sounding the alarm on "social justice warriors," who were largely the same people using the same tactics.

In contrast to these humorless and stuck up SJWs, the alt-right were remarkable for their humor. Much of it came from the exploding meme culture and a cast of cartoon characters such as Pepe the Frog and the Wojaks. Alt-right humor reminded me of the riotous, edgy stand-up comedy from before the industry went woke. Stand up was art as a celebration of free speech absolutism. The best comedians would mock and satirize the sacred shibboleths of society. Richard Pryor could find comedy in his perception of racial differences between Blacks and Whites. George Carlin could say all the naughty words you're not allowed to say on TV and deliver a biting critique of the U.S. military industrial complex.

A famous scene in *Lenny*, starring Dustin Hoffman, depicts Jewish stand-up comic Lenny Bruce delivering a shocking piece of social commentary during a stand-up performance, with Bruce reciting every racial and sexual slur in the American language, even to the point of saying "nigger" in front of a Black man.

The punchline insinuated that free expression could make the world a better place by desensitizing everyone to the words that are meant to hurt us. Bruce suggested saying words like "nigger" until it "didn't mean anything any more! Then you'd never be able to make some six year old black kid cry because somebody called him a nigger in school."

Alt-right political cartoons made fun of all the left-wing identity groups you weren't allowed to: Blacks, Asians, Jews, Muslims, gays, and women. It was refreshing to see that kind of rebellion against the stifling climate of censorship. A joke the authorities don't want you to tell is not just funny, it's an act of liberation. Most importantly, the alt-right meme culture *really was funny*! I never found any of the jokes I saw online as anything but mirth-inducing triumphs of free expression, certainly, in line with the racial humor heard in stand-up comedy acts going back to the 1970s from people like Andrew Dice Clay or Chris Rock. I tended to share Lenny Bruce's idealism about radical free expression and was not offended in any way by racial humor, even those using slurs. I felt the power of words to harm was overblown, and the greater danger was stifling speech to protect public sensibilities. This is not to say that I deeply understood the alt-right, how much more radical they were than I was at the time, and whether I should or shouldn't take them seriously. It was all new to me and I'd never even heard of terms like White Nationalism or Southern Nationalism. Never was this misunderstanding more disastrous than when I first heard of Richard Spencer and Mike Peinovich.

On November 19, 2016, Twitter was buzzing about an event they dubbed "Heilgate."

Apparently, there was a conference for something called the National Policy Institute where alt-right adherents would listen to speeches from their political leaders, including some fellow named Richard Spencer. At the end of his speech, he raised a glass and saluted, "Hail Trump! Hail our people! Hail victory!" A number of people in the audience responded by shouts of *Sieg heil!* (Hail victory!) and outstretching their arms in Nazi salutes.[33] One of the ringleaders was Michael Peinovich, better known as Mike Enoch, host of *The Right Stuff* (*TRS*) podcast.

I did not see the salutes as a genuine statement of affiliation with Nazism. I saw it as an extension of the humor culture I was a part of online and figured the salutes were satirizing prejudicial stereotypes about White people, namely, that all White people are racists and

---

[33] youtube.com/watch?v=1o6-bi3jlxk

Attendees salute Richard Spencer at the NPI conference known as Heilgate

Nazis. This could be compared to how Blacks took a derogatory term like "nigger" and co-opted it into the self-referential "nigga." This read was incorrect. In retrospect, I wanted to believe that someone like Spencer was the kind of august, genuine White civil rights leader that I had been looking for. I was explaining away red flags because I wanted to believe in the character and judgment of these so-called alt-right leaders.

I was not so much impressed with Spencer's ideas as I was with his associate Mike Enoch. Spencer was a little too dilettantish and ethereal for my tastes. He had a very effeminate, professorial, and self-serious way of explaining himself that never quite seemed to hit the right ideological targets for me. Enoch on the other hand was an impressive individual. The guy is a master polemicist, comedian, and online debate pugilist who verbalized a lot of incisive intellectual critiques of the culturally dominant racial theory that posited "white supremacy," and indeed "whiteness" itself as the source of all racial strife, villainy, and injustice in the world. Like many other alt-right personalities, he would point to the overwhelming data on higher rates of murder and violent crime among the Black population, or the rapes committed towards native Europeans by Islamic refugees, and illegal aliens. But Enoch's heaviest and most controversial critiques involved ideas about Jewish power and Jewish racism towards Whites. Indeed, some of his beliefs, including skepticism of the historicity of the Jewish Holocaust, are explicitly prohibited by law in many countries throughout the West. Critically, this is not true in America, where so-called "hate speech" is protected by the First Amendment to the U.S. Constitution.

The primary program on Enoch's *TRS* radio network is *The Daily Shoah* (*TDS*) podcast, a play on Comedy Central's *The Daily Show* and "shoah," a Hebrew synonym for the Holocaust. Within the alt-right subculture this would have been understood as a joke about the veracity of the Holocaust narrative of history and not a promotion of genocide. But clearly, it gives you a flavor of the dark, edgy humor proliferating in alt-right circles. The more serious accusation in Enoch's polemic is that Jews have an inherently racist evolutionary strategy of undermining majority White populations for their own ambitions. The most advanced articulation of this theory comes from a book by retired Professor Kevin MacDonald, *The Culture of Critique: An Evolutionary Analysis of Jewish Involvement in Twentieth-Century Intellectual and Political Movements*. MacDonald is an oft-cited and well-respected theorist within the alt-right movement. I met Spencer much earlier than Enoch, but we'll come to that later. It is important to keep in mind that during the critical events at question in this book, I did not understand or share the antisemitic beliefs espoused by Enoch and many of the other attendees at UTR. I now have a much more nuanced position after studying the incredible power wealthy Jewish oligarchs, activists, and Zionists have had on world events during the last two centuries. As you will see in the chapters detailing the legal fallout from the rally, I was hit head-on by a Jewish financed and supported lawsuit from the heavily connected Democratic attorney Roberta Kaplan, a Jewish lesbian. Seeing the

IT HAD TO HAPPEN TO SOMEONE . . .

power arrayed against us financed by Jewish oligarchs in Silicon Valley, litigated by Jewish attorneys, and promoted by Jewish celebrities like *That 70's Show*'s Topher Grace, helped me understand the wealth and coordination behind this most feared ethnic coalition.

I vividly remember staining decks as a side hustle in the run-up to the 2016 U.S. presidential election. Everyone was on fire over Trumpism. I listened to "mainstream" pundits like Bill Mitchell for statistical analysis of the race. Folks like Stephan Molyneux were in my rotation for analysis of Trumpism and racial disparities in IQ or rates of crime. Enoch and his *TDS* were occasionally in the mix when I felt like being challenged by something more radical.

One of the most indelible memories of my life was staining a back patio deck in Charlottesville on the day of the 2016 presidential election. As the results rolled in and it became apparent Trump could actually win the election, the energy in the air seemed to be kinetic. Trump's victory clearly created a "disturbance in the force" in Hillary-supporting, liberal Charlottesville. A chaos energy seemed to ignite every particle of the air, even as everything still remained eerily calm. The action potential for momentous events was on the horizon.

When I created the first iteration of my website, originally JasonKessler.net (now JasonKessler.us),[34] it was not a forum for my politics. I saw how toxic and combative social media sites like Facebook and Twitter were becoming, along the fractious Republican/Democratic divide, and tried to avoid it. Instead, the site, billed as Jason Kessler's Mad Dimension, was host to my creative writing and poetry. That all changed in the fall of 2016.

---

[34] My original website was deplatformed after the rally by the host, a San Francisco-based company called Weebly. Together with *The Daily Caller* deleting all my articles it became impossible for the public to get my side of events.

WES BELLAMY

In the summer I had been doing more shit-kicking odd jobs to stay afloat. This time I was cleaning junk out of the backyard of an older fellow named John Heyden, with a wooden cane, hunched back, and a long white beard. He had an open trailer which I loaded trash and brush onto before taking several trips to the dump.

It was during this dreary work that John and I began discussing local Charlottesville politics. It was the first time I heard about Vice-Mayor Wes Bellamy and his crusade against a monument to Confederate General Robert E. Lee in downtown Charlottesville, across the street from the brick walking mall and adjacent to the public library.

Bellamy wasn't the first to call for the monument's removal. That was his mentor, City Councilor Kristin Szakos, a liberal White woman, who spoke out against the overwhelmingly popular monument back on March 22, 2012.[35] Things really started rolling on March 19, 2016, when a morbidly obese 15-year-old Black girl named Zyahna Bryant created a petition calling for the statue to be removed, and Lee Park to be renamed.[36] If that seems like a strange preoccupation for a 15-year-old girl to have, the heavy rumor around town was that she had been put up to it as part of a political operation by Bellamy and Szakos.

The monument itself was commissioned in 1917 by philanthropist Paul G. McIntire, and unveiled on May 21, 1924,[37] in a ceremony

---

[35] archive.ph/2022.09.21-063811/https://dailyprogress.com/news/szakos-decries-response-to-statue-comments/article_2c62aadd-9c17-5fd1-9416-d892102037ef.html
[36] change.org/p/charlottesville-city-council-change-the-name-of-lee-park-and-remove-the-statue-in-charlottesville-va
[37] archive.is/YeFHQ

Unveiling of Charlottesville's Lee monument (May 21, 1924)

attended by 15,000 residents of Charlottesville and the surrounding area in their Sunday best.

Growing up, I didn't have a particular reverence for Confederate history, although my ancestors include both Confederate and Union soldiers. On the paternal side, my 3rd great grandfather, James L. Amiss (1818-97) from Albemarle, Virginia, served in the 46th Regiment, Virginia Infantry and my 3rd great grandfather, John Kessler (1840-1920) from Green, Indiana, served in the Union's 89th Regiment, Indiana Infantry. On my maternal side, my 3rd great grandfather, Abel Henry Holliday (1837-99) from Greenbrier, Virginia, served the Confederacy in the 14th Virginia Cavalry, and my 3rd great grandfather, Solomon Rhoades (1830-90) from Pike County, Indiana, served in the Union's 58th Regiment, Indiana Infantry.[38] The way that it breaks down is that both of my grandmothers were descended from Southern Confederate stock and my grandfathers came from Union stock. My stepfather Moses was a huge American Civil War buff, and his home displayed numerous gorgeous art pieces by Civil

---

[38] I found this out during my research for this book, using my Ancestry.com results and cross-referencing with the National Park Service's Civil War Soldiers and Sailors system.

War artist Mort Kuntzler. He had bought every collector's piece in the Franklin Mint Civil War chess board set with Lee and Grant as the kings. And he took our family to several Civil War reenactments during my childhood. But, until after the rally when I re-evaluated things, my stepfather and I didn't get along too well. We made up in the last years of his life when he was stricken with cancer.

What connected me to the Robert E. Lee monument, besides the fact that I often sat under the shade of a tree in Lee Park, library book in hand, was that I immediately sussed the attack on Robert E. Lee as an attack on "whiteness," and the proud history of the European diaspora in America.

There were hints of the same happening to other White historical figures for many years. In Charlottesville alone, there was also a simmering hatred of Charlottesville patron saint Thomas Jefferson. Extremists radicalized by left-wing professors at UVA began to take the position that Jefferson was nothing more than a slave master and racist. Long alleged, but unproven, allegations of a relationship between Jefferson and his African slave Sally Hemings added fuel to the fire, along with an accusation among the radicals that Jefferson was also a "rapist." Bellamy called on UVA to "re-evaluate" its relationship with Jefferson, and recently instigated a pressure campaign against a White UVA economics professor named Douglas Muir. Muir's crime? He had the audacity to post on his private Facebook account that, "Black lives matter is the biggest rasist [sic] organization since the clan." Bellamy also led a protest of an Italian restaurant Muir owned near the Downtown Mall. (I walked through their picket line to buy a fresh pasta, which I proceeded to eat in front of them while exclaiming how delicious the food was.)

A crucial thing to keep in mind throughout all the events in this book is that I was significantly motivated by my passionate, naïve, and idealistic belief in radical free speech.

Speech is the most fundamentally human mode of creative expression we have. No other animal has language like we humans. To me, speech is a sacred thing because it articulates the stirrings of our souls: whether through language, song, poetry, or theater. It helps us understand one another and even ourselves. Those who can criticize their government, or express dissenting opinions without fear of reprisal, live a qualitatively better and freer life. On the other hand, governments who forbid writing or speaking on certain topics are tyrannical. To constrain a man's innermost expression is subjugation of his soul. It is a fearful condition where dissidents of government policy have no hope of redressing their grievances through lawful appeals to their fellows. I idealized historic free speech cases like the one depicted in the 1996 film, *The People vs. Larry Flynt* starring Woody Harrelson as pornographer Larry Flynt. Or better still, the ACLU Jews who were so religiously committed to free speech that they defended the right of the National Socialist Party of America to conduct a demonstration in the heavily Jewish town of Skokie, Illinois. So, when I saw Bellamy and his collaborators attempting to hound poor Doug Muir out of a job, it triggered my sense of injustice.

As fate would have it, the Thomas Jefferson Center for the Protection of Free Expression announced a symposium on free speech with various professors, authors, and celebrities, including Kelly Carlin, the daughter of stand-up comedy legend George Carlin.[39] Another important attendee was Dahlia Lithwick, a Jewish U.S. Supreme Court (SCOTUS) correspondent for *Slate* magazine. Crucially, Lithwick was a Charlottesville resident at the time and attended the same synagogue as all of the most powerful Charlottesville Jews such as then-mayor Mike Signer. Lithwick had many high-profile connections nationally, particularly in the Jewish legal community. More on that later. It seemed like the timing of the symposium was in response to the woke mob attempting to cancel Muir, but they didn't expressly reference the controversy publicly.

I attended the October 13, 2016, symposium to stand up for Doug Muir. In reality, the event was an appalling disappointment. The speakers seemed to live in an alternate reality where all of the censorship was happening exclusively to leftist activists and racial minorities.

---

[39] web.archive.org/web/20190714192909/https://dailyprogress.com/news/uva/free-speech-panelists-say-college-campuses-need-dialogue/article_f5a577b0-4058-5f0e-b086-821cf39632ef.html

Kessler addresses a "free speech symposium" (October 13, 2016)

Local reporter Hawes Spencer (no relation to Richard) was in attendance. In his book, *Summer of Hate: Charlottesville, USA*, Spencer recalls how Carlin "remarked that her father would no longer be welcome on America's college campuses. Yet nobody mentioned Muir—even though the discussion took place during Muir's classroom exodus."

I couldn't allow that omission to stand. I was on pins and needles until the Q & A when my hand shot up like a bolt. Despite four or five audience questions being taking before me, I kept desperately raising my hand at every new opportunity. Just when I thought there might not be any hope, I was called on for the very last question of the Q & A.

> Well, let's be clear about who is having the problems with free speech in society, and it's the right wing. The right wing is being discriminated against; you've seen it with the guy Douglas Muir, the UVA lecturer who brought up the point—which is a valid point which can be debated —that Black Lives Matter is a racist organization. Now, we could have that debate or we could fire and shame and silence somebody like that. And, in order to have the discussion that's really going to enrich society, we have to have a

diversity of viewpoints. Is anybody on the panel a Donald Trump supporter? No, you're all center-left politicians quoting center-left media people, and I appreciate the points that you're bringing up—I appreciate them; they're good points—because I'm not necessarily a right-winger. I am a free speech person who is sick and tired of the left pouncing and shaming and trying to destroy people's livelihoods. And where is the diversity of intellectual debate on college campuses? 87% of professors are liberals; 13% are conservatives. We need a conservative person up here; we need a right-wing person. If you don't know Milo Yiannopolous you need to Google Milo Yiannopolous and be listening to people like him. We need right-wingers in this debate, or there's no free speech, period.[40]

Shockingly, even the director of the Center, Josh Wheeler, was unwilling to defend Muir. In response to a question from a local reporter about Muir, Wheeler claimed "Muir's apparent willingness to stand down diminished any claims about speech issues." So, because Muir was forced by the cancel mob to quit his job there was no free speech issue? *That was the free speech issue.* The cowardice and hypocrisy of the panel was infuriating and I argued vociferously with both Wheeler and Carlin after the symposium ended. It was clear to me they only cared about protecting speech of liberal Democrats. "I've been interested in free speech back when it was under attack by right-wing Christians and now it's being attacked by left-wing social justice warriors and PC police," I told them.

Although Bellamy and his fellow travelers attacking Muir and the Robert E. Lee statue claimed to be "anti-racists" standing up to the institutional power of "white supremacy," I saw something else. I saw a government official who *was* the "institutional power," using his position of power, not to unite, but to persecute the White people he nursed a vendetta against.

---

[40] youtube.com/watch?v=ZRf4KQnYSx0; bitchute.com/video/i7OegJF9zzDN

CHARLOTTESVILLE AND THE DEATH OF FREE SPEECH

Former Charlottesville Vice-Mayor Wes Bellamy, Department Chair Virginia State University

The majority of people in Charlottesville were opposed to the removal of the monument, but like John Heyden, held no power. So much for the underdog anti-racists against the institutional power of "white supremacy."

To test my theory about Bellamy's true motivations, I came up with an idea that struck me like a thunderbolt from the gods. Bellamy was also on Twitter and had been there for a number of years. I searched Bellamy's tweet history for the keyword "white," and boy was I surprised at what I found!

In honor of@MsWineFine niggaz gotta do it. #liesfemalestell 'I can count on 1 hand all the niggaz I had sex wit'>yea x3 lyin cunt

I HATE BLACK PEOPLE who ACT WHITE (B U NIGGA) - Jeezy Voice! I DONT LIKE WHIT PEOPLE SO I HATE WHITE SNOW!!!!! FML!!!!

I really #hate how almost 80% of the black people here talk white….# petpeeve. #itstheniggainme. #dontjudgeme

This nigga just said he don't have 2work as long as its white women walking the Earth. Lmaaaaaaaoooooo. That's some VA shit.

I hate seeing White people in Orangeburg #thos…

Word…RT @TAXSTONE: Eat it while she sleep if she moan it aint rape

White women=Devil RT @cjsdaillest:As a conspiracy charge, and her credit a2 RT @1RL1: @cjsdaillest @WesBTV that MTO joint was serious yo smh

Black Man RT @Mz2euceBOSS: Question: would you be more comfortable with a white man or a black man as your boss/superior?

So sad seeing these beanpole body white women in these sundresses smh…

Forgot why I never go out in Charlottesvill…the fact that I've literally seen less than 10 black people (and I'm w/ 2 of them) is crazy.

Lol funniest thing about being down south is seeing little white men and the look on their faces when they have to look up to you.

Lol people in here calling Thomas Jefferson a White Supremacist…. making a lot of valid points proving the accusation. Interesting…

Wes Bellamy, M.Ed
@ViceMayorWesB

In honor of@MsWineFine niggaz gotta do it. #liesfemalestell 'I can count on 1 hand all the niggaz I had sex wit'>yea x3 lyin cunt

9:11 PM - 9 Oct 2009

> **Wes Bellamy, M.Ed**
> @ViceMayorWesB
>
> I HATE BLACK PEOPLE who ACT WHITE!!! (B U NIGGA)-Jeezy Voice!
>
> 1:20 PM - 17 Nov 2009

> **Wes Bellamy, M.Ed**
> @ViceMayorWesB
>
> I DONT LIKE WHIT PEOPLE SO I HATE WHITE SNOW!!!!! FML!!!!
>
> 6:05 PM - 20 Dec 2009

> **Wes Bellamy, M.Ed**
> @ViceMayorWesB
>
> I really #hate how almost 80% of the black people here talk white....#petpeeve. #itstheniggainme. #dontjudgeme
>
> 12:43 PM - 30 Mar 2010

> **Wes Bellamy, M.Ed**
> @ViceMayorWesB
>
> This nigga just said he don't have 2work as long as its white women walkin the Earth. Lmaaaaaaaoooooo. That's some VA shit.
>
> 2:16 AM - 27 Jun 2010

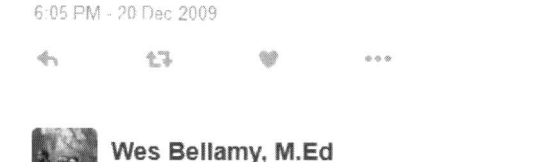

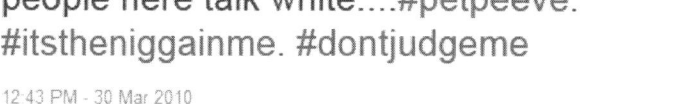

Wes Bellamy, M.Ed
@ViceMayorWesB

I hate seeing White people in Orangeburg #tho...

6:01 PM - 13 Feb 2011

Wes Bellamy, M.Ed
@ViceMayorWesB

Word...RT @TAXSTONE: Eat it while she sleep if she moan it aint rape

2:09 PM - 4 Oct 2011

Wes Bellamy, M.Ed
@ViceMayorWesB

White women=Devil RT @cjsdaillest:As a conspiracy charge, and her credit a1 RT @1RL1: @cjsdaillest @WesBTV that MTO joint was serious yo smh

RETWEET
1

9:24 PM - 3 Mar 2011

Wes Bellamy, M.Ed
@ViceMayorWesB

Black Man RT @Mz2euceBOSS: Question: would you be more comfortable with a white man or a black man as your boss/superior?

2:47 PM - 25 May 2012

Wes Bellamy, M.Ed
@ViceMayorWesB

So sad seeing these beanpole body white women in these sundresses smh...

6:31 PM - 18 Jul 2012

Wes Bellamy, M.Ed
@ViceMayorWesB

Forgot why I never go out in Charlottesville...the fact that I've literally seen less than 10 black people (and I'm w/ 2 of them) is crazy.

11:09 PM - 21 Sep 2012

Wes Bellamy, M.Ed
@ViceMayorWesB

Lol funniest thing about being down south is seeing little white men and the look on their faces when they have to look up to you.

11:12 AM - 13 Oct 2012

Wes Bellamy, M.Ed
@ViceMayorWesB

Lol people in here calling Thomas Jefferson a White Supremacist....making a lot of valid points proving the accusation. Interesting...

7:53 PM - 14 May 2014

Bellamy had also supported raping a sleeping woman. In response to a tweet suggesting, "Eat it while she sleep if she moan it aint rape," Bellamy retweeted the message with his own commentary: "Word." In Black culture, "word" is used as slang for agreement, endorsement, or acknowledgement.

Clearly Bellamy's anti-White tweets were validation of my hypothesis about his true motivation for attacking the Robert E. Lee monument and Doug Muir. I was righteously angry.

Additionally, online researchers later noted that the dates and times Bellamy put out his sickening anti-White and pro-rape tweets corresponded to when he was on duty as a teacher in the Albemarle County school system, around vulnerable, young White students and girls.

For a scoop of this monumental importance, I decided to use my creative writing site to host the investigative research. I wrote up the article including Bellamy's anti-White tweets and posted it over the 2016 Thanksgiving holiday. At the time, one of the big gathering points for local conservatives was on Facebook. People would post dissenting facts and comments on the Facebook posts of the local news outlets like *Daily Progress*, NBC 29, and CBS 19.

As a burgeoning political activist, I would immediately friend request other conservatives in the comment section. In this way I came to know Confederate heritage groups like the Virginia Flaggers who were fighting to preserve the Robert E. Lee monument, as well as others around the state. Their most well-known activity was smiling and waving the Southern cross at peaceful protests on roadsides or near Confederate historical sites. On one occasion they flew a massive Confederate flag on private property in Stafford County, Virginia, until the Virginia Department of Transportation invoked eminent domain to seize the property and remove the flag. I reached out to Susan Hathaway, leader of the Virginia Flaggers, with my article on Bellamy and it began spreading like wildfire across social media. Everyone in Charlottesville was talking about it. It wasn't long before national outlets like *The Washington Post* were reaching out to me for comment on the story. My position was that if Bellamy was a White man, he would have lost his job in a heartbeat. If we were going to have a society where people are treated equally, regardless of skin color, he should be removed from the Charlottesville City Council.

At first, there were some signs that the pressure was working. Then-Virginia Governor Terry McAuliffe, a devoted apparatchik in the Bill and Hillary Clinton network, removed Bellamy from a position which he'd appointed him to on the Virginia Board of Education.[41] It could only be progress to keep someone with Bellamy's toxic, racist views about White people and their history from deciding the school curriculum for little kids. But why were radicals like him appointed to these positions in the first place? Then something happened which I did not expect. In my rose-colored, MLK-inspired understanding of racial ethics, Bellamy would have lost his job if he were a White man. Hell, Bellamy himself had just supported UVA firing professor David Muir for what he claimed was a similar reason. However, none of the other members of the Charlottesville City Council called for his removal. Not one. This defiance was a slap in the face to their White constituents who were being treated with a racist double standard. I was outraged. What more could I do? I put on my little-worn suit

Kessler City Council speech (December 5, 2016)

---

[41] washingtonpost.com/news/education/wp/2016/12/01/virginia-board-of-education-member-resigns-after-vulgar-tweets-surface

jacket and decided to confront the tyrants during public comment at the Charlottesville City Council meetings.

On December 5, 2016, I signed up to speak, and when my time drew near, I took out my portable boom-box and walked to the podium like a pro-wrestler with Tom Petty and the Heartbreakers' "I Won't Back Down" blaring as my personal entrance music.

> My name is Jason Kessler and I am here on behalf of over 900 petitioners to demand that Wes Bellamy be removed from his office as a councilor for the City of Charlottesville because of his anti-women, anti-White, and pro-rape statements, which he assigned to the official Twitter account of the Vice-Mayor, have disqualified him from a position on council. When you Google the name Wes Bellamy, it is now synonymous with vile and derogatory hate. Unacceptable for an emissary of our city. Frankly, the lies and misinformation coming from both Bellamy and Szakos are unbecoming of the office. It has been well documented how Szakos first issued a statement about Bellamy being hacked, then deleted and issued a second statement, claiming the information I provided was false. When the veracity of my article was proven by *Cav Daily*, *Daily Progress*, and *The Washington Post*, among other news outlets, Ms. Szakos finally fell silent. Silent on, "It ain't rape if she moans." Silent on a gay slur. Silent on, "White women smell like assault charges and deli meat," and many other outrageously racist and offensive statements. In fact, Ms. Szakos and the other councilors have betrayed their every liberal, progressive value to secure the incestuous relationship between Ms. Szakos and her disgraced protégé. Mr. Bellamy and his allies continue to assert the easily falsifiable lie that his statements were made in his early 20s. I know the Vice-Mayor is not a math teacher, but he used to be on the board of education. So, let's see if he can follow some simple arithmetic. He is now 30 years old. All

of the tweets were made in the last six years, the most recent coming in 2014. That means all the tweets were made between the ages of 24 and 28, not early 20s, even by the most charitable standards, despite what you told *The Washington Post*. Even one of Bellamy's tweets would have forced his resignation a week ago if he were a White man. (a supporter in the crowd yelled "Amen") Consider this tweet which Bellamy wrote just a few years ago, while employed as a teacher in Albemarle County school system: Lol funniest thing about being down south is seeing the look on faces of little white men when they have to look up to a black man. Imagine if the reverse had been true. A White man, in a Black city like Detroit, is employed by the school system, and writes: "My favorite thing about being in the ghetto is seeing the look on the faces of little, Black men, when they have to look up to a White man." Wes Bellamy is a Black supremacist and a rape fetishist, and among other things (unintelligible)

The crowd became so raucous, the conclusion of my speech was drowned and then my time expired. As always in Charlottesville, I faced a hostile crowd which jeered, booed, filmed, taunted, and stared eyes into the back of my head with contempt.

On another occasion, when I explained to City Council, "I'm here for White people, because they need civil rights right now," I was warned by Bellamy's mentor, Councilor Kristin Szakos, that, "Mr. Kessler you are getting dangerously close to hate speech, which we do not allow." It's an indication of how out-of-control, anti-White bias has driven left-wing ideology that merely calling for White people to have civil rights is viewed as a form of "hate speech."

So-called "hate speech" is of course protected speech under the U.S. Constitution. It was an extremely inappropriate thing for a government official to say during a public comment. One of the big lessons of UTR is that protected speech is in fact effectively censored and banned by the Woke Left, by means other than technically making the speech illegal such as invasion of privacy, workplace harassment, smear campaigns, and lawfare, all the way up to threats and physical violence.

Several far-left belligerents surround and scream at Kessler during a City Council meeting

The New Jacobins

Around this time, I started a small group called Unity and Security for America, which met around town at various places like the public library or Miller's Bar on the Downtown Mall. The declared purpose of the group was the protection of Western civilization. It included a few political allies like former Jefferson Area Tea Party leader Jim Moore, Trump-supporting Republicans, and a very few alt-right inclined individuals.

It was during these meetings that we would become familiar with the stalking and intimidation tactics of left-wing groups in the area. Our primary antagonist was a group called Showing Up for Racial Justice (SURJ), essentially an Antifa or antifascist cell claiming to support "marginalized" non-White races, but whose membership was almost entirely extremist Caucasians and Jews. The ringleaders, Joe and Pam Starsia, were not working-class Marxists, but part of the wealthy and privileged set within Charlottesville. Pam is an attorney representing, among others, then-Vice-Mayor Wes Bellamy. Her husband Joe, also an attorney, is the scion of Dom Starsia, a famous UVA lacrosse coach who won NCAA national championships in 1999, 2003, 2006, and 2011.

Pam Starsia succinctly explained their modus operandi to *C-ville Weekly*: "White supremacists should not be allowed to move quietly in public spaces."

The rest of SURJ was a hodgepodge of these elitists and a literal freakshow of unhinged, mentally-ill misfits. There was Sara Tansey, who we referred to as the "Bearded Lady" for being an extremely ugly woman, likely taking male hormones, who had grown the spotty facial hair of a pubescent boy.

THE NEW JACOBINS

Joe Starsia (right) stalking the perimeter of an alt-right protest (May 13, 2017) and Antifa attorney Pam Starsia during a SURJ harassment campaign on the Downtown Mall (below)

CHARLOTTESVILLE AND THE DEATH OF FREE SPEECH

*Sarah Tansey aka The Bearded Lady in the former Lee Park
and Veronica Fitzhugh conducting an unsolicited nude protest in Lee Park
for Occupy Charlottesville (below)*

The "Fat Lady" Veronica Fitzhugh, was the only Black person, or racial minority for that matter, who was a regular activist with SURJ. Despite being horrendously obese, and possibly mentally retarded, Fitzhugh was known around town as an exhibitionist wearing neon wigs and using any stupid excuse to publicly disrobe.

A critical incident on the road to UTR occurred on February 11, 2017, when GOP gubernatorial candidate Corey Stuart visited Lee Park to voice his support for the preservation of the Confederate monument. He was confronted by an extremely aggressive SURJ. Joe Starsia, wielding an electric amplified bullhorn, stood inches from Stuart shouting: "Hey, hey, ho, ho, white supremacy's got to go." He was so abusively loud that no one could hear the speech Stuart tried to give.

I was in attendance livestreaming the behavior on Twitter using my cellphone.

The "Bearded Lady" did not like that one bit. She rushed me, jerking the phone out of my hands, and trying to escape with the device cradled under her arm. Joe Draego, a local conservative, caught her

Virginia gubernatorial hopeful and Prince William Board of County Supervisors member Corey Stewart during a campaign stop in Lee Park (February 11, 2017)

Kessler livestreaming during the Corey Stewart event (February 11, 2017)

and wrested the device from her hands before she could escape. In an example of Charlottesville "justice," Draego was charged with assault for his Good Samaritan deed.

During an incident on May 20, when I was sitting on the Downtown Mall with political friends, disturbing no one, a large group of SURJ protesters including Fitzhugh and Pam Starsia appeared, screaming expletives at us and chanting "Nazis go home" ad nauseum.[42] Fitzhugh got so close in my face I could smell her stank breath. When that didn't work, she grabbed the back of my chair and began violently shaking it. When the police arrived, Fitzhugh knelt on the ground with performative crying and accusations that she was being oppressed by racist police. Only an on-call, in-person intervention by Wes Bellamy saved Fitzhugh from being arrested for disorderly conduct (although she was later charged with assault).

On June 2 of that year, while the activists with Unity and Security

---

[42] bitchute.com/video/d10iZKmFy0Gu

for America were engaged in low-key conversation over beers at Miller's Bar, we were spotted and informed on by Jeff Fogel, a far-left Jewish "civil rights" attorney. He placed a call to SURJ, and soon about a dozen activists including Pam Starsia, were chanting and harassing us. Some of them went inside and asked the bar's management to deny us service. Ultimately, we were forced to acquiesce and were followed by an expanding and near-riotous mob as we departed. Fogel himself was arrested for pushing one of my friends. The temperature was rising and it felt like the pot boiler would explode any moment.

Things were exploding even more violently around the country. SURJ were part of a larger movement called Antifa (short for "antifascist") which took center stage during riots coinciding with the inauguration of U.S. President Donald Trump. These groups had apparently been feuding with White nationalists in America for decades, although they were formerly known by other monikers such as "anti-racist skinheads." For instance, one of the "anti-racist skinheads" named Jon Bair fatally shot and murdered 21-year-old Erik Banks, an alleged neo-Nazi, on January 1, 1993.[43] Though this rivalry between so-called "racists" and "anti-racists" had existed for decades, it was an underground niche phenomenon, largely unknown by the public.

I attended the inauguration of Donald Trump on January 20, 2017, but stayed within the vicinity of the tight police cordon protecting the event. Just outside that perimeter, masked, black-clad left-wing extremists were setting cars on fire, pulverizing ATMs, and throwing bricks and trash cans through windows. It was a coordinated riot.

The Washington Post interviewed one of the rioters, Thomas Massey of Philadelphia Anti-Racist Action, who would go on to play a critical role in the riots at UTR. "I think there should have been more violence yesterday," he told reporters. When asked if he engaged in violence he replied coyly, "There were some rocks thrown." But he hoped future riots would be "more successful. I'll get to punch a Nazi. I didn't get to do that yesterday. The police stopped me."

---

[43] opb.org/article/2021/10/08/portland-oregon-history-political-violence-skinheads-antifa-murder

Antifa conducted rampant acts of violence during the inauguration of Donald Trump (January 20, 2017)

However, other antifascist goons were more successful. During the inauguration, alt-right leader Richard Spencer, sporting a Pepe the Frog lapel pin, was giving an interview to journalists from Stateless Media and the Australian Broadcasting Corporation, when a black hooded and masked Antifa militant lunged forward, punching him square in the jaw before fleeing into anonymity on the streets of Washington, D.C.[44] This became a seminal moment in violent antifascist propaganda, with the video clip of the punch posted ubiquitously across the Internet and memed, along with the slogan "Punch a nazi," all part of the ideology and propaganda that would fuel the disastrous anti-speech riot in Charlottesville seven months later.

In a tragic pattern, few of these rioters were charged by either the federal government or the liberal Washington, D.C. police department. Most of those who were, quickly received pro-bono legal defense

---

[44] abc.net.au/news/2017-01-21/richard-spencer-national-policy-institute-punched-abc-interview/8200270

from left-wing NGOs like the National Lawyers Guild (NLG), and had their charges dropped. NLG would act as self-appointed "civil rights monitors" at large-scale events including UTR, but would only look out for the left-wing side and turn a blind eye to conservative victims. NLG was founded by Jewish-American communist Victor Rabinowitz.

THE BATTLE OF BERKELEY

Another critical vector in the national emergence of Antifa occurred throughout 2017, at a series of events in Berkeley, California, colloquially known online as "The Battle of Berkeley." Critically (and perversely, given ensuing events), Berkeley is often referred to as the "birthplace of the 1964 Free Speech Movement." The inception point of the conflicts was a planned speech by conservative gadfly Milo Yiannopolous on February 1. A "black bloc"—black-clad and masked anarchists who wanted to break windows, trash cars and, in some cases, engage in street fighting

An Antifa black bloc rioting in Berkeley, California (April 15, 2017)

with the police—of approximately 150 Antifa militants joined an already agitated protest outside the venue, and carnage ensued.

According to Wikipedia:

> The interrupting protesters claimed to be antifa activists and members of the left-wing group By Any Means Necessary. The group of interrupting protestors set fires, damaged property, threw fireworks, attacked members of the crowd, and threw rocks at the police.[45] Within twenty minutes of the start of the violence, the Yiannopoulos event was officially canceled by the university police department due to security concerns, and protesters were ordered to disperse. The interrupting protesters continued for several hours afterwards, with some protesters moving into downtown Berkeley to break windows at several banks, a Starbucks, a Target, a Sprint store, and a T-Mobile store. Among those assaulted were a Syrian Muslim, who was pepper sprayed and hit with a rod by an interrupting protester who said "You look like a Nazi," and Kiara Robles, who was pepper sprayed while being interviewed by a TV reporter. One person was arrested for failure to disperse, and there was an estimated $100,000 in damage.

The mutation into the first actual "Battle of Berkeley" occurred on April 15, surrounding a pro-Trump free speech event held in Martin Luther King Jr. Civic Center Park by the Oath Keepers, a group of ex-cop and military veterans purportedly dedicated to defending the Constitution. The event included popular dissident right livestreamers like Brittany Pettibone and Lauren Southern, whose livestreams vastly increased public viewing of the event and injected an intriguing dose of sex appeal. This was also the first public event I'd noticed incorporating elements of the alt-right, who could be recognized by things like cardboard signs depicting Pepe the Frog, or defensive

---

[45] nytimes.com/2017/02/02/us/university-california-berkeley-free-speech-milo-yiannopoulos.html

shields emblazoned with a Black Sun, or *sonnenrad*, an esoteric symbol from Germanic folklore which was later used by SS-leader Heinrich Himmler.

What should be understood is that this was the most radical tip of the dissident right spear. There were many others in the milieu who could be described as conservative Republicans, MAGA Trump supporters, and many derisively referred to as "alt-light," who agreed with many of the alt-right's critiques of anti-Whitism and "social justice," but whose rhetoric was much more moderate on Blacks, Jews, and other racial groups. At most times depicted in this book, I fell squarely into the latter group.

An Antifa black bloc arrived at Martin Luther King Jr. Civic Center Park intent on disrupting the demonstration by any means necessary, including violence. The event exploded into what appeared to be a war zone live and in color on an American street. Fireworks, smoke bombs, pepper spray, and other projectiles were flying and exploding everywhere, while hundreds of cell phone cameras livestreamed the action from every angle, sometimes running down the street like the camera in a Hollywood war film. According to the *Los Angeles Times*: "Both groups threw rocks and sticks at each other and used a large trash bin as a battering ram as the crowd moved around the perimeter of the park." Eleven people were injured, six of whom were hospitalized, including one person who was stabbed. Police "seized a handful of cans of peppers [sic] spray, some knives, and dozens of sign and flag poles, skateboards, and other blunt objects" from members of the crowd. Twenty people were arrested.[46]

Two individual incidents of violence were particularly noteworthy and deserve attention here. The first was an attack involving a radical Diablo Valley College professor named Eric Clanton. Wearing a black hoodie and sunglasses, with his face covered in a bandana, Clanton approached a right-wing protester addressing the media and smashed him over the head with a metal bike lock. The victim collapsed, bleeding profusely. Spoiler alert: Clanton received no jail time, only

---

[46] latimes.com/local/lanow/la-me-ln-berkeley-trump-rally-20170415-story.html

probation, for what was unarguably an act of attempted murder. Every alt-right and alt-light protester in the country saw that—if they were still brave enough to attend protests in 2017—they needed to take precautions to keep from being murdered by the growing army of Eric Clantons attacking protesters at public events.

The second incident involved a dreadlocked antifascist woman named Louise Rosealma, but better known online by the nickname "Moldylocks." Moldylocks was throwing glass bottles into a packed crowd of humanity when a sharp-dressed young man lunged out of the crowd and punched her square in the jaw, stopping the attack. That man was Nathan Damigo, leader of the most prominent alt-right and White Nationalist group in the country, Identity Evropa (IE).

After repeated incidents of violence against nonviolent speakers, several Batman-like heroic vigilantes emerged to fight back against Berkeley-area Antifa, e.g., John Turano (aka Based Spartan), a muscular behemoth in replica Spartan armor and Corinthian helmet. The most popular was Kyle Chapman (aka Based Stickman), another jacked, muscular dude who wore a breathing mask and carried a (you guessed it) large stick which he used to beat back Antifa assailants.

Following the success of my exposé on Wes Bellamy, I began freelance writing for several conservative outlets including Chuck Johnson's GotNews, Peter Brimelow's VDARE, and Tucker Carlson's *The Daily Caller*. In my ambition to raise my value as a journalist, I flew myself out to Berkeley, California, to cover a planned Ann Coulter speech at UC Berkeley originally scheduled for April 27. It looked primed to be the next explosive flashpoint. Although Coulter's speech was ultimately canceled due to threats of violence, I attended an alternative rally set up where comedian Gavin McInnes read Coulter's planned speech. It was also a networking opportunity to meet Lauren Southern, McInnes, Damigo, Based Stickman, and prominent *TRS* podcast network host John Ramondetta, known by the sobriquet of Johnny Monoxide.

Although no riots broke out, hundreds of Antifa arrived to disrupt the rally. The tension was palpable. Across the street from the plaza, a long line of Berkeley Police stood between them and us. Both sides

Kyle Chapman aka Based Stickman (April 27, 2017)

amassed on the sidewalks opposite one another, like two ancient armies on the cusp of battle. Occasionally, projectiles and pepper spray made their way from one side to the other, but the danger was exciting and there were clearly a lot of young men having a great time facing down their foes in the streets. There was an exciting sense on those streets, that free speech was not some dusty old platitude but something living and vibrant that patriotic young men would face danger to preserve. It seemed like we had the moral high ground and the claim to American values and tradition. I think of the words of Hunter S. Thompson describing the end of the hippy movement in *Fear and Loathing in Las Vegas*:

"So now, less than five years later, you can go up on a steep hill in Las Vegas and look West, and with the right kind of eyes you can almost see the high-water mark—that place where the wave finally broke and rolled back."

That wave we were riding was about to crash . . . hard . . . and recede back into the ocean.

My most significant contact during the trip to Berkeley was with Ramondetta, who I got together with for beers and conversation. Ramondetta was co-host of a show called *The Paranormies*, hosted on Mike Enoch's *TRS* radio network. Ramondetta's schtick was paranormal and conspiracy theory mixed with White Nationalism. He would go on to be one of the invited speakers at UTR.

Meeting Richard Spencer and the DeploraBall

The story of how I met Richard Spencer is so incredible it had to have been fate. One day, I casually mentioned Spencer and the alt-right to Phoebe Stevens, my girlfriend at the time, when she revealed that not only had she met Spencer but she also had his phone number. Apparently, she had attended the same UVA alumni event as Spencer. True to his reputation as a philanderer, he had hit on her and she ended up taking his number. According to her it never went any further. Regardless, I convinced her to share the number with me. I don't know that I ever would have contacted Spencer without this freak occurrence. In any case, I remember steeling myself to call him up out of the blue one afternoon and introducing myself. I explained who I was and why I was calling. He was terse and suspicious. He apparently did not remember Stevens, but acknowledged that the encounter sounded like something he would have done. The story probably sounded suspicious but, in any event, truth is sometimes stranger than fiction.

I happened to be planning to attend a MAGA event by Cernovich called the DeploraBall at the National Press Club in Washington, D.C. on January 19, 2017. Knowing that Spencer's apartment was above a chocolate store nearby in historic Old Town Alexandria, Virginia, I suggested this would be a good opportunity to meet up and discuss shared objectives. He agreed and I left the conversation excited that I might finally meet the Great White Hope I'd been searching for.

As the DeploraBall approached there was drama surrounding Project Veritas' exposure of an amateur terror plot by the D.C. Antifascist Coalition. After publication of the Veritas video, the Metropolitan Police Department of the District of Columbia (MPDC) arrested Scott R. Charney, 34, of Northwest Washington, for conspiracy to commit assault for a planned "acid attack." Charney's apparent plan was to sabotage the sprinkler system in the National Press Club to release butyric acid instead of water. Butyric acid is commonly used by the Anarchist Cookbook types to make stink bombs but, according to the World Health Organization, can cause potentially serious symptoms such as blisters, labored breathing, abdominal pain, shock, or collapse. It is also a combustible chemical, which could have tragic consequences in proximity to candles or cigarette lighters.

In any case, I drove up to Alexandria in my best cheap suit and called Spencer after a quick lunch at a local Indian restaurant. Old Town was a cute little neighborhood with trendy restaurants, lots of White people, red-bricked Colonial-era architecture, and lefty politics. In other words, it was a lot like Charlottesville. I walked around the side of the Blüprint Chocolatier on King Street, the main drag in Alexandria. Behind the sweets shop was a locked gate with security cameras beaming down from overhead. It was easy to see why someone paranoid about his privacy and safety would want to live there.

I was nervous like I always am when meeting new people and it was very unlike me to speak with someone who had been lauded with rounds of Nazi salutes. The meeting was not particularly eventful and I didn't get a good impression of Spencer. He was, as usual, dressed sharply. He sported the now-infamous hairdo, known as "the fashy" (a play on fascist), close shaved around the side of the head with a medium length crop of side-combed hair on top. Despite planning the visit with him in advance, he had set up a simultaneous video interview with two journalists, one of whom I now recognize as alt-right broadcaster James Allsup. Pretty much the entire time Spencer was preening and pontificating for Allsup's camera. I sat on the stairs in his apartment but barely said but a few words to Spencer. What I did say, Spencer did not seem to care about. I got the sense he was a cold and narcissistic person. On the other hand, like most narcissists, he was quite confident in himself, which is often a prerequisite for a movement figurehead. He also seemed intelligent, although I didn't agree with most of his positions, which seemed rather cold and heartless to me. The incident where Spencer was punched happened the very next day during the inauguration. Since Spencer said he was being interviewed by "two journalists from Stateless Media" at the time, I suspect this was Allsup and his cohort.

When I arrived outside the National Press Club for the DeploraBall that evening, there was a virtual army of angry, black-clad anarchists outside the venue howling at the thin line of MPDC protecting the entrance. It was like the crowd of Jews and Romans demanding Pontius Pilate hand over Jesus Christ, or maybe a bit of the orc hordes preparing for war in Lord of the Rings.

An Antifa mob gathered outside the DeploraBall at the National Press Club (January 19, 2017)

But a very small number of police was, for the most part, able to keep them from attacking attendees, a notable exception being a fist fight that broke out with Proud Boys founder Gavin McInnes. Inside the opulent soiree filled with booze and hors d'oeuvres, I met Mike Cernovich, firebrand "pharma bro" Martin Shkreli, numerous conservative journalists, and had my first actual conversations with Lauren Southern and the aforementioned McInnes. Not bad.

THE ALT-RIGHT'S SYRIAN MISSILE STRIKES PROTEST

On April 4, 2017, a chemical weapons attack occurred in the Syrian town of Khan Shaykhun, which killed at least 89 people and injured more than 541. Various governments including the U.S. and Israel attributed the attack to the government of Syrian president Bashar al-Assad. Assad, along with allies such as Russia, vehemently denied the charges and blamed U.S.-backed rebel groups. Whatever the case might be, to many of us who voted for Trump in large part because we didn't want the U.S. involved in foreign conflicts with limited strategic interest to our country, we saw echoes of the Iraq War WMDs canard. On April 7, the Trump administration launched 59 Tomahawk cruise missiles at the Assad-controlled Shayrat Airbase in Syria. Many in the alt-right, including myself, were outraged and concerned about mission creep into yet another Middle East war.

Enoch and Spencer announced they would be holding an anti-war protest at Lafayette Square on April 9, and I decided to go cover the event for *The Daily Caller*. Although the *Caller* ended up already having journalists on the scene with dibs on coverage, I posted the report to my website. Here is a portion:

> Spencer, a proponent of ethnic nationalism, invited attendees by Twitter and YouTube to Lafayette Square in front of the White House for a "peaceful gathering against further

Richard Spencer and Mike Enoch protest in Lafayette Square

military intervention in Syria." Spencer emphasized that the 59 Tomahawk missiles fired by the Trump administration into the Shayrat military base in Syria could be only the beginning and that voters should, "tell Donald Trump unequivocally: not in our name. No more Neocon wars" before it's too late.

When asked by reporters and Spencer himself about their perspective on the missile strikes, various Antifa protestors declined to comment. One Antifa supporter told me that he did not support the missile strikes but also did not support the alt-right because, "they actually support Assad and support the genocide." When asked what his solution to the Syrian conflict would be the Antifa activist replied, "Implement full Communism . . . seize the means of production." When asked how Communism could be implemented during a full-blown civil war he declined to comment. Another attendee on the Antifa side was infamous Disrupt J20 activist Paul "Luke" Kuhn who was caught on tape by Project Veritas planning to gas the

DeploraBall with butyric acid. He also declined comment and ran from the camera.

During the rally Spencer and the alt-right chanted "America first," "Take a shower," "Fire Kushner," and "Build walls, not wars." The Antifa counter-protestors shouted back "Fuck you, Nazis" and "No Nazis, no KKK, no fascists USA."

Towards the end of the rally events turned violent. One Antifa protestor broke through Spencer's line of bodyguards to throw glitter on his face and shoulders. An alt-right supporter tackled the Antifa to the ground and exchanged blows.

As Spencer and his associates made their exit from Lafayette they were chased down the street by Antifa. At one point Spencer made it into a cab only to be assaulted by a mob beating on the windows with their fists. One man opened the trunk of the vehicle and tried to reach for Spencer before Spencer's crew exited the vehicle and ran for a mile or more from pursuers before finally making their escape in another cab.

The alt-right supporter who tackled the glitterbombing Antifa was a short, stocky young man sporting a fashy haircut. Like other members of Damigo's Identity Evropa, he donned a white collared shirt and khaki pants at public events. Elliott Kline, or as we knew him at the time, Eli Mosley, would turn out to be an absolutely critical player in the UTR story, although omitted from the mostly clueless mainstream narratives of what transpired.

After a pulse-pounding taxicab escape from Antifa pounding on car windows and blocking street thoroughfares, Spencer, Enoch, Mosley, and a crew of about 20 supporters reconvened back at Spencer's Alexandria apartment for an after-party. The vibe at Spencer's pad reminded me of the UVA fraternity parties I used to drive up from Richmond to attend during my college years. There were plastic cups and cheap beer cans strewn around the apartment. In lieu of Bob Marley or drinking game posters at Spencer's apartment, a single

German Chancellor Adolf Hitler during a planning conference at the Berghof (July 1940)

poster of Hitler and his entourage at the Berghof in July 1940 adorned a wall in the kitchen next to a shelf with various books for sale from authors like Jared Taylor and Kevin MacDonald. (By this point there was no denying that the alt-right had an affinity for Nazism. Although I found it distasteful, I did not take it seriously. These were Americans engaging in constitutionally protected speech activity, some of which I strongly agreed with. There is no equating the alt-right with individuals who actually prosecuted World War II (WWII) in in my opinion. Along with my commitment to free speech, I fatefully pressed forward with our alliance.) The top floor exited onto a spacious open-air balcony with a fantastic view of Downtown Alexandria. There were lots of both men and women drinking and having a great time. Spencer and Enoch posed for photographs together in what seemed to be the best of times for the two men.

But I continued to get a bad vibe from Spencer. It is perhaps to my eternal damnation that I did not listen to my gut. There was something cold, elitist, and sociopathic about him, like a shark. I recall standing in a circle with him on the balcony and expressing my displeasure with the impact mass immigration from the U.S.-Mexico border was having on blue-collar, White Americans like myself. Spencer waved my concerns off dismissively: "I'm not concerned at all about those people. Who cares about workers with some shitty minimum wage jobs. I'm concerned about the White-collar tech jobs we're losing to people from India."

It was on this occasion that I first became acquainted with Mosley, who presented himself as an intelligent, enthusiastic, and hyper-ambitious alt-right organizer and foot soldier. He spoke a mile-a-minute with excitement about all the attention he was getting for his tackle of the glitterbomber for which he was being memed online and receiving plaudits from influential leaders like Spencer and *The Daily Stormer* founder Andrew Anglin. Mosley seemed to be incredibly status conscious. It didn't take long for him to brag about his credentials as a pseudonymous writer for Anglin's *Stormer*, and his importance as an indispensable consigliere to both Spencer and Enoch.

Spencer and Mosley were abuzz with excitement about booking speaking engagements at various college universities. He had one coming up at Auburn University and was looking for more students and organizations to invite him to other campuses. When I had a free moment, I suggested to Mosley that there was a lot of potential in making hay about the Charlottesville monument issue and Bellamy's tweets. To my shock, he had already discussed plans for a protest in Charlottesville with Spencer. Once again, it seemed like a kind of destiny. What were the chances?

I arranged to cover their upcoming protest in May for *The Daily Caller* and was allowed into a group chat where they discussed the event. But there would be three more major milestones before the alt-right first came to Charlottesville.

Richard Spencer Speaks at Auburn University

Richard Spencer had been invited to speak at Auburn University in Alabama on April 18 by graduate student Cameron Padgett. The university attempted to bar Spencer from speaking and were hit with a First Amendment lawsuit in federal court, filed by renowned White Nationalist Sam Dickson. U.S. District Court Judge W. Keith granted an injunction, citing in his ruling that, "While Mr. Spencer's beliefs and message are controversial, Auburn presented no evidence that Mr. Spencer advocates violence."

During a two-hour speech, Spencer talked about things like the danger of diversity as "a way of bringing to an end a nation and a culture." "There would be no history without us," he said, prompting shouts from the crowd. "The alt-right is really about putting Humpty Dumpty back together again."

In response to a question from a Black female student, Spencer replied: "You have an identity. You're part of a story that I can't understand. And I'm part of a story that you can't understand. We're fundamentally different and that's what makes the world beautiful. I don't want to turn everyone into just some individual. I want you to have your history. I want you to have your meaning. That's true diversity. That's what makes the world beautiful. But part of what makes the world beautiful is Whites understanding who we are. What makes us special."

Hundreds of protesters congregated outside the venue in Foy Hall. There was some violence and three arrests, but police protected the event and Spencer was allowed to speak.[47] Joining him at the event were Mosley and Enoch, who was also allowed time to speak.[48] Referencing the protests outside Enoch asked: "Why are these people out here getting so violent just because White people want to stand up and say we have a collective interest? We have a collective right to represent our interests and we're going to do it. Why of all peoples are we uniquely denied this right? And we're not going to be denied it anymore."

---

[47] cnn.com/2017/04/18/politics/auburn-richard-spencer-protests
[48] vimeo.com/249497013

The Nationalist Demonstration in Pikeville, Kentucky

The most hardcore right-wing and antisemitic groups who would go on to attend UTR had another major demonstration in Pikeville, Kentucky, on April 29, 2017. League of the South (LoS), Traditionalist Worker Party (TWP), National Socialist Movement (NSM), and Vanguard America, were collectively known as the Nationalist Alliance. These groups differentiated themselves from the alt-right, which they saw as too moderate and bourgeoisie, with the moniker of Hard Right.

From left: Michael Hill, Matt Heimbach, and Jeff Schoep in Pikeville, Kentucky (April 29, 2017)

Several of the speakers at this event would be in attendance at UTR: for example, TWP leader Matthew Heimbach, NSM leader Jeff Schoep, League leader Michael Hill, and radio shock jock Christopher Cantwell, host of the program, *The Radical Agenda*.

The most important thing that came out of the Pikeville protest was a sense that small-town authorities were capable of handling controversial protests. Police kept the demonstrators safely enclosed behind barricades where they waved flags and gave speeches. Counter-protesters shouted at them from the sidelines but never came close enough to engage in violence. This gave everyone involved a high degree of confidence in the right, and ability, to safely protest leading into Charlottesville.

The Battle of New Orleans

An important but oft-forgotten milestone on the action-packed 2017 road to Charlottesville was a series of protests on May 7, 2017, in Louisiana known as The Battle of New Orleans. The key players in this drama were the City of New Orleans (NOLA), Antifa, and radical Black activists who were trying to remove Confederate monuments on the one hand, and Confederate heritage groups and activists on the other.

New Orleans Mayor Mitch Landrieu had ordered the removal of four Confederate era monuments back in 2015, egged on by radical anti-monument groups like Take 'Em Down NOLA. Early on the morning of April 24, 2017, under cover of night, masked construction workers broke in half and carted away three statues starting with The Battle of Liberty Place monument. The area around the statue was fenced off, guarded by a New Orleans Police Department squad and protected by overhead snipers. After they were done, even the names inscribed at the base of the statue to commemorate the dead had been chiseled away, leaving only a blemished stump of concrete. After this incident, dedicated monument defenders began guarding other NOLA Confederate monuments day and night, in hopes they could prevent the city from destroying them.

Hostilities broke out on May 1, 2017. As Brad Griffin wrote in *Occidental Dissent*: ". . . the Battle of New Orleans was provoked by the truckload of Antifa who showed up to attack Black Rebel, Arlene Barnum and the Confederate heritage activists at the Jefferson Davis monument last Monday. They also vandalized the P.G.T. Beauregard monument on May Day and wrote an article about it on ItsGoingDown.org to celebrate their triumph." Andrew Duncomb, aka "Black Rebel," was a controversy-loving Black Confederate heritage supporter who was unafraid to throw down with Antifa. Arlene Barnum was a Black female Confederate heritage supporter. Fearless of controversy herself, she was perhaps less able or willing to engage in the same fisticuffs as Duncomb. A contingent of Antifa militants arrived to confront the monument protesters gathered around the mid-city Jefferson Davis monument in a large green military truck with a banner reading, FUCK OFF NAZI SCUM!

Throughout an evening-long protest, dozens of Confederate heritage supporters, mostly White, came and went from the front of the Jefferson Davis monument. Left-wing protesters were throwing bottles and other projectiles from the other side of a police protection line. But some more explosive brawls did break out. At one point, a White male protester lunged into the Confederate side and grappled for one end of a flag pole. After several seconds of vicious struggle,

Antifa militants from New Orleans in an armored military truck (May 1, 2017)

Black Rebel came in from the side and threw a hail-Mary punch against the side of the Antifa's face. "Cut it out!" a man in the crowd shouted. A thin, White man with a long white beard wearing a Confederate battle flag t-shirt shouted to a fat, White female protester: "You don't like freedom of speech now!" "That doesn't mean anything anymore!" she shouted back.[49] Antifa burned Confederate flags and the Confederates burned Antifa flags right back at them. A pro-monument demonstrator, Eileen Marcinkowski, whose pelvis was crushed in a May 4 car accident and was bound to a wheelchair, was maced by Antifa. "This woman comes across the road screaming and spraying mace. There was no provocation and she didn't seem to be trying to spray anyone in particular. I felt an extreme burning that I never felt before in my life. My lips today are still tingling and swollen." Eileen went on to explain that one protester also threw a broken glass bottle that bounced off the side of her wheelchair. Five arrests were made that evening, for charges ranging from disturbing the peace to crossing a police cordon and public intoxication. Two of those arrests were from the Confederate supporters. None of the arrests were due to vandalism or the assault on the wheelchair victim.

The online community exploded in outrage. Several dueling protests were scheduled surrounding the NOLA Confederate monuments on May 7. Two of the most prominent were organized by the Antifa group Take 'Em Down NOLA and a rival patriot event by the Alt-Knights, a group affiliated with Kyle Chapman. Once the Internet became involved you had the full carnival sideshow of online political culture: patriots, Antifa, Confederates, livestreaming White rapper and Trump booster Baked Alaska, angry Blacks, and Marxist liberals alike. The Battle of New Orleans even had its own version of Based Spartan, wearing plastic Roman-style body armor and draped in an American flag cape. The wannabe Roman centurion was dubbed the "Cuck Knight"[50] after getting into a brawl with monument supporters. Although he initially appeared to be anti-Antifa, he bizarrely began

---

[49] youtube.com/watch?v=v4wmpCko4UI
[50] Cuck is a term popularized online for Whites who had sold out their people and culture.

improvising anti-racist speeches about his Jewish ancestry, biracial children, and how everyone should ditch Confederate symbolism and unite under the American flag. The Cuck Knight seemed to be chasing Internet celebrity because he had traveled all the way from California and had a friend filming him as he gave this pompous Captain America LARPing[51] speech. The Confederates mercilessly taunted the self-important buffoon until he became so angry that he charged into them like a rhinoceros and tried to damage a Confederate flag. The good ol' boys with the flags promptly knocked him on his ass, where he curled up clutching his bleeding head. Some of these country-strong good ol' boys were League of the South members, an organization that would end up playing a critical role at Charlottesville.

League of the South, originally The Southern League, was formed in 1994 in Tuskaloosa, Alabama, by 28 Southern partisans including Michael Hill, professor of British history at Stillman College, a historically Black university. Its charter is Southern Nationalism and it advocates for the secession and independence of a free South. The League is an unapologetically pro-White organization, which begs the question why Dr. Hill taught at a Black university. When I asked him this directly, he responded that he simply, "needed the money." Fair enough. The League's manifesto notes that "in a time when all cultures are celebrated and protected and considerable social pressure is brought to bear on anything that resembles racism, Southerners are still routinely portrayed as 'rednecks' or 'crackers' in movies and on television, and it is still socially acceptable to refer to them as such." LoS boasted having around 10,000 members in 20 states, including Virginia, and I'd become acquainted with several members who were also active with the Virginia Flaggers. It was my impression there was a wide variety of ideology and temperament within the group, from pretty mainstream to quite radical. Both Hill and his top lieutenant Michael Tubbs were in attendance at the May 7 event in NOLA.

---

[51] LARP = Live Action Roleplaying

THE ALT-RIGHT COMES TO CHARLOTTESVILLE

The May 13 demonstration was envisioned as a three-part event with a daytime demonstration in Jackson Park, a night-time demonstration in Lee Park illuminated by torchlight, and a luncheon the following afternoon on May 14.

The daytime event included speeches by Spencer, Enoch, Damigo, and Georgia attorney Dickson, who was riding high after representing Spencer in his successful Auburn University injunction case. Dickson was of an older generation than the other attendees and had been an intellectual powerhouse of the White identity movement for years, for example, in his role as keynote speaker at every one of Jared Taylor's *American Renaissance* conferences since they began in 1994.

The first alt-right torch demonstration in Lee Park (May 13, 2017)

What's more, Dickson was a proud Southerner whose papers, including "Shattering the Icon of Abraham Lincoln," were foundational works of historical revisionism in the Southern Nationalist cause. Mainstream detractors criticize him for defending members of the Ku Klux Klan (KKK), but these criticisms highlight the hypocrisy at the heart of the American "justice" system. Aren't even the most despised deserving of a vigorous legal defense? Hearing Dickson's account of how these trials played out as nothing more than corrupt show trials, one must surmise the answer is "no."

Most of the more than a hundred protesters in attendance were members of Damigo's Identity Evropa. They wore the formal Identity Evropa uniform of white polo shirts and khaki pants for men, and white sundresses for women. Some carried Confederate flags, Betsy Ross flags, or picket signs with an image of the Robert E. Lee monument. Some had even printed out large copies of Wes Bellamy's anti-White tweets on placards. Some laughs were had by the group as they marched past Lee Park, which ironically was holding a multiculturalism festival called Festival of Cultures. When they arrived in Jackson Park, some of the Identity Evropa activists unfurled a banner that said You Will Not Replace Us and set off colored grey and green smoke flares for dramatic effect.

Spencer spoke first: "Ladies and Gentlemen, we are here for two reasons. We are here to say no . . . no more attacks on our heritage, on our identity, no more attacks on us as a people. But we are also here to say yes . . . yes, we are going to occupy space. You will not replace us." And later: "I want to live in a world of gods and heroes like Robert E. Lee and Stonewall Jackson. I want to live in a world of White men who created our civilization." Damigo implored the crowd to remember the stakes: "This fight is essentially a demographic struggle for the future of Western civilization."

A local Black alt-right activist named Emerson Stern was in attendance and took selfies with Spencer and the others. When asked why he was taking selfies with a White Nationalist, Stern told me: "Spencer speaks what everyone is thinking but afraid to say out loud." I knew Stern as "Meme Alert," a YouTube and Twitter personality online. For those wondering why a Black man would be a fan of the alt-right, I can only say that Stern was a strange bird indeed. He was either a self-hating Black or a mischief maker addicted to aggressively trolling the humorless moral authorities in Charlottesville. He was a friend and collaborator but he could also be a major pain in the ass. One time he created a YouTube video with a parody song that an opening title card claimed was "written by Jason Kessler." The video involved a very dark-skinned Black man in an orange prison jumpsuit being compared to an ape. This caused *Cville Weekly* journalist Lisa Provence to take this as literal and publish an article claiming that I was comparing the Black prison population to simians. Eventually this was taken down but not before critical damage was done to my reputation by the media smear machine.

Speaking of memes, a humorous and embarrassing moment occurred for Spencer when I took a photo of him during the assembly and posted it to Twitter. I'd intended it to hype the event in all seriousness but the photo unintentionally appeared to show Spencer looking bloated with an uncomfortable grimace on his face. This image took off like wildfire and was memed to make Spencer look more absurd, for instance by elongating his cranium to look like a conehead. I, and many others, have had enormous laughs over it ever since.

As the meeting wound down, I noticed SURJ leader Joe Starsia slinking around the periphery of the event. This could only mean he was calling in his thugs for reinforcement. "You have an Antifa coming here now," I warned. The crowd immediately turned to face him with a chant of, "Cuck! Cuck! Cuck!" rousing in unison. But perhaps their second chant, "Trust fund commies, off our streets!" was even more apropos. He was soon joined by the "Bearded Lady," Sara Tansey. After getting a whiff of her hormone-intensified body odor, the crowd humorously regaled with chants of "Take a shower! Take a shower," to the beat of the snare drum slung around IE member Dave Reilly's shoulders.

Around 8:30 PM, that night, a group consisting of perhaps 200 activists regrouped in McGuffey Park about a block away from Lee Park in downtown Charlottesville. Everyone was still clad in their

CHARLOTTESVILLE AND THE DEATH OF FREE SPEECH

Spencer looking uncomfortable in Jackson Park (above)

The Spencer "conehead" meme

white polos and sundresses, but with the unique distinction of also carrying tiki torches, which were lit as the demonstrators solemnly, but enthusiastically, grouped in a marching line. I, however carried my smartphone rather than a tiki. I was not an activist at this demonstration but covering it in my capacity as a journalist for *The Daily Caller*.[52]

There has been much controversy surrounding the use of tikis, likening it to Klan or Nuremberg rallies. However, the tikis were the brainchild of Identity Evropa activist Evan Thomas, who explained to me at the time that they symbolized, "a torch-lit funeral procession for the fallen dead. This has a long and rich tradition in European cultures."

As the demonstration kicked off and the march began to historic Lee Park, the beauty of my city by candlelight had never been more striking. As the roughly 150 demonstrators filed into the park, there was an electric feeling of being part of history and a bit of that mischievous joy children feel playing hide and seek games in the dark. The Lee monument had never looked more impressive than it did that night in the flicker of torchlight. With the demonstrators gathered round, there was an air of some ancient ritual taking place, perhaps with the bronze statue as an altar to the old gods of Europe. Dickson spoke first, the flames of sacrifice roaring around him. He decried "brother wars" like the American Civil War and called for Whites to unite in brotherhood and unity. It was a stirring call to action. Dickson, who speaks fluent Russian, criticized the notion that America's foreign enemies are more significant than the enemies within. This led the crowd to spontaneously chant, "Russia is our friend!" Other chants heard that night were, "No more brother wars!" and "You will not replace us!"

As the event was about to end, there was a scare of violence and some drama. A few harmless passersby had stopped to witness the rally, including *Daily Progress* reporter Alison Wrabel. Less welcome was a dirty, foul smelling Antifa named Jordan McNeish. McNeish, who has a criminal record a mile long, and a documented history of heroin abuse, stormed into the park reeking of booze.[53]

---

[52] archive.is/tugLb
[53] c-ville.com/finding-the-helpers-locals-offer-addiction-support

CHARLOTTESVILLE AND THE DEATH OF FREE SPEECH

Attorney Sam Dickson (left) addresses protesters

Mugshot of Antifa Jordan McNeish after his arrest for assault (May 14, 2017)

Likely, he'd been drinking and doing drugs around the bars downtown when he heard the chanting and saw the flames. He rushed up to one of the demonstrators and chest bumped him, screaming in his face like he was about to explode. McNeish threw a punch and was immediately smashed over the head and shoulders by several tiki torches until he retreated in a punch-drunk daze. The entire incident happened so fast that few observed it, and it has generally been forgotten in accounts of the demonstration that night.

The press coverage from Wrabel, my reporting in the *Caller*, and livestreams of the event caused an international sensation. Even then, the local authoritarians were calling on the demonstrators to be jailed based on a twisted interpretation of Virginia's former cross burning statute prohibiting "burning an object with intent to intimidate." But City spokesperson Miriam Dickler shot that interpretation of the law down as wishful thinking: "While we prefer protesters get permits like any other event, such assemblies are protected by the First Amendment, and we do not interfere unless we perceive a legal or safety issue."

That night a wild party was held at an Airbnb home at the end of a quiet cul-de-sac on Ramblewood Drive in Charlottesville. Enoch was there holding court as his admirers listened to him wax philosophical about his political beliefs. Spencer, as always, seemed to be trying to relive or recapture his college days with heavy drinking and casual sex. Mosley's girlfriend at the time, an IE activist named Samantha Froelich, was in attendance and ended up going home with Spencer that night instead of her boyfriend. It was a constant pattern with Spencer of disrespecting his subordinates by stealing their girlfriends.

The most significant and infamous moment of the night occurred after a rendition of "Tomorrow Belongs to Me," a song from the hit TV series adaptation of Phillip K. Dick's *The Man in the High Castle*. The premise of the show is depicting an alternate timeline where the Nazis won WWII and control America.

A representative passage of the song goes:

Oh, Fatherland, Fatherland show us the sign
Your children have waited to see

The morning will come when the world is mine
Tomorrow belongs, tomorrow belongs
Tomorrow belongs to me

Dozens in the crowd sung in unison; drunken, sloppy, but passionately. At the end of the song, so overcome with emotion was the crowd they spontaneously burst into chants of *Sieg heil! Sieg heil!* with arms outstretched into Roman salutes. Spencer was among them, so enthusiastic that his once carefully manicured hair swung violently around his head. The chants were so loud that I worried about the neighbors hearing it and calling the police.

For my part I was deeply embarrassed. I was pro-White but had no affinity for Nazism. Nor was I really what you'd call an antisemite at that time. For many years I believed I was the only one in that crowd who did not participate in the chants. My head was down and I hid inside myself until it was over. Years later I'd come to find out that Identity Evropa member Dave Reilly also abstained and, in fact, surreptitiously recorded the chants using his cell phone.[54] It would not be the last time Reilly secretly recorded Spencer engaging in embarrassing activity. The party was eventually broken up when the police did indeed respond to a noise complaint due to the raucous chanting.

I was well and truly in way, way over my head and I knew it. But I needed bodies in the streets for my longed-for White civil rights movement. I naively thought these people had enough self-control to bottle up their less palatable extremist tendencies and advocate for the one thing that was a net positive in everyone's self-interest: White wellbeing. How foolish I was.

On May 14, the following afternoon, there was a luncheon organized by Mosley and Identity Evropa in a nearby park. There was a catered lunch buffet and several speeches by notables including Spencer and Dickson. At the time, I truthfully did not know who Dickson was, besides his legal victory for Spencer at Auburn.

---

[54] bitchute.com/video/iTWCQJAqWDZJ

Nevertheless, I was given a paper with a brief introductory speech by Mosley and asked to read it at the podium. Fake it till you make it, I thought. I read the speech convincingly and appropriately, I would retroactively endorse all of my remarks. It was also the first time I recall thinking about inviting the alt-right back to do another rally in Charlottesville. I was straddling a political chasm between the alt-right and the MAGA Republicans. On the one hand, I very much agreed with Peinovich and Spencer on the growing mistreatment of White people. But on the other hand, I wasn't yet convinced, or even interested in, their theories about Jews. I was in a similar position with the Republicans. I liked how under Trump they were moving to be anti-war and a better friend to the blue-collar and working-class White men no one else in politics seemed to give a damn about. I particularly agreed with Trump's views on immigration restriction. We are losing our cultural and ethnic heritage because of socially devastating levels of foreign immigration. The demographic replacement of White people during my lifetime has been frightening. Not because there is anything wrong with these people necessarily. Many of them are very nice, I am sure. But they are coming in in such numbers that they're like an invasive species that will overwhelm the native population. We cannot take in this many foreign peoples simultaneously in every White nation on Earth and survive as a people demographically. No other people are subjugated to this treatment without charges of ethnic cleansing. Today, I might compare it to the occupation of Palestine by the Zionist Jews in Israel. The local Arabs were displaced by civilizationally transformative foreign immigration of Jews—from Europe, the U.S., and Russia, which spans the continents of Europe and Asia—until they became an oppressed second-class race living incarcerated on the wrong side of the ever-encroaching Israeli border.

However, the Republicans refused to actually talk about White people in the way that they would pander to every other identity group on Earth. Trump and the Republicans would make open appeals to Black voters, Hispanic voters, and even gays, but they would never explicitly claim to have policies to help blue-collar

White families, despite them being the plurality of the Republican voting base. So maybe if they could meet in the middle on the issue of White people standing up for their rights and heritage, we might have a Goldilocks area where things are just right: the alt-right restrains some of its more extreme political positions, and the Republicans act a little more bravely on behalf of their constituency. My original conception of the rally was to mix alt-right figures like Spencer with some more moderate alt-lighters like McInnes and Chapman.

Emerson Stern (right), a Black alt-right troll poses with Richard Spencer (May 13, 2017)

Mob Violence in Lee Park and a Wrongful Arrest

The evening of May 14, after the alt-right had all gone home, Charlottesville's left-wing activists including Bellamy, a local BLM leader named Don Gathers, and Joe Starsia led a candle-lit counter-protest against the alt-right in Lee Park. There was likely over 1,000 people in attendance, considering the entire park was so full the crowd overflowed into the streets, effectively shutting off the Downtown Mall to traffic that night. The activists had slung a large sheet over the Lee monument reading, Fuck White Supremacy! and many carried candles with lit flame. I watched it from the comfort and safety of my apartment, thanks to Emerson Stern, who was inside the crowd livestreaming the event with his smartphone. Going anywhere near that congregation would have been suicidally dangerous, like Frodo marching alone into Mordor to confront a horde of orcs.

But then the unexpected happened. One of the White leftists in the crowd recognized Stern, perhaps from the selfies he'd been taking with Spencer the day before. "Hey, that's Jason Kessler's friend!" one of them shouted to alert the others. Soon he was beset by several rabid members of the mob, faces contorted with anger and hatred, their bodies tensed in aggressive postures mere inches from Stern's face like a pack of gorillas about to strike. Many of the speeches that night had centered on platitudes like, "Love overcoming hate" and contrasting the "peace" of their candlelit protest with the alleged violence of our rhetoric. But, of course, there could only be peace with these people so long as they had absolute control and there was no longer even a single person with a minority viewpoint they could bludgeon into submission with harassment. I'd thought that by virtue of being a Black man, Stern would be immune from the danger within a woke mob. But as the livid White male leftists circled around him, I realized I was wrong and that he might be in grave danger. I'd been communicating with Stern online and sharing jokes for months. He was like a little brother to me. Without thinking of the danger or my personal safety, I swung my megaphone strap around my shoulders and marched out the door for Lee Park.

I arrived around 5-10 minutes later and walked a direct line in through the throngs of people to the center of the mob where Emerson was located. All of what transpired that night from this point forward was captured on video by Stern's livestream. There were murmurs in the crowd from those who recognized me and Stern caught wind: "Kessler's here!" he exclaimed. The first thing I said to him was: "I came for you, Emerson," and "We need to get you out of here." I tried to say more about how I had been watching his livestream and was concerned for his safety, but members of the crowd were shouting over me, trying to drown me out. This was what I had brought my electronic bullhorn for. I clicked the button and started speaking, even louder than the hecklers this time. But then they started getting handsy and frantic. Some of them tried to smother the front of the bullhorn while others were much less squeamish about using force and started slapping at me and the device. It wasn't like I was trying to give a political speech. I was just trying to talk with my friend. But these people weren't about to let me say *anything*. It was a physical manifestation of a cancel mob and they wanted to censor my ability to say anything ever. I had another problem in that Stern did not seem to understand we needed to leave the park and I got separated from him by the surging crowd. The clear path of escape was backwards towards the Lee monument. But once I turned in that direction, I saw the despicable FUCK WHITE SUPREMACY! banner they'd hung from

Kessler attempting to speak in Lee Park; Tyler Magill screams behind him

Lee, and was filled with righteous anger. In that moment I knew how Jesus must have felt when he saw moneylenders in the temple and wanted to turn over their tables. I grabbed one corner of the sheet and tugged it down like a sailor heaving the sail from a large mast. There was an audible gasp from the crowd. Another jolt of fury surged through the crowd and they rushed towards me. Immediately policemen stepped forward and declared that everyone had to leave the park. But it didn't seem like they had a plan beyond this to deal with crowd control.

There was basically only one direction that had any give whatsoever and that was in the direction of the public library. So, I crossed the street out of the park, but once I came to the outer wall of the library, I ran out of room and the crowd had boxed me in. With nothing else to do, I picked up my megaphone and started talking again. More slapping, pushing, and shoving at my device. I eventually saw a gap in their line and squeezed through, but no sooner had I made it out onto the street than a group of about 10 leftists locked arms and marched shoulder-to-shoulder, forming a human circle around me and trapping me inside. I had to escape, but how? I saw a small gap between two of the activists just large enough for me to squeeze through. I ducked and sprinted through but they constricted the circle on my way out to squeeze me and try to prevent me from leaving. I pulled through and then two Charlottesville Police officers grabbed me, twisted my arms behind my back, and cuffed me.

The "love not hate" and "fuck the police" crowd cheered when they realized I was being placed under arrest. They saw what it looked like when the state used its power to lock up their political enemies, and they liked it. The joy on their faces and ecstasy in their voices, to me, betrayed a totalitarian fanaticism to purge dissent. As I was in this defenseless state, the booze-soaked Antifa from the previous night, Jordan McNeish, walked up and spat in my face.

They said I was under arrest. I wanted to know what for! "Why am I being arrested?" I demanded. Neither of the officers seemed to be able to tell me, though I asked repeatedly. I was placed in the back of a squad car and driven to the jail just outside the city limits in Albemarle County. I partly wondered if they might have arrested me for my own safety or to prevent a riot. In fact, Stern had mused about the same theory towards the end of his livestream. As I sat there in the holding area waiting to be booked into the jail, I started getting the first weak excuses about why I had been arrested. The whole thing was very sketchy. The first explanation was that I had been arrested for using the megaphone because the decibels were too high. This didn't make sense because all of the politically powerful leftists like Bellamy, Gathers, and Starsia were also using electric bullhorns. It was clear to me that I had been arrested because of illegal criminalization of my speech and the reaction of the hostile crowd.

Regardless of whether the charges were "real" or not, they took my mugshot, which was very real. The same media that often refuses to show the mugshots of Black robbery and murder suspects had no such reservations about posting mine everywhere. It was front page on *The Daily Progress*, which was then re-used by other regional and national outlets, and the *Cville Weekly*, a free weekly newspaper distributed throughout the Charlottesville area.

This was the first attempt to smear me and associate me with criminality, or as an enemy of the state. The open, one-sided contempt the local media had for me was like Soviet propaganda towards a hated

The original flimsy rationale for Kessler's arrest was that using an electric bullhorn constituted a "noise violation," although Gathers, Bellamy, and Starsia used them the same night

dissident. Over the coming months and years, the media's belligerent propaganda painting me as a villain would gradually convince most of the city, even many conservatives, that I was always wrong or guilty in every situation. No more contemptible villain had ever walked the streets in Thomas Jefferson's city.

I posted bond and was able to return to my apartment later that night. In the coming days, the rationale for my arrest had apparently changed to some blend of "disorderly conduct" and, to my shock, "assault." Not only was this bizarre, vague charge against me real, but they had a leftist woman coming forward to say that I "shoved her to the ground." They showed me two conflicting police officer's reports. One, based on the officer's personal experience, backed up my story that I was surrounded by a hostile mob and was trying to escape. The other report, incorporating the leftist's testimony, claimed I had pushed the woman to the ground. I couldn't believe it. Emerson Stern had video recorded all of my activities around the park that night on his livestream. How in the world could they accuse me of something that didn't happen and could be disproven by videotape?

Some weeks later the charge would be declared *nolle prosequi* —Latin for "unwilling to pursue"—due to lack of any evidence whatsoever backing up the phony accusations. But by then, my First and Fourteenth Amendment rights had already been violated and I'd been branded a criminal in the media, who quietly swept the affair under the rug and didn't ask cops any tough questions about the bizarre made-up and dropped charges.

Unite the Right
is Conceived

I decided to call the upcoming event Unite the Right based on the fact that different segments of the American right-wing could come together around some shared principles. As I saw it at the time, White Nationalists were a little too extreme in some ways, like their coarse language and hostility to other racial groups, and the MAGA Republicans were motivated by a lot of similar issues, like illegal immigration, but were weak on explicitly defending White people. I felt like the two could meet in the middle in defense of White history and group interests, without necessarily attacking other races like Blacks and Jews. Originally, I wanted the speakers to include more moderate personalities like Gavin McInnes and Based Stickman, both Civic Nationalists. But all of the speakers who weren't explicit White Nationalists were scared to appear on the same ticket with more controversial personalities like Richard Spencer. In the end, my speakers were a who's who of the most controversial, attention-grabbing White Nationalists on the scene at the time. I didn't really know any of them that well or what they represented. I just thought they would create a good spectacle and be unafraid of advocating explicitly for White people and their history.

Throughout the month of May, I continued networking with individuals in the alt-right, Hard Right, alt-light, MAGA, and patriot movements about my plan for a united front free speech rally in Lee Park. My speakers' list was as follows:

- **Richard Spencer**, head of the National Policy Institute, niche

Internet celebrity and de facto leader of the alt-right.

- **Mike Enoch**, founder of *The Right Stuff* radio network and host of *The Daily Shoah*.
- **Augustus Sol Invictus** (born Austin Gillespie), one of the few personalities I have not mentioned up to this point. Invictus was a former 2016 Libertarian U.S. Senate candidate from Florida. He was then a leader in Kyle Chapman's Alt-Knights. Invictus was in many ways the most normal and likeable of our speakers. He was married with a family, employed as an attorney, and didn't have as big of an ego as some of the others.
- **Anthime Gionet (aka Baked Alaska)**, by far the most bizarre and cartoonish of the speakers. A White rapper with a mullet, living meme, and former BuzzFeed writer. Baked Alaska made his living from viewer donations made to his livestreams, including when he attended the Battle of New Orleans. Originally, Baked Alaska was an assistant to alt-light figures Yiannopolous and Cernovich. Shortly before the rally he made a hard right turn, associating with Spencer, making explicit appeals to White identity, and trolling Jewish activist Laura Loomer with memes of Trump executing her in a gas chamber. I only recall talking to him on the phone once before the rally. He

Internet personality Richard Spencer

UNITE THE RIGHT IS CONCEIVED

Mike "Enoch" Peinovich, host of The Daily Shoah

Attorney Augustus Sol Invictus (born: Austin Gillespie)

Anthime Gionet aka Baked Alaska

suspiciously kept asking me if I was "full 1488" like him. 1488 is code for the Fourteen Words and Heil Hitler. The Fourteen Words—"We must secure the existence of our people and a future for White children"—is a famous expression by militant, White Nationalist David Lane. 88 refers to H being the 8th letter of the alphabet, so HH means Heil Hitler. Gionet had previously participated in some shady online operations like creating memes telling Black, female Hillary Clinton supporters they could vote in the 2016 presidential election via text. A collaborator named Douglass Mackey would later be convicted of criminal election interference for this behavior, while Gionet was left alone. Following Charlottesville, Gionet would infamously attend the January 6 (J6) protest and storm Nancy Pelosi's office. The fact that Gionet was by far the most famous individual to breach the U.S. Capitol, and had also attended Charlottesville, seemed like a surefire indication he would be harshly prosecuted to make an example of him. Curiously, while others who entered the Capitol were levied multi-year sentences, Gionet received only a 60-day slap on the wrist. It soon became apparent why, when court transcripts revealed Gionet had agreed to cooperate with federal investigations of other protesters in exchange for the lenient sentence.[55] In reality, he'd already done more than anyone else to help the Federal Bureau of Investigation (FBI) apprehend J6 protesters. Still images from his livestream identifying protesters inside the Capitol building were printed on the sides of billboards and bus stops all around the Washington, D.C. area for months following J6 and posted online with calls for information leading to arrests. Ironically, given all this information, Gionet's most famous viral hit as his Baked Alaska persona was an autotuned rap called "We Love Our Cops." The lyrics go like this:

> *When I'm in a jam, when I'm in a jam*
> *I know that I can call up the Man*
> *Can call up the Man with the plan*

---

[55] x.com/MajstcSeagull/status/1592314753061646336

> *When I'm on the run, when I'm on the run*
> *All I gotta do is dial 9-1-1*
>
> *We love our cops, our law enforcement*
> *We love our military, they're important*

- **Pax Dickinson**, computer engineer affiliated with GotNews, an outlet I had written some articles for in the past. He had an outlaw swagger and caught my attention when he was photographed giving the middle finger while wearing a red Trump MAGA hat (very Johnny Cash at San Quentin prison). Dickinson was certainly the most alt-light of the bunch. The inclusion of Dickinson in the speakers list is sort of a vestigial tail of an evolutionary fork in the direction of White Nationalism and the American right generally. Prior to UTR, I was on a much more mainstream political trajectory with guest stints on programs like *InfoWars* and the *Gavin McInnes Show*. I was immediately attracted to writing for Chuck Johnson's GotNews because of his expose on *Rolling Stone* magazine's UVA rape hoaxer Jackie Coakley.[56] At the time I wrote now-prescient conservative articles on how Russia did not have to be a geopolitical enemy of the U.S. and President Trump could bring about a golden age of relations through his soft touch with strong men like Vladmir Putin. Johnson placed me in a Slack chat with a number of public and private powerhouses at the intersection of alt-right/alt-light politics and technology. Dickinson had joined Johnson ventures GotNews and WeSearchr, a crowdfunding platform, after leaving his position at Business Insider in 2013. Also in the chat were various influencers like Baked Alaska, Cernovich, and MIT Media Lab top 150 ranked social media influencer Douglass Mackey (aka "Ricky Vaughn").[57] Mackey was a writer and political operative for Anglin's *The Daily Stormer*, which is what is meant when mainstream conservative defenders like Alex Jones and Tucker Carlson refer to Mackey as a "conservative journalist." In addition to

---

[56] thecollegefix.com/judge-jackie-coakley-not-covered-patient-counselor-privilege-rolling-stone-defamation-suit

[57] apnews.com/article/influencer-mackey-conviction-hillary-7ca8f2bcb487a89f80a24029aeb3ee58

UNITE THE RIGHT IS CONCEIVED

information gathering and commentary, the group including Mackey, Dickinson, and a Vietnamese computer programmer named Hoan Ton-That, were developing groundbreaking facial recognition software called SmartCheckr, now known as Clearview AI, which could either help law enforcement identify criminals or help the FBI and Antifa dox participants at a right-wing protest. Mackey's boss at SmartCheckr, and then Clearview AI, was Jewish political operative Richard Schwartz, who co-founded the company. Schwartz was never in the Slack chat, to my knowledge, and I only learned about him after the fact. I did not understand the technology or its significance at the time; I was just a reporter working a very different beat. As of the writing of this book, the two biggest cause célèbres of mainstream conservatism are the J6 defendants and Mackey. Mackey was charged and convicted for election interference for a hairbrained scheme with Baked Alaska to disseminate images prompting Black Hillary Clinton supporters to "vote by text" instead of at the voting booth. Since then, Mackey has been depicted as something of a "free speech Jesus" by the conservative movement, ironic since his SmartCheckr technology has been used to dox and prosecute attendees at the J6 protest.[58] A full explanation of why that happened, and why individuals like Mackey and Dickinson ended up viciously turning against UTR participants in the aftermath of the government sabotage is beyond the scope of this book. But the inside baseball of White Nationalist and alt-light politics is that PayPal co-founder and billionaire Peter Thiel was one of the funders of SmartCheckr and is a major shot-caller on which influencers get financing and public support campaigns and which don't. Post-Charlottesville, the bridge was burned to separate influencers like Mackey, Anglin, and up-and-coming stars like Nicholas Fuentes from the rest of the alt-right who went to Charlottesville. A brutal "optics war" ensued led by Vaughn, Fuentes, Dickinson, Anglin, Jewish computer hacker Andrew "Weev" Aurenheimer, and other Thiel-connected White Nationalist politicos. They tried to depict Charlottesville organizers as reckless and their

---

[58] nytimes.com/2021/01/09/technology/facial-recognition-clearview-capitol.html

CHARLOTTESVILLE AND THE DEATH OF FREE SPEECH

Pax Dickinson, former chief technology officer for Business Insider

Matthew Heimbach

actions leading many protesters to getting arrested. Again, ironically, Fuentes and Anglin later encouraged their splinter movement to attend J6, where many more protesters were doxed by SmartCheckr and arrested.

- **Matthew Heimbach**, founder and leader of the TWP, a graduate of Towson University, renowned for creating a White Student Union on campus. He was the subject of a 2013 documentary by Vice Media (the hipster news outlet originally founded by McInnes and Shane Smith) where he is seen patrolling campus with his student union looking for crime.[59] I did not know Heimbach prior to inviting him to speak at the rally. He was suggested to me by Mosley. I felt a lot of pressure to invite certain people who represented different wings of the alt-right so as not to offend anyone. What research I did do into the White Student Union did not seem inappropriate to me, and I also found Heimbach could be quite elegant as a defender of both Confederate history and White rights. The downside is Heimbach had drifted into a bizarre Strasserite philosophy. It was Heimbach who brought in even more problematically controversial people like Schoep and the NSM. The whole thing quickly spun out-of-control and I tried unsuccessfully to disinvite the NSM when I realized how bad it would look for the rest of us to be associated with such a group, although in theory I still supported their free speech rights as well. After the rally, Heimbach would make several startling shifts in ideology. First, Heimbach linked up with a White former Islamic extremist turned anti-extremist researcher named Jesse Morton (now deceased). Morton reached out and made contact with a number of UTR participants including myself, Heimbach, and Schoep. Heimbach made several videos with Morton's organization Light Upon Light featuring himself renouncing "white supremacy" and making friends with a Black man named Daryl Davis. Later, Heimbach turned on Morton and briefly resumed his activism as a member of NSM before they kicked him out for his extreme socialist views. I bring this up because of an accusation about Heimbach's conduct during UTR

---

[59] youtube.com/watch?v=GJ_MHp8iqtQ

made by Morton. Morton was Heimbach's confidante during the period of his "deradicalization." During my research, Morton told me that Heimbach revealed he was in communication with the FBI prior to UTR. In fact, there are news articles preceding August 12, 2017, in which Heimbach discusses taking late night phone calls from federal agents since at least 2015.[60] Allegedly, Heimbach was against going to the rally, but his handlers talked him into going and keeping tabs on events. He agreed in exchange for financing TWP's travel and the production of shields and equipment. Heimbach denied these allegations during the *Sines* civil trial.

- **Christopher Cantwell**, right-wing shock jock. In 2017 he hosted a program called *The Radical Agenda*. Cantwell started out as a very radical libertarian whose exploits included camping out near speed traps and warning passersby about the cops. Originally from Stony Brook, New York, and sporting a very distinctive Long Island accent by way of *Family Guy*'s Peter Griffin, he'd moved to Keene, New Hampshire, as part of the Libertarian Free State project. Over time, Cantwell's views had drifted into the racialist sphere, though he retained his intense capitalist and free market views. Incredibly smart, articulate, funny, and charismatic—but also a mentally unstable hot-head—Cantwell had developed a massive following within the alt-right and his black and white *Radical Agenda* t-shirts were ubiquitous in White Nationalist circles in the summer of 2017. Following the rally, the press would dub Cantwell the "Crying Nazi" because of bursts of sobbing in public and around recording equipment. He would also do time in maximum security prison for threatening to rape the wife of a political rival.[61] Cantwell was another example of me getting in way over my head by inviting people I knew very little about. The first time I'd listened to a Cantwell podcast in full I was going for a run around downtown Charlottesville wearing my headphones. Cantwell went into an extremely offensive satirical mockery of the Holocaust. My heart beat faster after I heard his

---

[60] web.archive.org/web/20150726210941/https://projects.aljazeera.com/2015/07/hate-groups
[61] nbcnews.com/news/us-news/crying-nazi-christopher-cantwell-found-guilty-extortion-rape-threat-case-n1241263

language than from the jogging. There was no way I could spin it if Cantwell starting talking like that at the rally. It would make everyone, myself included, look bad. On the other hand, as a free speech absolutist, it would be a powerful free speech statement to have a talented provocateur like that in the mix. It would be what it would be. It was only after I had invited Cantwell and the others to the rally that I started to learn anything about them. You may say I didn't do my due diligence, a fair criticism, but I have never before or since accidentally invited so many mentally unstable people into my orbit. I never could have imagined so many could exist in such a

Christopher Cantwell

small social circle. I will never forget listening to an interview Cantwell did before the rally with the SPLC where he talked about his extensive drug abuse and a suicidal podcast where he cried uncontrollably after breaking up with his Hispanic girlfriend over an abortion. Cantwell freely admitted to the SPLC "that he has abused a host of drugs in myriad and unusual ways—everything from chocolate drenched hallucinogenic mushrooms to meth injected up his anus."[62] Because of Cantwell I came to know that "boofing" is the slang term for injecting methamphetamine up one's anus. He had even taken nude photos of himself in the act and posted them all over the Internet!

- **Michael Hill**, founder of LoS and a former professor of British history.
- **Johnny Monoxide**, host of *Paranormies* and a beloved comedic relief act in the *TRS* radio universe.

In retrospect, after the August 12 event turned into a riot, a lot of people asked about why I would have wanted to hold the event in a place like Charlottesville in the first place, as thoroughly infiltrated as it was with radical leftists. However, the events surrounding Unite the Right legitimately shocked me regarding how far gone my city had become. As a boy I knew it as a fundamentally conservative city in many respects and I always thought the good citizens of the city furtively wanted to reject the revolutionary radicals making so much noise around the university and in city hall.

I saw the radicalization as a recent phenomenon which wasn't fully complete. I thought there was still a majority of good people in Charlottesville who would reject the radical Jacobin types. I had no idea how thoroughly the transformation had already taken place beneath the surface. I would imagine a similar process has played out in many cities, particularly college towns, across the country.

On Tuesday, May 30, 2017, around 11:30 AM, I walked into the Charlottesville Parks and Recreation Department on the Downtown Mall and filled out a special event application request in order to

---

[62] splcenter.org/fighting-hate/extremist-files/individual/christopher-cantwell

UNITE THE RIGHT IS CONCEIVED

League of the South president Michael Hill (center) with Ike Baker (right)

John Ramondetta aka Johnny Monoxide

obtain a permit for a "Free speech rally in support of the Lee Monument." The application was four pages, cost $25 and included a crudely sketched diagram of where speakers, sound equipment, and potential event tents would be arranged in the park. The original request application was for a permit between 12 PM and 5 PM on August 12, 2017. However, I returned a week or two later, and with the permission of Parks and Recreation Director Michelle Christian, moved the time up to 10 AM, sealed with my initials.[63]

The wait for approval was excruciating. Every day that transpired indicated that something was seriously wrong. Why was it taking them so long to approve it? I worried about having a legal fight on my hands. By June 5, I was told the permit was being provisionally approved. Not that they had much choice. Permits were deemed granted if not explicitly denied within 10 days. But when receiving this good news, I also received a sour, unwelcome surprise. The Loyal White Knights, a KKK group from North Carolina, had also apparently applied for a permit to protest in Jackson Park on July 8, and the City very strategically announced both events to the public on the same day, seemingly drawing a connection between them. I was deeply disturbed by the revelation. In my mind there was a high likelihood this supposed Klan group could be a controlled operation to make us look bad and associate UTR with the KKK. As it turned out, this was a validated fear since, in the aftermath of both rallies, the media would often run incendiary photographs of men in Klan robes from the July 8 event when discussing my August 12 event. There are other reasons why the impact of the Klan event may have been a major factor in why UTR turned into a disaster, as we will discuss later.

The permit was officially granted on June 13. To prepare a way for organizers to stay in contact with public attendees of the rally, Mosley had fellow Identity Evropa member Erica Alduino create a chatroom on the Discord gaming server. Different channels were created including a General chat and higher security channels like

---

[63] jasonkessler.us/wp-content/uploads/2023/11/Unite-the-Right-Permit-Application.pdf

Leadership Chat. Channels were created for the various regional groups, for discussing different aspects of protest like chants and signage, making major announcements and so forth. General invitation links were distributed across all the rowdy right-wing forums on the Internet. Some of the links could be copied and pasted by third parties into even more obscure corners of the net. In short, there was very little quality control of the people outside the Leadership Channel. Since I am a free speech absolutist and we were doing an explicitly "free speech" styled event, there was minimal moderation of what people posted in the chatroom. So, intermixed with serious discussions about issues related to the protest you would also have trolls making extremely offensive and racist jokes and talking quite liberally about preparations to defend themselves in the event the rally was attacked by Antifa. In retrospect, this would turn out to be a major strategic error, as after the event turned into a disaster, our enemies would use the loose talk and outlandish rhetoric as an attack vector to smear the organizers and blame them for the violence. Every embarrassing comment by anonymous trolls would thereafter be attributed to "organizers" of the rally, whereas the completely businesslike Leadership Channel would never see the light of day. A series of Operational Orders were distributed to leadership on the Discord. The first, released on June 11, outlined proposed speakers, activist roles including Propaganda Coordinator, Lodging Coordinator, Intelligence Section Coordinator, and Medical Team Leader, and an ambitious schedule for the planning and promotion of the rally.[64] The document succinctly reiterated the stated objective of the rally:

> The right wing must stand united to defend free speech, and the main attack on free speech is the left's intolerance to have pro-White or anti-SJW points of view. Coming together to support each other at this event will be an important show of strength and unity regardless of our disagreements.

[64] jasonkessler.us/wp-content/uploads/2023/11/OpOrd1_LeadershipOnly.docx

CHARLOTTESVILLE AND THE DEATH OF FREE SPEECH

In other words, there is nothing in any way vindicating the media and Jewish activist narrative that it was planned violence masquerading as a free speech event. The amount of planning and coordination, internally and with police, renders that argument nonsensical.

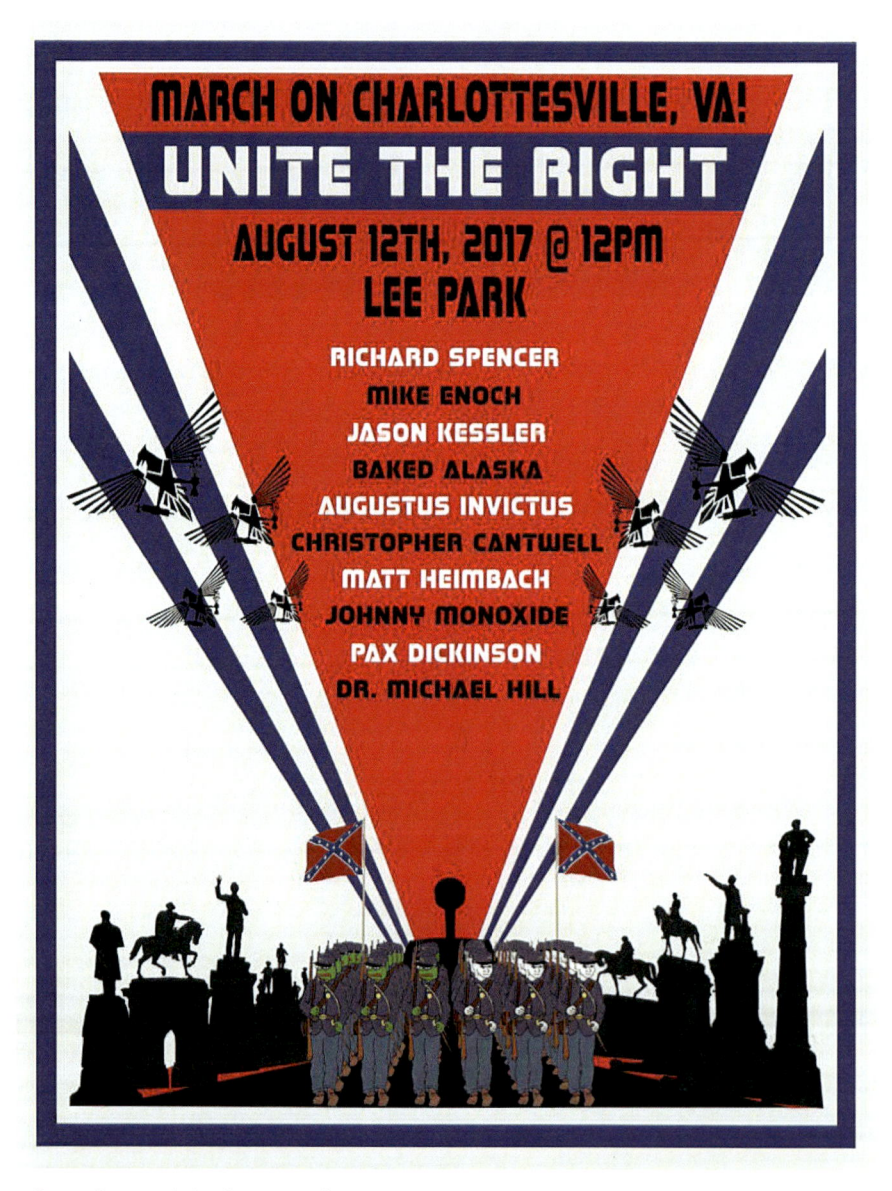

One of two original posters for the event labeled "fascist" by the left-wing media

"FREEDOM OF SPEECH RALLY" AT LINCOLN MEMORIAL IN WASHINGTON, D.C.

A harbinger of what the lost UTR speeches might have looked like occurred on June 25. Spencer ally Colton Merwin had booked a "Freedom of Speech Rally" in front of the Lincoln Memorial on the National Mall facing the Lincoln Memorial Reflecting Pool and the Washington Monument. Many of the prospective speakers from UTR were featured headliners, including Spencer, myself, Enoch, Cantwell, Baked Alaska, and Augustus Invictus. Interestingly, the counter-protest to this event did not come from Antifa but a group of slightly more moderate right-wingers in the alt-light. Led by Jack Posobiec, the "Rally Against Political Violence," held in front of the White House, featured Laura Loomer, Cassandra Fairbanks, and Proud Boys member Kyle Prescott.[65] The event page claimed the intention of the rally was to condemn "political violence such as the attack on Steve Scalise and US Congress recently, as well as depictions of gruesome displays of brutality against sitting U.S. national leaders. All sides must join together to condemn violence and the violent rhetoric that inspires it!" If the two events seemed in any way unrelated, this was only to observers without any context of the situation. Posobiec was originally slated to speak at the Merwin event until he learned Spencer would be a co-speaker and pulled out.

---

[65] archive.is/uVdSZ

Spencer took to Twitter to accuse Posobiec of being a "cuck," and the speakers at his event "a collection of liars . . . perverts . . . and Zionist fanatics."[66]

It was during this feud that I made one of the worst strategic blunders of my nascent career. At the time I was a rising star in right-wing media circles. I'd guested on Alex Jones' *InfoWars* a couple of times as well as McInnes' show, and *The Daily Caller*. My association with Spencer would cost me everything, while gaining nothing in return.

I had recently written an article on Antifa for GotNews and created a companion video for the article on my YouTube channel. To my surprise, Posobiec had created a video ripping me and my article off word for word. I was even able to sync up the two videos we'd made showing Posobiec and me reading the exact same script from my article. The problem was that Posobiec hadn't given me any credit whatsoever. Posobiec and I had exchanged several Twitter messages about the incident and he had apologized. I also received an apology by phone from Ezra Levant, the owner of *Rebel Media* where the Posobiec video had been published. When Posobiec started feuding with Spencer, I backed up Spencer by publicly airing my plagiarism accusations, forever burning the bridge between myself and the alt-light camp. In retrospect, Posobiec had more influence and proximity to consequential power brokers like Donald Trump than Spencer ever would. Second, Spencer did not reward my display of loyalty in kind. As we will see, in subsequent actions, Spencer would take control of UTR from my leadership, desert me, and present me as the scapegoat in the aftermath of UTR. The more prudent course would have been to graciously accept Posobiec's apology and call in a favor from him at a later date.

During the event I carried a Confederate battle flag on a dowel rod and had friends photograph me on the steps of the Lincoln Memorial, relishing in the symbolism of standing triumphant with the flag in that location. A Black man named Don Folden took notice

---

[66] twitter.com/RichardBSpencer/status/875959139582840832

and began relentlessly heckling me. I gave it right back at him. Don, I would come to learn, was the clout-chasing owner of DC Black Tours, known for holding up signs with messages like STOP HATING EACH OTHER BECAUSE YOU DISAGREE in front of media spectacles like the trial of Trump advisor Paul Manafort. I was riding high then and in no mood to debate someone I considered a troll. But, in subsequently more humble years, I would see Folden again and form a friendship based on mutual respect and debate.

As per usual there was another drunken frat-style party back at Spencer's pad above the chocolate shop. A man from his security detail pseudonymously named "Sacco Vandal" was there playing an acoustic guitar, while another Brian Brathovd (aka Caerulus Rex) bragged about his Islamic kill count in Afghanistan. The men were also minor celebrities who hosted *The War Room* on the *TRS* radio network. While I personally found Sacco to be genial and fun to be around, he was an advocate of Anglin's White *Sharia* policy, in other words, enforcing Islamic strictures onto White women. He was a notorious skirt chaser who would intentionally try to impregnate as many women as possible, all to drive up the White birth numbers. This was just a taste of the demented scene that was the alt-right in 2017.

THE KU KLUX KLAN RALLY IN JACKSON PARK

In the weeks leading up to the Klan rally I looked up the Loyal White Knights website and found the contact number for their leader Chris Barker, a man of dubious reputation within the White Nationalist community due to his activity as an FBI informant.[67] I pleaded with him to call off his rally; it would only stir up tensions before my much larger and what I considered to be a more significant event. And, truthfully, I did not want my event to be associated in any way with the Klan. He turned me down because his group had apparently already taken off of work and booked travel arrangements.

All of the radical-left groups like Charlottesville BLM and SURJ were in attendance to "counter-protest" the rally on July 8, but I was not. However, there was later some confusion on this issue because my Twitter account was livestreaming from the event. This was because Dave Reilly happened to be in town and borrowed my phone in order to livestream. I thought it would be humorous to confuse the enemy into thinking I was actually there.

About 40-60 members of the Klan group were escorted by CPD past a crowd of about 1,500-2,000 counter-protesters. At about 3:16 PM several arrests were made when about a dozen agitators locked arms and threw their bodies across the entrance to the park in an attempt to block the rally from taking place. Additionally, the militant

---

[67] dailyprogress.com/kkk-leader-was-fbi-informant/article_5a15bb04-f88c-5f87-854d-985bc83b5027.html

crowd was geared up in body armor and gas masks with walkie talkies and other military accoutrements. At about 3:45 PM, the Klan marched in with CPD in a narrow corridor of separation from the counter-protesters created by the VSP.

The setup done by CPD allowed violent Antifa in unnecessarily close proximity to the Klan. The mob repeatedly surged against the barricades in torrents of anger, launching apples, oranges, tomatoes, water bottles, and other projectiles over the barricades at the permitted demonstration.

Things really got ugly after the event was over. The police evacuated the Klan to the Juvenile and Domestic Relations Court parking garage at around 4:30 PM, where they were followed and surrounded by a crowd of hundreds. When CPD was finally able to clear enough of a path through the crowd blocking exit from the garage, the Klan's escape vehicle was pounded on with weapons as others tried to block it from driving away.[68] With the Klan out of sight,

The Loyal White Knights walk past counter-protesters to Jackson Park

---

[68] Heaphy p. 58

Counter-protesters grapple with police at July 8 Klan event

the activists turned their fury on the police. Several officers were injured in fights, for example CPD Officer Eric Thomas who was sent to the emergency room after being kicked in the groin. "Cops and the Klan go hand in hand!" shouted the furious mob. Three warnings were given for the increasingly-violent crowd to disperse before CPD finally deployed tear gas to subdue the crowd around 5:07 PM. When confronted by an angry Chief Thomas about why he deployed tear gas against the rioters, Major Pleasants responded: "You are damn right I gassed them, it needed to be done." To his credit, the crowd did disperse after the deployment of tear gas and without police having to physically confront them. Police arrested 22 violent, unhinged counter-protesters and no KKK attendees, and were flummoxed because all the KKK had done was speak and leave, giving them no reason to make arrests. Of course, this led to accusations the cops favored the Klan in some way. Due to left-wing political pressure, the majority of the 22 people arrested at the event had their charges dropped.

What came next was one of the single biggest factors in what led UTR to spin out of control. A flurry of left-wing legal groups including Legal Aid Justice Center, NLG, ACLU, and the Rutherford Institute, wrote to Governor McAuliffe, Charlottesville City Councilors, City Manager Maurice Jones, and Chief Thomas criticizing what they called an "outsized and militaristic governmental response."[69] They were particularly upset about the deployment of tear gas to disperse the violent crowd and encouraged police to use "de-escalation" training rather than responding to violence at protests like riot police.[70] The letter alleged that the police "prior to any clear and present danger of violence, descended on the scene dressed in riot gear, driving armored vehicles, and carrying weapons typically used only in war zones." Instead of violating the Klansmen's rights to appease the mob, "law enforcement may have played a role in provoking the unrest that ensued, and certainly made those demonstrating against the Klan feel like enemies of the state." The letter said the Constitution "obliges law enforcement to refrain from tactics that intimidate and chill non-violent counter-protest, even when the target of protest is law enforcement itself." Additionally, pressure was put on Charlottesville Chief of Police Alfred "Al" Thomas for the deployment. He was called to testify before the Charlottesville City Council but he refused. However, the damage had been done. Left-wing political pressure inside and outside City Hall had caused police to second guess the appropriateness of using any force whatsoever to contain the actions of left-wing rioters. This reticence to exercise crowd control would yield poisonous fruit on August 12.

On July 11, I received an email from a whistleblower within CPD using a burner account.[71] "I am taking a risk by sending you this email," wrote my CPD Deep Throat. "There are many of us at CPD that would love to speak out about 'things' but our first amendment rights do not always extend to matters in the work place . . . Be careful with the chief. He and Bellamy are very very tight. He defends Bellamy rigorously throughout the department." There was a follow up on July 12th: "The chief is scared to death of losing his

---

[69] dailyprogress.com/news/in-letters-to-city-and-mcauliffe-aclu-others-question-police-tactics-at-klan-rally/article_d7cfa266-6b32-11e7-a085-5b80fc7a95f1.html
[70] *Cry Havoc* p. 152
[71] jasonkessler.us/wp-content/uploads/2023/11/Emails-from-CPD-Whistleblower.pdf

job. He publicly stated it was the commanders on the ground that made the decision to use tear gas, simply trying to insulate himself but yet 'supporting' the decision . . . Be prepared for the city to offer you a different venue. Prepare your argument for that, if you haven't already." That was the last email I received from my Deep Throat, but the prophetic quality of his intel confirmed to me his legitimacy. Several months after the rally I tried to email him again about just what the hell had gone wrong, but I received a bounce-back notification informing me the email account no longer existed.

PRESS CONFERENCE WITH THE WARLOCKS MOTORCYCLE CLUB

After the Klan business was finally over, I decided to shift attention to my rally by holding a press conference in front of City Hall and the Charlottesville Police Department on July 11, 2017. Realizing that such a feat would be dangerous in the violent post-Klan rally political environment, I reached out to a local tattoo artist who led the Warlocks Motorcycle Club for protection. About a dozen tough, pierced, and tattooed bikers kept anyone daring to disrupt at bay.[72]

"We have a serious double-standard in this community and across this country where people who are White are not allowed to advocate for their own interests," I said. I pointed out that people of "every other persuasion—homosexual, Muslim, Jewish, Black, Hispanic, whatever" are able to advocate for themselves without fear of violence or government repression. "There is no one who is protecting White people, and that's absolutely unacceptable. If people really care about diversity, if they really care about values like equality, you have to be allowed to have White people advocate for their own interests. People need to be able to come to America and see a majority European country because this is a country that was founded by European Americans,"

---

[72] web.archive.org/web/20200710004206/https://dailyprogress.com/news/local/kessler-discusses-kkk-unite-the-right-rallies-and-his-political-beliefs/article_610ca84a-66a0-11e7-af48-1389a3205b81.html

CHARLOTTESVILLE AND THE DEATH OF FREE SPEECH

Kessler and the Warlocks outside the Charlottesville Police Department (July 11, 2017)

Trans Antifa Edward Gorcenski aka "Emily"

I continued. ". . . it's absolutely unacceptable for these liberals to have displacement-level policies which are removing the indigenous people from the country."

For some reason, local Antifa activists like Edward "Emily" Gorcenski—a pockmarked Asian transexual—began spreading rumors the Warlocks were the intended security for the rally itself.

They tried to sow panic among decision makers in Charlottesville City Hall that the rally could turn into another Altamont, a 1969 rock concert featuring The Rolling Stones which turned into a deadly riot after Hell's Angels bikers acting as security began fighting with the crowd.

The actual plan was always dependent on CPD separating both sides as police had done in Pikeville. To the extent we had internal "security," it was just friends walking with the speakers and watching their backs to make sure they weren't an easy target for assaults by the crowd. Unbeknownst to us, even as I was negotiating the details of this arrangement with law enforcement, Chief Thomas had already decided not to abide by the plans. After July 8, 2017, during a zone commanders debrief from the Klan rally, Chief Thomas told his subordinates: "I'm not going to get [alt-right] in and out" during the UTR rally.[73]

Chief Thomas' meaning was clear. In a departure from the successful Klan rally plan, UTR speakers were going to be left without protection from violent assaults by counter-protesters on the way into the venue. CPD told third party investigators that during this time they had been ordered not to engage over "every little thing"; not to "go in and break up fights"; not to interrupt "mutual combat"; and officers were not to be sent out among the crowd where they might get hurt. A primary conclusion of the third party report by former federal prosecutor Tim Heaphy, found that, "Rather than engage the crowd and prevent fights, the CPD plan was to declare the event unlawful and disperse the crowd." So, there was never any intention of allowing us to speak as there had been for the Klan rally. The leadership of the

---

[73] Heaphy pp. 64, 97

Police Chief Al Thomas (left) gets cozy with radical Reverend Seth Wispelwey

City who endorsed this policy, like Maurice Jones and Chief Al Thomas, were only too aware a police stand-down would lead to a riot. I obtained an email between the two men where they shared a news article about how a Berkeley protest turned into a riot after a stand-down by city police earlier that year.[74]

Nevertheless, I proceeded to jump through various planning and logistical hurdles placed in front of me by the City. I was told I needed to get Port-A-Johns so that demonstrators could use the bathroom without having to wade through an army of counter-protesters to use facilities on the Downtown Mall. But as soon as I booked a contract, harassment from left-wing activists caused the company to break it. Similarly, I was asked by Parks and Recreation Director Michelle Christian to obtain insurance for the gathering, which I promptly did. Once again, activists, including the transexual Gorcenski, applied a pressure campaign which successfully caused the company to cancel my insurance policy. Fortunately, and to the dismay of the activists, the government is actually prohibited from restricting First Amendment activity to those who are able to pay for insurance.

---

[74] jasonkessler.us/wp-content/uploads/2020/05/Highlight-Beat-Each-other-bloody.png

PRESS CONFERENCE WITH THE WARLOCKS

The next thing the anti-speech extremists tried was submitting permit applications for their own events in McGuffey and Jackson Park, both within a block or two of UTR and scheduled for an overlapping time. The applications were submitted on July 13 by one of UVA's radical anti-White professors and racial theorists, Walter Heinecke.

Heinecke claimed he filed the permits "to allow assembly for citizens protesting the white supremacist groups that will occupy Emancipation Park." However, "Heinecke met with Christian and Captain Lewis in advance of August 12, and it became clear that the true focus of the Justice and McGuffey events was to use the parks as staging areas for counter-protesters" to attack the UTR rally.[75] Unlike UTR, which was predicated on proximity to the Lee monument, there was no reason for these counter-protesters to need to be so close to my rally when the crowd size could become a major public safety hazard.

Militant Black supremacist Don Gathers (center) raises black power fist; with far-left UVA Professor Walter Heinecke (right)

---

[75] Heaphy p. 77

On July 30, around 8:59 PM, I texted CPD Captain Wendy Lewis my concerns:[76]

> Kessler: "What's going on with the Jackson and McGuffey Parks? It's going to be a safety issue for my attendees having two Antifa rallies on either side of Lee Park. It would pretty much be impossible to segregate foot traffic with 3 event[s] clustered in such a small area. **My people are already concerned about being ambushed on their way to the event.**" [Emphasis added]
>
> Lewis: "I'm not sure if they approved it or not but we did decline providing any resources if they do. We have nothing to give them. I will call your security team later this week. You need to get the word out for everyone to come in from the east."

Despite vague references to a plan to "come in from the east," no specific plans were ever formalized with police. One time, while visiting the office of Captain Lewis, she momentarily showed me a cardboard printout of an aerial view of Lee Park with red lines indicating proposed flow of foot traffic by groups and coordination of police officers. But I was told it was secret and not to let anyone else know she had shown me. I was not able to take a photograph, but assumed I would be fully briefed on the implications of this vague plan before the event. On the contrary, disastrous decisions by the political leadership of the Charlottesville government would soon conspire to bar CPD from even talking to me about what the plan for the rally was going to be.

---

[76] jasonkessler.us/wp-content/uploads/2023/11/Wendy-Lewis-Text-1.jpg

THE SECRET CLOSED-DOOR MEETING

A mysterious closed-door meeting was scheduled for City Council on August 2. While the topic wasn't announced, it was clearly top-secret discussions about the rally. Bellamy showed up carrying a backpack depicting the Marvel Comics character Black Panther, clearly a coded message for people on the black supremacy wavelength. At the time, the contents of the meeting were a complete mystery to the public, including me. But with the release of his book *Cry Havoc* in 2020, former Mayor Mike Signer described what went on. Signer, who is Jewish, had an adversarial and very sensitive reaction to criticism of his Jewish heritage from both the left and right. Following the rally, he would go on to become a fierce partisan for the Jewish ethno-state of Israel. Signer was also a pompous ass with delusions of grandeur. On January 31, 2017, after the election of Donald Trump, Signer called a vainglorious press conference to announce that Charlottesville was the "capital of the resistance."

The event stirred up divisions within the community with its blatant disrespect to the conservative minority in the town. The only purpose seemed to be to gain publicity for his political ambitions. Perhaps it was this excessive pride mixed with Signer's desire to shut down perceived criticism of Jewry which led him to taking an active role in trying to get the rally in Lee Park cancelled and moved to McIntire Park, miles away from the Lee monument. Rally planning should have been handled by police for a safety plan free of political bias and sabotage, but Signer took a heavy hand in injecting his

Wes Bellamy bringing a Black Panther backpack into the secret closed-door meeting with Szakos where rally sabotage was planned

political agenda into the process by retaining the powerhouse law firm of Boies Schiller Flexner LLP at a cost of $30,000, paid for by the Charlottesville taxpayer, to advise him on how to legally relocate the rally. Even though the law firm warned that moving the rally would likely be unconstitutional, Signer ignored their advice and began lobbying his other City Councilors hard to adopt his relocation plan.

The August 2 meeting began with a threat assessment from VSP which "mostly focused on the far left and the specific threats that violent Antifa members might present to law enforcement. They went into the black bloc technique in depth and discussed devices that could be thrown at police." Signer was enraged the police had identified violent leftists as the primary threat vector, but "said nothing about the possibility of violent, organized militias invading the city."[77] He wanted police to investigate the permitted demonstrators and spend less time trying to protect the event from violent counter-protesters. Chief Thomas vehemently opposed relocating the rally and changing the security plan at the last minute. According to Signer: "He again responded that if he had received the request six weeks earlier, it would be a different story, but now too many resources had gone into the strategy they'd decided to use." The hot shot attorneys from Boies Schiller also warned that City Councilors like Signer were overstepping their bounds by trying to implement a decision that was under the authority of the police chief and city manager. "But we still had to formally stay out of the decision to pass legal muster," Signer wrote. "In other words, the attorneys were united in advising us that we could not actually make the decision.

Mayor Mike Signer at his "capital of the resistance" rally (January 31, 2017)

---

[77] *Cry Havoc* p. 176

We could just tell Jones it was the decision we wanted him to make." The attorneys further went on to advise that to the extent City Council was determined to move forth with a relocation strategy, it should be focused on "content neutral" rationales like safety hazards caused by too many attendees clustered in the downtown area. Tellingly, there was no discussion about relocating Heinecke's "counter-protest" rallies in Jackson and McGuffey or mention of my concerns about how allowing those parks as staging grounds for anti-speech militants would be a precursor to violence and chaos. No thought whatsoever was given to canceling their permits.

Information uncovered after the rally via the Heaphy Report, showed deep divisions between not just the City Councilors themselves, but between the council and other city government officials. In July, Signer was warned by a city attorney that involving himself in the rally location could expose him to personal liability. That same month, after a closed meeting where Signer and three other councilors pressured Jones to move the rally, a councilor sent an email reminding Signer of their requirement to "seek advice from the city's professional staff." Less than 10 minutes after the email, the city attorney emailed Signer, warning him he was entering "into operational details of city government."[78] Signer kept diverting police attention to his own pet priorities like alleged antisemitic tweets he received online and requests for the Virginia National Guard to be assigned to his synagogue.[79]

---

[78] *Summer of Hate* p. 104
[79] wset.com/news/local/leaked-memo-poor-communication-contributed-to-chaos-in-charlottesville

A Rush of Meetings and the Permit is Revoked

My primary concerns continued to be counter-protesters occupying the park the night before the rally, refusing to allow anyone entry, blocking Market Street and violently attacking demonstrators on their way into the venue. I was especially concerned that Jackson (aka Justice) Park would be used as a staging ground for the most violent militants who were coming to disrupt the event.

My police contacts were hedging on giving specific details about the plan for August 12. With no clarification on how authorities intended to deal with these issues and protect public safety, I shot off a desperate August 4 email to Michelle Christian:[80]

> Michelle,
> I'm aware that there are plans to do concurrent demonstrations in MacGuffey [sic] and Jackson Parks at the same time as Unite the Right. I have some concerns about these events interfering or causing safety concerns for my event. Please give me a cal[l] . . .
> Best,
> Jason Kessler

---

[80] jasonkessler.us/wp-content/uploads/2023/11/Michelle-Christian-Email.jpeg

She responded by inviting me to a meeting in her office at 11 AM the next day, and when I arrived, Christian led me into a meeting room with Captain Lewis and City Manager Jones. I quickly realized I'd been led into an ambush.

It was my first time meeting with Jones, a sweaty and obsequious bureaucrat, torn between being White-presenting and higher than average intelligence, and his credibility as a Black man.

Bellamy was constantly gut checking him on the latter whenever he didn't perceive Jones was making decisions based on his Black identity first. Jones was a dumpy former sportscaster for local TV station NBC29, before he received the appointment to Charlottesville city manager out of nowhere. Since he didn't have any relevant experience, one can only guess the snooty White liberals and Jews running the local government decided they liked the thought of appointing a Black executive, qualifications be damned.

I sat down and *again* voiced my concerns about dangerous, armed Antifa thugs obstructing Main Street and attacking supporters

City Manager Maurice Jones

of the permitted demonstration. Once again, I was given no clear answers, only platitudes of assurance the City "had a plan." But Jones continued to press me hard on the number of attendees for the rally. I had estimated 400 on the application but I freely admitted to them I had no way of knowing for sure since the event was open to the public. Jones kept asking me loaded, probing questions about a Facebook event page which had received perhaps a thousand people selecting that they either would attend or were considering attending the rally. Obviously, Jones was fishing for evidence he could use in court to say, "We should be allowed to cancel the permit because too many people are coming." I stood firm on my estimate of 400. I did not believe anonymous clicks on a public Facebook event page were an accurate estimate of who was actually coming. By the way, according to attendance totals reported by NPR, my estimate may have turned out to be pretty accurate. Throughout this interrogation I kept asking Jones what the maximum safe occupancy was for the park. If they could give me a firm number, I could try to limit attendance to that amount. He didn't even hazard a guess. The "attendance problem" was a loose and flexible attack on my political speech, not a serious, fact-based critique of how many people could safely attend the event.

Although the city claims that no audio recordings of the meeting exist, I was able to obtain notes made by Jones about my conversation with him that night through a Freedom of Information Act (FOIA) request.[81] He wrote things like:

> "has a right for people to speak"
> "1,000-2,000 says he didn't say that"
> "Passing through a mob"
> "traveling from one park to another"
> "Concerned about people causing violence"
> "Barricades around the park"
> "Waiting on final presentation from the police department"

---

[81] jasonkessler.us/wp-content/uploads/2023/11/Maurice-Jones-Notes-from-Meeting-with-Jason-Kessler.pdf

That reveals a pretty vivid picture of the overlap between my account and one posited by an adversarial party like Jones. It was quite a lot, most importantly that I wanted to know specifics about how we were going to keep attendees safe.

At the time I was given several concrete promises that turned out to be lies:

- There would be eight squadrons of police assigned to keep the peace at the protest. Officers would be embedded at both the front and back of Lee Park for this purpose.
- There would be 200 officers stationed in the back of the park to assist with entry of speakers. On the day of the rally I would accidentally try to enter from the back and side of the park before being turned away.
- Officers would be stationed at the entrances to the park to prevent disruption from violent agitators.
- Undercover officers would be embedded throughout the crowd, breaking up fights, making arrests, and keeping the peace.

In a 2018 deposition of Jones, conducted under oath for one of my civil lawsuits against the city, Jones verified many of these promises that had been made to me. He also acknowledged that during the meeting I repeatedly expressed fear about the police standing down as they had before riots earlier that year in Berkeley, California.[82]

Attorney: ". . . did [Kessler] express concern about the police standing down as they had in Berkeley, California?

Jones: I believe he mentioned something about that, yes.

Attorney: Did Mr. Kessler request that demonstrators and counter demonstrators be separated by the police department?

Jones: I believe he did, yes.

Attorney: Did Mr. Kessler express concern about the streets surrounding Emancipation Park?

---

[82] jasonkessler.us/wp-content/uploads/2023/11/Maurice-Jones-Deposition.pdf

A RUSH OF MEETINGS AND THE PERMIT IS REVOKED

Jones: He did.

Attorney: Being blocked off by counter protesters?

Jones: He did.

Attorney: Did Charlottesville, in fact, station police officers at the front and back of the park?

Jones: We had officers that were prepared to provide support and escort in and out of the park . . .

Attorney: But they didn't actually deploy to those areas?

Jones: I don't know.

I left that meeting and started walking home. An email notification reached my inbox. I opened it to find a formal letter in City of Charlottesville[83] letterhead informing me:

> The City has decided to approve your application for a permit to hold a demonstration on the day and at the times requested, provided that you use McIntire Park, rather than Emancipation Park,[84] for your demonstration . . . If you are unwilling to use the McIntire Park location, the permit for Emancipation Park is hereby denied . . .

This was complete nonsense and political spin, of course. For one thing, the permit for Lee Park had already been approved. City law outlines that permit applications will be "deemed approved" if there is no word to the contrary after 10 business days. It had been almost a month and a half. Second, the proposed relocation to McIntire Park was obviously aimed at diluting the potency of the rally's political symbolism by removing us from proximity to the Lee statue which was the focus of the protest. The letter outlined its rationale for denying the permit thusly:

> Your permit application states that the demonstration will consist of approximately 400 people. However, in recent

---

[83] jasonkessler.us/wp-content/uploads/2023/11/Denial-of-Permit-Letter.pdf

[84] Like Jacobin revolutionaries, the City had recently renamed Lee Park to "Emancipation Park."

days it has come to the City's attention that many thousands of individuals are likely to attend the demonstration. Because Emancipation Park is a relatively confined space of just over one acre in a densely populated urban area with limited parking space, it is unable to accommodate safely even a peaceful crowd of this size.

This rationale was bunk for several reasons:

- No distinction was made between crowd size based on attendance in support of my demonstration versus the counter-protesters we were likely to be outnumbered by. Canceling the permit based on the number of counter-protesters would have been tantamount to a heckler's veto.
- The denial of the permit based on "crowd size" was obviously disingenuous and masking an attempt to censor my political viewpoint. The City did not have a problem with the May 14 event led by Bellamy which had so many thousands of attendees that the park overflowed into the streets for hours on end. Nor did they have a problem with the "between 3,500 and 4,000" who attended the May 14, 2016, Festival of Cultures event in Lee Park.[85]
- Perhaps most importantly, the City had not canceled the two counter-protest rallies in McGuffey and Jackson Parks. If they were only concerned about crowd size, why had they ignored my pleas for help about the very dangerous proximity of the much-larger counter-protest assemblies? The City actually thought it was okay to cancel my original event and allow the counter-protests to go ahead. I imagine they were licking their chops thinking about banishing my assembly to a vacant field in a park miles away while the left-wing revolutionaries were "taking" Lee Park for themselves in front of the international news media cameras and the humiliating propaganda coup it would have been.

---

[85] jasonkessler.us/wp-content/uploads/2023/11/Fesitval-of-Cultures-attendance-article-NBC-29.pdf

As reported by *The Washington Post*,[86] I declared moving the venue was a no go: "The genesis of the entire event is this Robert E. Lee statue that the city is trying to move, which is symbolic of a lot of issues that deal with the tearing down of White people's history."

I called Captain Lewis to find out just what the hell was going on. It was clear the City was not playing straight with me. I brought my concerns about safety to them, and instead of listening, they pretended to listen while gathering intel for their bogus legal suppression campaign. Lewis informed me I was being invited for a meeting with Chief Thomas himself that afternoon.

Thomas, a light-skinned 60-something Black man with a pencil-thin moustache, spoke calmly and with the deceptive gentility of a Southern accent. He shook my hand when I entered the office and, at the time, had me fooled that he was shooting straight and doing his best to keep the event safe. Through FOIA requests, I was able to obtain an audio recording of the meeting surreptitiously recorded without my knowledge by Captain Lewis. I opened the meeting with a statement of my position:

> So, I mean, I really wish that we could have talked about this before this decision was made because I think this makes everybody a lot less safe. We at least had a security plan beforehand. We had a way that no one's First Amendment rights were going to be violated. The people in the permitted rally in Lee Park were going to be able to do their free speech and there was going to be a zone for the counter demonstrators to express their First Amendment rights. Now, we have sort of a free-for-all situation where no one knows what to expect. I mean, we're going to be challenging this decision in court, but we are planning to go to the park no matter what. This is a civil liberties issue, this is a constitutional issue for us, and we're not going to back down.

---

[86] washingtonpost.com/local/charlottesville-readies-for-a-white-nationalist-rally-on-saturday/2017/08/10/cff4786e-7c49-11e7-83c7-5bd5460f0d7e_story.html

With the knowledge we now have publicly available about the internal dialogue within the Charlottesville government and the exchanges in the "closed-door meeting" on August 2, we now know conclusively that Chief Thomas was not being genuine when he presented the proposed change of venue to McIntire as his idea and what he considered the "most safe" option:

> Well, that's our goal is nonviolence on every side. That's our goal. We feel that we can better accomplish that in a larger venue. [Thomas claimed through gritted teeth.] Again, if that turns out to not be the case for whatever reason, then I agree with you. I still think it's imperative that we continue to work together for safety, for safety purposes, for everyone. I still think we need to continue to have that dialogue. I know you've spoken with the captain on several occasions. I don't expect that to change throughout. So whatever venue ultimately this takes place, our focus is safety. Our focus will be safety. [Thomas shifted nervously in his chair.] **I'm not sure what the plan will look like as this evolves. We have very short notice now to start working on this** and focusing likely on both parks, it looks like, potentially. [Emphasis added]

Thomas assured me that whatever happened, there was a plan in place to protect the event at Lee Park. I was concerned that without the permit in place the City would rescind law enforcement resources necessary to keep the peace. "Again, today, based on this conversation, it sounds like we need to be prepared for both locations," he told me. "Maybe that changes as we go through the week. We're not going to protect an area and leave another area unprotected unnecessarily. That's not the plan. I can assure you of that. We will have an adequate plan for either location."

I was adamant that resources should not be split between McIntire and Lee. We had no intention of going to McIntire:

This is called a heckler's veto in First Amendment law, where you talk about people who want to threaten an event and create violence at an event, being able to shut it down. That's what they've done, essentially. If these people weren't bothering us, we would just go, we would speak our mind and we would leave. *Look, these individuals have permits for McGuffey, for Jackson Park. They are calling on thousands of people. I did not call for thousands of people, as Maurice Jones said. They explicitly have, but yet their events are not being shut down. My people have never attacked police officers. My people have never done any of these things their people have,* so it doesn't make any sense to me why I'm being targeted, except for the kinds of views that we plan to express. [Emphasis added]

*Charlottesville police in riot gear under an inflammatory sign
placed by the City for the rally*

*UNC-Chapel Hill Professor Dwayne Dixon (left)
with members of Redneck Revolt*

Antifa Brent Betterly unleashes a stream of bear mace

From left: Dave Reilly, Elliot Kline aka Eli Mosley, James Fields

*Tom Massey (left) brawls with an unidentified protester,
a weapon of some kind in his left hand*

Activist Joseph Jordan aka Eric Striker engaging in civil disobedience

Unite the Right 2 (August 12, 2018)

Michael Tubbs (center) of League of the South

A banquet inside the National Press Club for the DeploraBall

Gavin McInnes at the DeploraBall

Kessler counter-protesting as hostiles try to cover his bullhorn (May 14, 2017)

Kessler attempts to speak at a press conference (August 13, 2017); Brandon Collins (right) would later be convicted of assaulting him

The "Fuck White Supremacy" banner placed on the Lee monument during the May 14 protest

Former Louisiana State Representative David Duke drew significant international media attention during his appearance at UTR (August 12, 2017)

Kessler walks towards Lee Park with the security detail which protected him August 11-12, 2017

A rioter clutches a balloon, which may have been filled with biohazards like paint, urine, and feces. Rioters coming prepared with masks shows pre-planning the use of tear gas and other irritants

Vice-Mayor Wes Bellamy gives a Black power salute during a Charlottesville City Council meeting (September 11, 2017)

ENTER THE ACLU

After the meeting was over, I returned to my apartment and separately contacted both Dickson and Spencer. I hoped they might provide good counsel based on their experience with the Auburn University heckler's veto case. Both men recommended contacting the ACLU. On August 8, 2017, at 1:15 AM, I sent a direct message to the ACLU of Virginia's Twitter account: "Charlottesville City Council canceled my permitted Unite the Right rally in Lee Park in clear violation of my first amendment rights I need legal representation right away!"[87] By 7:33 AM they responded: "Please go to our website and fill out our intake form. You'll find it under the Get Help tab." I followed their advice without delay. "I did. It said it would take four weeks for a response but I need to file something in court by Wednesday." "Thanks. Trust us we know how to triage for time sensitive matters," the ACLU representative assured me. By 2:29 PM, the ACLU, together with the Rutherford Institute, had fired the first public salvo of the legal battle. A missive on the ACLU of Virginia website stated: "ACLU OF VIRGINIA AND RUTHERFORD INSTITUTE CHALLENGE CHARLOTTESVILLE'S DECISION TO MOVE PLANNED 'UNITE THE RIGHT' DEMONSTRATION."[88]

According to the article, "Today the ACLU of Virginia and the Rutherford Institute sent a letter to Charlottesville City Council asking them to reverse their decision to move the 'Unite the Right' demonstration planned for Emancipation Park this Saturday to another,

---

[87] jasonkessler.us/wp-content/uploads/2023/11/Kessler-ACLU-Twitter-Messages-1.png
[88] acluva.org/en/press-releases/aclu-virginia-and-rutherford-institute-challenge-charlottesvilles-decision-move

larger park a mile away from the statue that was to be the focus of the demonstration."

Citing a number of serious First Amendment concerns, the letter concluded:

> The City must act in accordance with the law, even if doing so is distasteful to members of the community who disagree with the views espoused by the "Unite the Right" organizers. At the very least, the City must explain in more than just generalities its reasons for concluding that the demonstration cannot safely be held in Emancipation Park. It must allow the organizers the opportunity to dispel fears or concerns about the rally. Otherwise, it appears that the City's revocation of the permit is based only upon public opposition to the message of the demonstration, which would constitute a violation of the organizers' fundamental First Amendment rights.

My principle contact at the ACLU during this time was Virginia Director Claire Guthrie Gastanaga. In his book, *Cry Havoc*, Signer reveals he was also in contact with Gastanaga at this time and considered her an "old friend of mine from Virginia Democratic politics."[89] Once word got out that I was being represented by the vaunted ACLU, butt cheeks tightened within the City of Charlottesville government.

I was called back for another meeting, this time with Captain Lewis and Captain Victor Mitchell. Once again, Lewis was surreptitiously recording the meeting and I retrieved a copy of that recording through FOIA. The full-court press was on to make me submit to Signer's unlawful relocation plan which Chief Thomas knew full well was throwing safety planning into chaos.

"I think that we've been . . . we have been at this point our plan is changing based on the fact that you don't have a permit," Lewis

---

[89] *Cry Havoc* p. 152

told me. "We will need to look at security at McIntire Park and plan for that security there."

"So, we're not going to be able to keep the security in place at Lee Park?" I asked. "That was my understanding from the meeting with Chief Thomas yesterday because I mean just realistically we have no interest of doing a demonstration at McIntire Park. It's going to be at Lee Park and the permit is probably going to be reinstated before then."

What became abundantly clear was that yesterday Chief Thomas was playing the "good cop" who just wanted everyone to get along and be safe. But today he sent in his stooges to be the "bad cops" who would make it clear the City was not going to talk to me about the alleged plan for security at Lee Park because I "didn't have a permit."

"Are we going to file an injunction?" Lewis asked.

"Yes," I answered resolutely. "So hopefully when that happens, we will go back to our plan and *be able to share that with you but only if that happens with the injunction*."[90] [Emphasis added] "That's the whole thing that is so crazy for me is that ostensibly they're canceling the permit for safety reasons and this has made the situation so much less safe. It only seems like it was done for a political reason," I sighed. "I mean obviously everybody knows how City Council feels about me and about the demonstrators. I mean there's no doubt that there's a political bias in place. I just I wish that police could put their foot down on these politicians who think that this is creating a safer environment. It's not going to create a safer environment. The plan that we had originally in place was creating the safest possible conditions for the rally. Now this uncertainty is going to change that."

"Well, the fact that it would have been a safer environment had you gone to McIntire. But if you're not going to McIntire you're absolutely right," Lewis responded.

"Well, what's going on with these two events in McGuffey and

---

[90] This alleged "plan" for Lee Park was never shared with me, even after securing the injunction.

Jackson? They still have their permits?" I asked.

"As far as I know," Lewis responded.

They never had a good answer for that one.

"But if the permit is reinstated, you're saying can we talk about that plan [for Lee Park]?" I pressed her.

"Yeah we already had that in the plan. We had the van coming up that service sidewalk behind the statue. And you'd be able to park that right there right behind the statue where the barricades would go around. We already have plans for ingress and egress for speakers."

Once again, I left another meeting with only vague reassurances about a "plan" that officials refused to share with me in any detail. I was forbidden from hearing what exactly was expected of me or my attendees in order to comply with this mysterious "plan."

The Mutiny From Within

What follows is a critical account of how elements of the alt-right turned against me while my attention was divided with research and preparation for the ACLU legal case. The main instigator was Mosley, my primary co-organizer. I prefer not to dwell too much on the toxicity that made "Unite the Right" anything but. However, it is absolutely critical to our understanding of what transpired because, for one thing, it climaxed in Spencer calling off police escorts for the speakers—not a trivial matter. Much of what follows in this section has been reconstructed after the fact. Due to the legal discovery—the mandated process of gathering and exchanging information between parties involved in a legal case—that occurred during the *Sines v. Kessler* civil trial, I have access to private Discord messages, texts, and other materials which were not available to me at the time of the rally. But they are enormously useful in piecing together duplicity and scheming that might not otherwise have ever seen the light of day.

Mosley was a megalomaniacal, status-obsessed, pathological liar of the most sociopathic variety. He built his "brand" within the movement as a no-nonsense political strategist who ran his protests like a military operation. He used a lot of military lingo and constantly asserted his credentials as a U.S. Army veteran who had been deployed to front-line combat in Iraq. He sometimes guested on Sacco Vandal's *The War Room* podcast where he bragged about his alleged exploits as a merciless killer of Muslims in combat. "I was in the Army and I got to kill Muslims for fun. I'm not sure which is better: watching niggers and spics cry that they can't feed their little mud-children or watching Muslims' brains spray on the wall."[91] The following year after UTR, he was exposed in a *New York Times* investigation as a fraud. In fact, he'd never been deployed to Iraq, and his claims of overseas combat duty were stolen valor.[92] He was confronted by Emma Cott, a reporter with *The New York Times*, whose piece he erroneously thought would bolster his credentials within the alt-right:

> I explained that I had gotten his official records from the Army and the National Guard.
> "So did you go to Iraq?" I asked.
> "I was in Kuwait," he said. "I told you that before."
> "You told me you went to Kuwait and then you went to Iraq."
> "Basically, it's very similar the way it works," he said.
> We talked for a while longer and his story kept changing, but he did not back down. He wavered between blaming a military clerical error and saying that a military form he would send me would clear up the confusion once and for all.

Mosley was a member of the Pennsylvania National Guard, but no one from his unit was ever deployed to Iraq.

At the time of the rally, Mosley became concerned about whether he was getting enough credit, and decided to marginalize me while my back was turned. The primary piece of evidence for this fact were text messages between Mosley and Spencer, turned over for discovery in *Sines v. Kessler*.[93] In one text exchange, Spencer wanted to know if I was still making decisions:

---

[91] rawstory.com/2018/02/called-alt-right-lieutenant-caught-lying-killing-muslims-fun-iraq
[92] nytimes.com/2018/02/05/insider/confronting-a-white-nationalist-eli-mosley.html
[93] jasonkessler.us/wp-content/uploads/2024/05/Richard-SpencerDiscovery-Materials_compressed.pdf

"Did Kessler make the call?"

"No, I did," Mosley responded.

"Good call."

"I've removed Kessler from all operational calls starting today," Mosley assured him. "All the security and leadership are getting orders from me . . ."

👍 Spencer responded with a thumbs up emoji.

According to Samantha Froelich, the girlfriend who cuckolded Mosley with Spencer, Mosley's immediate objective was to "make an army for Richard" but that he ultimately wanted to "kill Richard and take over all of it."[94] In another text exchange, Mosley presented Spencer with phony ancestry "research" in an attempt to discredit me by "proving" Jewish heritage. Mosley sent Spencer a profile from a website called MyHeritage.com of a woman named Evelyn Goldberg (born Kessler), who lived between 1940 and 2002. "He's Jewish. This is his grandma lol," Mosley wrote. "And Laura didn't want me to figure it out but I did. [To this day I have no idea who this "Laura" is.] I don't even think we need to spread it. It's a good enough sword to hold over his head to go away after this." At that time both of my grandmothers, Patsie Holliday Cutright and Winnie Norvelle Kessler, were still alive. Mosley's disgusting smear was false. For the record, I had an Ancestry.com DNA test done, just for my own edification. The results identified me as 58% English and Northwestern European, 21% Welsh, 12% Irish, 6% Scottish and 3% German.[95]

"Cameron is always right," Spencer responded, in an apparent allusion to his assistant Cameron Padgett also claiming that I was Jewish.

"I'm actually laughing so hard that we had a natural reaction to a crypto lolol," Mosley said, referring to the term "crypto Jew," or one who disguises their Jewish heritage.

Spencer's immediate thought was noticing that I was the only

---

[94] thedailybeast.com/far-right-leader-elliott-kline-discussed-raising-an-army-and-killing-jewish-people
[95] jasonkessler.us/wp-content/uploads/2024/01/Kessler-DNA-Results.jpg

one not performing a *Sieg heil!* at the May 13 afterparty: "I was right to see his lack of sieg heiling as a sign."

"And the beady eyes that were clearly hiding something and trying to be all Jewy to get in with us. What's hilarious is I bet his funder doesn't know lolol," Mosley laughed.

In another example of fraudulent research, Mosley presented to Spencer an image of one of my random Twitter followers named "Jimmy Fry" with this message: "We figured out who we think is giving Kessler money. It's not good. Some rich white guy who converted to Islam."

The depth of Mosley's smear campaign was massive in scope. According to a local Charlottesville woman, alternately named Hannah Zarski and Hannah Brown (she married and divorced men like others change their dirty underwear), Mosley had created a chat with her and several TWP activists up to and including Heimbach which was literally called "The Coup."[96] The purpose of this was to trash talk me and shift control of events on August 12 out of my hands.

"This coup is an official move now," Mosley told the other members of the chat. "I'm going to talk to Heimbach in a moment about Kessler." Later he confirmed the conversation went to his liking: "Heimbach and I are 100% on the same page."

A major flare-up involved an incendiary *Daily Stormer* contributor named Robert "Azzmador" Ray. The speakers list had already been conceived and I was comfortable the speakers were going to stick to White identity and monuments issues without going into an embarrassing Third Reich-style rant about Jews. Azzmador came to me demanding he be allowed to speak at the rally. My concern was he would say and do things which would be an embarrassment to the more moderate individuals I wanted to welcome into the UTR coalition, like patriots, Confederate heritage supporters, and Trump voters.

To give you an idea of how far off the reservation Azzmador

---

[96] jasonkessler.us/wp-content/uploads/2023/11/Coup-Chat.pdf

Robert "Azzmador" Ray (August 11, 2017)

was, he maintained his own Discord server, which he used to launch raids against the Charlottesville server. On his server, one cartoon Azzmador shared with his followers depicted a Black slave bound and gagged in a metal torture device where he was anally sodomized to the delight of approving White slave masters.[97] This was another example of evidence that came out after the fact during the civil trial. Something like that is cruel, sick, and has nothing to do with my politics, but it gives you an idea of why I didn't want this man to be a speaker. Nevertheless, Azzmador was a major threat because I had no way of controlling who could show up and associate themselves with the event. He was threatening to bring his fans from *The Daily Stormer* and disrupt UTR with a bunch of *Sieg heils!* and Nazi chants that I wanted nowhere near my event. Considering that this type of rhetoric still made it into the rally shows I was extremely naive about how much I could control the Overton Window of expression at a public rally.

---

[97] I saw this in court during the *Sines v. Kessler* trial.

The intended purpose of the rally was narrowly focused on the issue of historical monuments and the inherent righteousness of White people defending their heritage. But Azzmador, with assistance of his patron Andrew Anglin, were distributing incendiary fliers depicting a cartoon of Azzmador smashing a Star of David with a sledgehammer. This was clearly outside the purview of the rally and an attempt by the most radical elements to hijack the message. I fought against Azzmador and his minions vehemently.

Unapproved poster created by Azzmador and The Daily Stormer

THE MUTINY FROM WITHIN

On August 2, Mosley wrote to Azzmador (about me): "Yea he's a total faggot kike isn't he? Dealing with him the past 3 months has fucking sucked. The future of our movement is in you and daily stormer and your guys. Not fucking Jason Kessler lol."[98]

But apparently attempts to placate Azzmador's massive ego by offering him a speaking slot failed. A week later on August 9, he and Mosley were at loggerheads. "Dude the only one not friendly towards you or DS has been Kessler. That is it," Mosley wrote. "Everyone else has and we all conspired and mutinied to get you here and now you are throwing it back in our face because of the order at which you are slated to speak during one of the MANY security plans."[99] Apparently once given a speaking slot by Mosley, Azzmador was now unhappy about his order on the schedule.

Also in the mutiny loop was future IE leader Patrick Casey, who then went by the pseudonym "Reinhardt Wolff." "This is why Kessler must go," Mosley told Casey on August 2. "So I've heard," Casey responded, "and if you notice, the moment azz brought up the jew and crazy stuff he beant [sic]." "Yeah," Casey agreed.

Because Erica Alduino, who created the "Charlottesville" Discord channel, was an IE member, technically subordinate to Mosley, he was able to have her transfer ownership of the channel to him. He remade the chat in his image, bringing in more extreme voices and giving moderator powers to extremely questionable people like Michael Chesny, know alternately as "Tyrone" and "Bunker Santa" on Discord.[100] Chesny would become a constant problem in the Discord. I was warned by multiple people about Chesny posting violent or inappropriate things in the chat. Ultimately, I did not see anything but lawful speech from the guy, which was my main criteria for leaving someone in. However, his over-the-top rhetoric and jokes about violence became a huge liability for us after the rally and formed the basis of the litigation against us.

---

[98] jasonkessler.us/wp-content/uploads/2023/11/Mosley-Azzmador-Kessler-is-a-Kike.pdf
[99] jasonkessler.us/wp-content/uploads/2023/11/Mosley-Azzmador-Kessler-Doesnt-Like-Azzmador-Daily-Stormer.pdf
[100] aljazeera.com/news/2018/4/17/neo-nazi-tyrone-exposed-as-us-marine

Mosley was working hard not only to sully my reputation among the leaders of the alt-right but also to toxify the messaging with people like Anglin. In private Discord messages, Anglin and Mosley maintained a line of communication about me and the rally: "95% of the people (literally we did a poll) supported him in every way and we literally staged a mutiny against Kessler," Mosley informed Anglin. "I also fed Azzmador some realllllly bad dirt we have on Kessler to use afterwards."

After the rally was over, Mosley would go on to tell a supporter named "Wyatt" that, "I was in charge of the whole thing."

When I was attacked by a left-wing mob at a press conference on August 13, the day after the rally, Mosley gloated about it with Johnny Monoxide, who had always represented himself as a friend to my face.

"Kurt told me about Kessler. Lmaoooooo wtf," Monoxide gloated.

"Yaaa," Mosley responded.

"That's so great. Holy shit. What a self absorbed dumb shit,"[101] Monoxide said.

According to planned speaker Augustus Invictus: "There seemed to be a consensus that the Spencer camp was taking control of the event . . . they de facto took control."[102]

Following this extensive smear campaign, Mosley began holding break-away planning meetings for the rally with Spencer's inner circle in Alexandria, including Brian Brathovd, Allison "Jack" Pierce (aka Ajax), and Greg Conte (another subordinate Spencer had cuckolded). I confirmed this thanks to a whistleblower, a young alt-right woman who was, at the time, pregnant with Sacco Vandal's child. She was the note taker for these meetings and shared some of the notes with my attorney.

A central problem I faced was that, especially with the looming ACLU case, I just did not have enough time to manage everything. I had to delegate responsibility, but had few trustworthy people to rely

---

[101] jasonkessler.us/wp-content/uploads/2023/11/Mosley-Monoxide-Mock-Kessler.pdf
[102] *Charlottesville Untold* p. 48

on. I entrusted Brathovd and Pierce to help with the planning details like how to get our people into and out of the event safely. Crucially, I even introduced Brathovd and Pierce to my contact at CPD, Wendy Lewis. Brathovd was presented as general head of security and Pierce as head of security for Spencer. Both of these men were loyal to Spencer and Mosley. Once they had the in with CPD, I was kept out of the loop entirely. Many things Lewis and other officers said to these men, which they assumed were being transmitted to me, never were. They went to Mosley instead. There would be absolutely disastrous implications of this on the day of the rally itself as we will soon see.

VIOLENCE

The final days leading into the UTR rally were a potboiler of rage and threats of violence from the so-called "counter-protesters" towards the demonstrators, and these taunts were often thrown right back at them in equal measure. George Lindbeck M.D., Head of Emergency Medical Services for the UTR rally, recalled being briefed by law enforcement prior to the rally. Intelligence they'd gathered led them to believe Antifa felt humiliated after a defeat at the Battle of Berkeley and were counting on a gratuitously violent victory in Charlottesville to recapture momentum.[103] According to Lindbeck, it was understood that "some 'left-wing' groups felt an obligation to physically attend the protest, and to physically confront the protesters." And that the UTR demonstrators were "less likely to initiate violent interactions than counter-protesters."

Contrary to popular perception that "Antifa is not an organization," Antifa are generally organized in regional chapters like Antifa of the Seven Hills (ASH) in Richmond, Smash Racism DC in Washington, Philly ARA in Philadelphia, and South Side ARA in Chicago. They are united through several means, including an umbrella organization called the Antifa Torch Network (the umbrella organization uniting the regional Antifa chapters), and via media platforms through which they publish their propaganda and instructional materials on topics like sabotage, rioting, and executions.[104] The most prominent websites are "It's Going Down" and "Crimethinc." The secular black bloc Antifa

---

[103] bitchute.com/video/6wDepKaioh8U
[104] farleftwatch.com/far-left-militia-training-for-guerrilla-warfare

are backed up by ideologically aligned "antifascist" church groups whose primary focus is "Black liberation theology," "queer liberation," and "antiracism," rather than anything to do with Jesus Christ or the Ten Commandments. Members of Congregate Charlottesville, Solidarity Charlottesville, and Anarchist People of Color, reached out to Redneck Revolt, an explicitly communist paramilitary unit, to act as their armed security during the protest weekend. Redneck Revolt has a reputation among Antifa affinity groups for being proficient in a military theater due to their firearms training and distribution of instructional propaganda on "sabotage," "kidnapping," and "executions." Redneck Revolt is considered by many an anti-White terrorist group which has called for "death to the 'good' paternalistic white 'ally.'"[105]

During the spring of 2017, Redneck Revolt prepared for battle by setting up targets in a desert gun range depicting images of Pepe the Frog, a symbol of the alt-right, and shooting them with semi-automatic rifles.[106] They posted a "Call to Arms" on both their own website and "It's Going Down." They called for their members and allies in Antifa affinity groups to come to the UTR rally and "dust off the guns of 1921," referring to an incident in 1921 where armed communists murdered military and law enforcement personnel.[107] Redneck Revolt posted another "Call to Arms" on their Facebook page in which supporters encouraged them to "Punch a Nazi." Another user posted an image of a hanging noose and platform along with the caption, "The only platform a fascist should have." This comment was "liked" by the Redneck Revolt account. Redneck Revolt brought along several additional communist militias for the purpose of using violence and intimidation to shut down the UTR rally, including Socialist Rifle Association and the John Brown Gun Club. Additional groups included co-conspirators Philly ARA, South Side ARA, Metropolitan Anarchist Coordinating Council (MACC), ASH, Roanoke People's Power Network, the Revolutionary Communist Party, Carolina Anti-Racists, Workers World Party, Democratic Socialists

---

[105] archive.is/I9oXi
[106] bitchute.com/video/A5wwRDBIJNNH
[107] redneckrevolt.org/single-post/call-to-arms-for-charlottesville

of America, Refuse Fascism, Louisville ARA, New York City Antifa, and Nashville ARA. Most, if not all, of these groups aren't legitimate protest organizations but violent criminal gangs tracked by Homeland Security,[108] the U.S. Army,[109] and watchdog agencies like the Regional Organized Crime Information Center (ROCIC).[110] Most explicitly argue the "failure of nonviolence" and exist for the purpose of violently repressing speech, or "no platforming." For instance, the Philly Antifa website calls for "direct confrontation" at protests and falsely claims offensive violence is "completely legal" because "the best defense is a good offense." They call for rallies and marches to be shut down and their political opponents to be "completely neutralized on the streets." Further, "Antifa generally adhere to a 'no platform' policy for racists and fascists, meaning we would oppose their organizations attempts to speak in public, hold political demonstrations, or recruit openly."[111]

After the rally, there was much speculation from conspiracy theorists about whether either the left or right-wing groups were funded by Jewish-Hungarian billionaire George Soros. What can be said for certain is that Refuse Fascism, co-founded by Black American affirmative action princeling Cornel West, and Carl Dix of the Revolutionary Communist Party, is funded, at least in part, by Soros. Refuse Fascism is not its own nonprofit. It receives fiscal sponsorship from Alliance for Global Justice—which is indeed a Soros-funded group.[112] Picket signs made by Refuse Fascism were distributed to members of the Antifa Torch Network and used to beat UTR demonstrators at the rally. Co-conspirator Anarchist People of Color declared: "There's no Nazi we can't punch,"[113] and posted a picture of planned UTR speaker Spencer getting assaulted.[114] South Side ARA encouraged their members to punch planned UTR speaker

---

[108] muckrock.com/news/archives/2018/jan/08/fusion-centers-antifa
[109] propertyofthepeople.org/document-detail/?doc-id=5018795-2018-10-18-Army-Antifa-RL
[110] propertyofthepeople.org/document-detail/?doc-id=5769976
[111] phillyantifa.org/frequently-asked-questions-suggested-readingsvideos-start-here
[112] influencewatch.org/non-profit/alliance-for-global-justice
[113] facebook.com/AnarchistPOC/photos/a.692863637483831/960593390710853
[114] facebook.com/AnarchistPOC/posts/950632408373618

Spencer.[115] Torch Antifa Network posted: "No platform for fascism."[116] Smash Racism DC told members it was "All out to bash the fash" at UTR.[117] ASH posted: "#punchrichardspencer #punchanazi,"[118] and encouraged co-conspirators to, "Get your crews together to #SmiteTheRight #A12."[119] Edgar Brandon Collins told supporters and co-conspirators: "I am confident they will have their asses handed to them . . . possibly physically."[120] Joe Starsia put out an incitement to "Kick white supremacy's ass."[121] Starsia's group, Cville SURJ, reposted an "It's Going Down" article about UTR speakers with the message "Know a Nazi, see a Nazi, punch a Nazi."[122] ASH published an image with the names of UTR speakers Kessler, Spencer, Heimbach, and IE leader Damigo with an incitement to "Destroy white supremecy [sic] and its actors."[123] Trans activist Gorcenski assured "It's Going Down" co-conspirators that Antifa "would take serious action" against the UTR rally.[124] Gorcenski also revealed that his activities surrounding the planned sabotage of UTR got him placed under FBI surveillance. The FBI even called to try to stage an intervention. Gorcenski became unhinged in the lead-up to the rally, posting pictures of himself firing semi-automatic rifles and telling UTR demonstrators: "Antifa are watching you." Gorcenski created and published a hit list of the UTR speakers with boxes to check off for each target being attacked. Following the rally Gorcenski updated the list with symbols such as fire, indicating the victim had been successfully pepper sprayed or an "X" indicating a successful assault.[125] As Gorcenski stated during the 2020 George Floyd

---

[115] twitter.com/Chicago_ARA/status/866140378575011841
[116] twitter.com/TorchAntifa/status/805550390079000577
[117] facebook.com/AntifaDC/posts/1063934550409816
[118] twitter.com/ash_antifa/status/828399392688324608
[119] twitter.com/ash_antifa/status/891726523266461696
[120] facebook.com/brandon.collins.796/posts/1599400656745861
[121] web.archive.org/web/20190501153841/https://www.facebook.com/joe.starsia/posts/10155670075397122
[122] jasonkessler.us/wp-content/uploads/2023/11/surj-cville-twitter-see-a-nazi-know-a-nazi-punch-a-nazi-in-reference-to-an-article-about-utr-organizers.pdf
[123] twitter.com/ash_antifa/status/895661737793519616
[124] twitter.com/EmilyGorcenski/status/894942985531650050
[125] twitter.com/EmilyGorcenski/status/898209167097384965

riots: "I'm not against violence, by all means punch the Nazi, burn a cop car."[126]

He also threatened UTR demonstrator Hannah Zarski in a very *Fatal Attraction* way, saying: "I will ruin every good thing [you] have." Gorcenski appealed to the most violent left-wing extremist groups in the country by placing propaganda on the "It's Going Down" website encouraging the Antifa Torch Network groups to attend and "Defend Cville" from speech they considered offensive. These articles included links to Gorcenski's social media where he was promoting opposition to the UTR rally and providing links to a Solidarity Cville social media account.[127] [128] The "It's Going Down" website is not a venue for legitimate, legal political activity. It is a website which hosts tutorials on espionage, sabotage, rioting, and violence against political rivals. It is the premier website for publication of propaganda and recruitment

Hitlist created by trans activist Edward "Emily" Gorcenski

---

[126] https://web.archive.org/web/20200624061627/https:/twitter.com/EmilyGorcenski/status/1275674100137148420
[127] itsgoingdown.org/charlottesville-va-unite-right-plans-friday-surprise-torchlit-rally-uva
[128] itsgoingdown.org/nonewkkk-mobilize-defend-charlottesville-va

material by co-conspirators Antifa of the Seven Hills, Redneck Revolt, Solidarity Cville, and Louisville ARA. When cells in the Torch/"It's Going Down" network have completed illegal acts like sabotage of communication infrastructure[129] or railway lines,[130] vandalism, rioting,[131] and heckler's veto "direct actions,"[132] they publish propaganda on "It's Going Down" bragging about their criminal exploits.

In addition to the activity of groups and individuals identified, there was a deluge of the most violent threats possible from thousands of individual social media accounts online. A local left-wing musician suggested that Charlottesville residents find my home and burn it down. While sharing a post from the ADL, an Asian man named Kai Au suggested, "Send the UN swat team and gun them all down! Display their carcasses and skulls on stakes!"[133] A Facebook user named George Burrell posted about the rally that "It should be legal to shoot the nazies [sic] and the kkk, I'd run them over if they were in my town."[134] We were told we "wanted to get shot," "when AntiFa and others like us get there it'll be like shooting fish in a barrel. Time to wipe these racists off the map for good," and that "There can be no mercy, no quarter, the round ups must be whole families, wives, children, relatives of racists and white nationalists." There were a number of threats related to the prospect of demonstrators again using tiki torches during a demonstration as they had on May 13. Twitter user Mike Isaacson proposed, "If Nazis are carrying torches, douse them in gasoline!"[135] An anonymous Twitter user suggested how great it would be if alt-right protesters were set on fire by an "aerosol-hairspray-wielding phalanx of drag queens."[136]

---

[129] web.archive.org/web/20170620140612/https://itsgoingdown.org/fiber-optic-cable-sabotage-continues-into-california

[130] web.archive.org/web/20170620135904/https://itsgoingdown.org/olympia-wa-train-tracks-sabotage-stop-fracking-equipment

[131] web.archive.org/web/20170620140544/https://itsgoingdown.org/sabotage-actions-against-gentrification-solidarity-with-baltimore-rebellion

[132] web.archive.org/web/20190417162554/https://itsgoingdown.org/antifascists-won-battles-berkeley

[133] jasonkessler.us/wp-content/uploads/2023/11/Threat_Display-their-Skulls-Carcasses-on-Stakes.pdf

[134] jasonkessler.us/wp-content/uploads/2023/11/Threat_Shoot-the-Nazis_Run-Them-Over.pdf

[135] jasonkessler.us/wp-content/uploads/2023/11/threat-if-they-have-torches-douse-them-in-gasoline.pdf

[136] jasonkessler.us/wp-content/uploads/2023/11/may-14-reaction-use-aerosol-spray-on-torch-nazis.pdf

Seeing all these warning signs of violent danger at the rally, many organizers and attendees prepared to employ self-defensive violence, if necessary. At one point, I posted an announcement recommending attendees "bring picket sign posts, shields and other self-defense implements which can be turned from a free speech tool to a self-defense weapon should things turn ugly." At other points I put the situation in more hyperbolic terms: "But if we are forced into a street brawl . . . fight them with honor, stay within reasonable bounds of the law and whoop that Commie, anti-white ass all over God's green Earth." At the time, I was not advocating total non-violence. I believed using self-defense when necessary was the best strategy and I was willing to fight for my rights. What was the alternative, telling people they had to stand there and be punched in the face without defending themselves? That masochistic level of commitment is what it takes to be a strict Gandhian nonviolence practitioner.

We set up a channel in the Discord called VA Law where we would help to clarify things people could and could not bring to the rally. I posted the actual Virginia statute governing self-defense, which talked about the appropriate level of force allowed by law. The final OpOrd, or operational order, was released on August 10, two days before the rally.[137] It contained a series of rules related to violence and weaponry at the rally, which came directly from consultation with the police. We told people not to bring knives, to avoid using flags as a weapon, highly discouraged using pepper spray (because of the overspray risk to innocent parties), prohibited attacking counter-protesters with tiki torches, and set general rules of engagement, which read:

> **It is extremely important that we avoid extreme violence at all costs** outside of what is needed to defend our people. **Do not aggress towards the counter protesters or start any fights.** If you are carrying follow the state law of VA and realize that if you use your weapon there is a high

---
[137] jasonkessler.us/wp-content/uploads/2023/11/OpOrd3-Avoid-Violence-HIGHLIGHTED.pdf

likelihood the court will treat you harshly/unfairly. Allow the police to do their job. As we saw at the KKK rally the cops were incredibly hands on, and in our communications with them they know the left are the ones looking to do violence. [Emphasis added]

This information was passed on to the leaders of the various groups attending, and it was their responsible to transmit this information to people attending the event under their leadership. Additionally, many individual users in the Discord community promoted, not an idea of pacifism, but lawful self-defense. "PEACEFUL CIVIL DISOBEDIENCE," wrote SpencerReesh. And later, "No violence. We have to keep our anger in check." Erica Alduino wrote: "Come prepared, bring your friends, but plan to be peaceful." User Baeravon wrote: "Hold the line. Don't be surprised at violence. And also, know that this is going to be about impressions. Don't be the perpetrators. Be blameless." User Cacoethes wrote: "Anyone encouraging violence is stupid at best and a fed at worst."

Links to the Charlottesville Discord were distributed freely across every rowdy alt-right message board on the Internet. We would certainly get people in the chat who would encourage violence in an unproductive way and we tried our best to moderate and remove those comments. However, we were all very busy and from time to time, braggadocio about "cracking skulls" and the like would slip through. Even I used this rhetorical flourish on one occasion to describe a life-or-death, self-defense situation. Much of the rhetoric that got out of control came from one man: Michael Chesny, aka "Tyrone." In retrospect, we should have moderated more of his comments and booted him from the chat. A centerpiece of the *Sines v. Kessler* lawsuit filed against organizers was a post by Chesny about running over protesters blocking roadways. His meme included the caption, "Introducing John Deere's New Multi-Lane Protester Digestor." He also asked, "Is it legal to run over protesters blocking roadways?"[138]

---
[138] lawandcrime.com/race-relations/neo-nazi-tyrone-u-s-marine-fired-charlottesville

A meme placed in the Charlottesville Discord by Michael Chesny aka Tyrone

The conspiracy theory that formed the basis of Roberta Kaplan's lawsuit insinuated there was some kind of "shared purpose" between organizers and James Fields which included running over counter-protesters. There are a few points that I would bring up in our self-defense:

1. There was no indication that anyone agreed with, or even saw, Chesny's post. Chesny himself didn't even attend the rally.[139] Although he made some suggestions about organizing shuttles to get protesters to Lee Park, none of his ideas were used. He was not an organizer. Curiously, only people who planned to speak and march in Charlottesville were sued for his comment, not Chesny himself. Kind of curious if the intention is to punish a "conspiracy" rather than inhibit First Amendment activity, right?

2. Detective Steve Young, the investigating officer in charge of Fields' homicide case, testified under oath there was no conspiracy,

---

[139] jasonkessler.us/wp-content/uploads/2023/11/Tyrone-Did-Not-Attend-Charlottesville.pdf

or even communication, between Fields and the UTR organizers.[140] Fields was not in the Discord and there is no way he would have seen Chesny's post. This was the result of both an analysis of the phone Fields had on his person at the time of his arrest and computers the FBI seized from his home in Maumee, Ohio.

3. Even if someone had seen Chesny's comment, who would have taken it seriously that he planned to drive a combine tractor to the protest and gobble up Antifa? The notion is too absurd to be taken seriously.

4. At the time, there was a massively popular meme on social media lionizing people who drove cars into annoying left-wing protesters blocking traffic, which still exists to some degree even today. It was so common to see conservatives joking about running over protesters that Fox News and *The Daily Caller* even posted articles with a supercut of protesters being run over to the soundtrack of Ludacris' rap hit "Move Bitch."[141] Lyrics: "And you about to get ran the FUCK over/Move bitch, get out the way/Get out the way bitch, get out the way." These articles were subsequently deleted after the rally. But this was yet another reason not to take seriously, or even give a second thought to Chesny's absurd post.

5. The first time I was able to log into Discord after learning about the death of Heather Heyer, I was informed by one of the moderators (Wyatt) that "Tyrone" was laughing about the woman's death but that he couldn't be reprimanded because Mosley had given him moderator status. I immediately removed his moderator powers and banned him from the chat.[142]

To summarize, we received volumes of sadistic and murderous threats prior to the demonstration. We tried our best to address the prospect of violence in a responsible way. With hindsight 20/20, we should have more heavily moderated the chat. However, the outcome of a total police stand-down, leading to a riot and a car careening into

---

[140] storage.courtlistener.com/recap/gov.uscourts.vawd.109120/gov.uscourts.vawd.109120.1153.1.pdf
[141] archive.ph/2017.08.15-201311/http://dailycaller.com/2017/01/27/heres-a-reel-of-cars-plowing-through-protesters-trying-to-block-the-road-video
[142] jasonkessler.us/wp-content/uploads/2023/11/Kessler-Wyatt-Remove-Tyrone.pdf

a crowd of people, was completely unforeseeable and we were operating under the premise of allowing all legal speech. The fact there were young men amping themselves up for a potentially dangerous situation seemed normal and appropriate given the circumstances. Insinuating that we "conspired" with Fields relies entirely on inviting jury prejudice to those they perceive as "Nazis." How could we know we had to parse every comment in a chatroom for anything that could be even vaguely perceived as an invitation to call our motives into question? Does it make sense that we filed for a permit and invited the police to come watch us commit wanton assaults and illegal acts of violence? I think not.

AUGUST 10:
THE ACLU HEARING

The ACLU filed their complaint[143] on August 10, with the understanding we'd get a fast-tracked hearing with a ruling one way or the other by the evening of August 11. It was going to be a nail-biting photo finish all the way up until the end. The brief argued in part that:

> The City granted permits for demonstrations opposing Plaintiffs views to occur on August 12, 2017 in Justice and McGuffey Parks located just blocks away from Emancipation Park in the same downtown area. Those demonstrations are said to be organized to protest "the messages of racial intolerance and hatred advocated by" the persons attending the demonstration in the Park. Upon information and belief, the organizers of these other events have encouraged and expect an attendance of more than 1,000 persons. Despite their allegation that the decision to revoke Plaintiffs permit was not based on the views he wishes to express, but on the numbers of possible participants, Defendants have taken no action to modify or revoke the permits issued for demonstrations by those with opposing views. Thus, with his scheduled rally only two days away, Plaintiff does not have a permit enabling him to demonstrate in

---

[143] jasonkessler.us/wp-content/uploads/2023/12/Kessler-v-Charlottesville-ACLU-Case.pdf

Emancipation Park, and counter-demonstrators have two downtown permits and the ability to occupy Emancipation Park without permit.

Coming full circle, I was feverishly utilizing the social media research skills I developed in researching for my Bellamy tweet exposé to find exhibits for the ACLU's complaint. The purpose was to show City of Charlottesville officials had a hostility to the viewpoints associated with my rally and that "safety" was not the reason they were canceling my permit for Lee Park.

Responding to an Antifa campaign for "anti-racists" to "#DefendCville" the weekend of UTR, Bellamy wrote: "This is dope! #Resist." Mayor Mike Signer taunted that his "9th grade locker room was more manly & advanced" than the Proud Boys (who he believed would be attending the rally). Paradoxically, he later crowed that "even the 'Proud Boys' have disavowed the August 12 alt-right event for racist and bigoted content and speakers." This was a reference to Proud Boys founder McInnes posting a "disavowal" of the rally to the Proud Boys website.[144] Perhaps he felt compelled to do this because I had been a guest on the *Gavin McInnes Show* multiple times and had technically joined the Proud Boys. In spite of this, future Proud Boys leader Enrique Tarrio did attend the rally.

Besides the ACLU, the complaint was also supported by legal research from the Rutherford Institute, a libertarian civil rights organization in Charlottesville, and alt-right attorney Kyle Bristow, a friend of Spencer from Michigan. Bristow, through his nonprofit, Foundation for the Marketplace of Ideas, had communicated a blistering July 23 letter[145] notifying the "Charlottesville governmental leaders" that:

> The police cannot and must not stand idly by if interlopers attempt to shut down the Alt-Right rally by improperly seizing control of the venue or by intimidating or physically

---

[144] The article was later re-edited to remove the term "disavow."
[145] jasonkessler.us/wp-content/uploads/2023/11/Bristow-Letter.pdf

attacking the Alt-Right activists. Failure of the police to act in good-faith to maintain order and to safeguard the First Amendment rights of the participants of the Alt-Right rally amounts to a due process violation of the most basic sort.

Bristow cited a U.S. Court of Appeals for the Sixth Circuit case called *Bible Believers v. Wayne County* which would also be cited in the federal ACLU complaint. *Bible Believers* was the most strongly worded enunciation of the legal principle that police have an affirmative duty to "take reasonable action to protect from violence persons exercising their constitutional rights." The Sixth Circuit held that, "If the officers allow a hostile audience to silence a speaker, the officers themselves effectively silence a speaker and effectuate a heckler's veto." Like in the landmark 1977 SCOTUS case *National Socialist Party of America v. Village of Skokie*, at least one of the ACLU attorneys representing us in court, Victor M. Glasberg of Alexandria, was Jewish. The others were Hope R. Amezquita of Richmond, a Latina, and John Whitehead, a White man and founder of the aforementioned Rutherford Institute. On the other side, Charlottesville was represented by City Attorney Craig Brown, in consultation with the legal giant Boies Schiller.

On August 10, planned speaker Christopher Cantwell arrived a day earlier than the others and we decided to get lunch together at the colonial-era Court Square Tavern, which I loved for its European beers and bespoke sandwiches. I rode to the Downtown Mall in Cantwell's car, which had been fitted with a security camera under the rearview mirror, and he wore a body camera on the collar of his shirt for good measure. I was informed he was recording me. We discussed things like our predictions for the ACLU case and the big meeting the next evening at McIntire Park. There had been chatter in the Discord for some time about a potential sequel to the May torchlight demonstration. Although we'd been noncommittal for months about whether to actually go through with it, plans seemed to be solidifying due to the overwhelmingly enthusiastic response to the idea. If it was going to happen, we'd decide the next night at McIntire. Almost as a matter of passing, I mentioned to Cantwell I'd received an email from Vice News journalist Elle Reeve inviting me to be interviewed for a documentary about the rally.[146] I was too busy, but offered Cantwell to take my spot. We both understood she was doing a hit piece, but Cantwell seemed to take inspiration from the old saying, "there's no such thing as bad publicity," and enthusiastically accepted her invitation. This was one of those decisions in retrospect that I'd like to take back. Cantwell ended up harming himself and playing right into the media's designs to depict us as violent, sociopathic goons. Reeve followed him to a *Radical Agenda* meetup in McIntire Park which went well enough. He was filmed giving his no-holds barred incendiary responses to Reeve asking about things like, for instance, Donald Trump's Jewish son-in-law Jared Kushner. The real problem set in when Cantwell took Reeve back to his hotel room . . . which is not what you may be thinking. Cantwell was the most traditionally "conservative" of the UTR speakers in many ways, such as being militantly pro-capitalist and pro-Second Amendment. He took the opportunity of Reeve's visit to show her all the legally purchased firearms he'd brought with him to Charlottesville. It was a veritable armory of handguns and semi-automatic rifles that would look at home in a movie about Marvel Comics' Punisher. Among them, two AK-47 semi-automatic rifles, a Kel-Tec P3AT handgun, a .380 ACP, a 9-millimeter Glock 19, a Ruger LC9, and a knife. In short, it created vivid propaganda for Vice's audience of terrified liberals living in a nightmare world where they believed crazy, out-of-control, White male Conservatives with a gun fetish were akin to terrorists and responsible for the American mass shooting epidemic. It didn't matter whether Cantwell was a model gun owner, never credibly accused of using them for anything but lawful self-defense. The perception of Cantwell as a gun nut stereotype in the video, titled *Charlottesville: Race and Terror*, was clear and maybe even consciously invoked by Cantwell as part of his liberal triggering self-promotion strategy. The situation was only worsened by Cantwell's tone-deaf response referring to counter-

---

[146] bbc.com/news/business-68377742

protesters as "stupid animals," admitting he'd "lost track" of all the guns he'd brought, and worst, claiming "a lot more people are going to die before we're done here."[147] Cantwell's statements are all defensible from a certain perspective. People do die when political tensions are hot, not due to violent designs necessarily but as casualties of the happenstance and chaos of political tumult. This historic inevitability was almost certainly the intention of Cantwell's comment. However, giving that statement to enemy media was a strategic misread which veered significantly from controversial self-promotion into handing talking points directly to a bad faith propagandist determined to make the protesters look like terrorists.

---

[147] youtube.com/watch?v=RIrcB1sAN8I

AUGUST 11

There were so many unknowns going into August 12. Believe it or not, one of my biggest worries was that we'd get rained out and all our planning would be for naught. As it turned out the forecast was warm and sunny: a perfect summer day for a protest. The bigger issue was that we had hundreds of protesters on their way to Charlottesville, but no permit and no clear planning details from police; only the steely determination to enter Lee Park no matter what. Through the Discord we encouraged attendees arriving that evening to bring their own tiki torches for an evening protest. Additionally, Mosley was able to disperse some funds collected within IE for the purchasing of extra tikis for the unprepared. Our intention in not publicly announcing this aspect of the protest weekend was to avoid conflict with Antifa. We hoped, like on May 13, we could do a quick pop-up demonstration and leave before left-wing militants could mobilize. This avoidance strategy affected most aspects of the planning. For instance, anticipating that it would be too hot to reappear at Lee Park, I suggested the alternative demonstration point of the historic UVA Rotunda, which is a stunning example of Roman-inspired, American colonial architecture with a monument to third American president and Charlottesville icon Thomas Jefferson in its central plaza. As a fan of the Enlightenment and its free speech principles, I found much common cause with Jefferson as the patron saint of my hometown. Jefferson, like all of the Founding Fathers, was also what you might anachronistically call a "White Nationalist." In *The Autobiography of Thomas Jefferson, 1743-1790*, he wrote about African slaves that, "Nothing is more certainly written in the book of fate than that these people are to be free. Nor is it less certain that the two races, equally free, cannot live in the same government. Nature, habit, opinion has drawn indelible lines of distinction between them." The first United States Congress, during Jefferson's tenure as Secretary of State, specified that only "free white persons" could be naturalized.[148] Further, Jefferson expressed a preference for the aesthetic beauty of the White complexion: "Are not the fine mixtures of red and white, the expressions of every passion by greater or less suffusions of colour in the one [Whites], preferable to that eternal monotony, which reigns in the countenances, that immovable veil of black, which covers all the emotions of the other race?"[149]

I also wanted to make the point that it was more than just Confederate generals who were under attack. The anti-White left had already pledged to come after Founding Fathers like Jefferson and George Washington because they were slave owners at a time in which bondage was still commonly practiced around the world. We felt confident we were well within our legal rights to use flames as part of our demonstration on UVA campus. Carrying the tikis was clearly part of the message of the protest and thus covered by our rights to free speech and assembly under the First Amendment. This was due to things like the legal analysis[150] published by Charlottesville Commonwealth Attorney David Chapman, which confirmed it to be First Amendment protected, as well as an opinion proffered to us by attorney Bristow. I personally did not see anything untoward, malicious, or "hateful" about the use of torches in protest. They've been used throughout history by European peoples in a variety of contexts. The Scots use them during their New Year's festival of Hogmanay. European nations like Hungary and Estonia[151] utilize torches during anniversaries of revolution against and independence from communism. The Vikings marched with torches to commemorate fallen warriors, before

---

[148] *Alien Nation*, Peter Brimelow, p. 12
[149] "Notes on the State of Virginia," *Thomas Jefferson: Writings* (New York: Library of America, 1984), pp. 264-5.
[150] wina.com/news/064460-chapman-memo-to-jones-no-saturday-night-prosecutions
[151] news.err.ee/914193/gallery-ekre-torch-parade-on-independence-day

using them to set boats containing the deceased on fire for a funeral pyre at sea. This tradition continues to this day in the form of the Up Hella Aa festival every January on the islands of Shetland, Scotland.[152] *The Smithsonian* pinpoints the origin of American torchlight parades to 1858 in Hartford, Connecticut. These nighttime torchlight parades for the Republican Party became "entertainment of unprecedented scale that attracted the attention of men, women, and children." According to Wikipedia, "Before the American Civil War in the U.S. illuminated processions were held as a way of promotion of political parties. That includes mass torch light processions in 1858 at Hartford Connecticut, the Republican Party in New York City in 1860[153] and in Galesburg, Illinois in 1884."[154]

Torchlight parade for Abraham Lincoln, New York City, October 3, 1860, published in Harper's Weekly

---
[152] theatlantic.com/photo/2023/02/photos-up-helly-aa-viking-fire-festival/672911
[153] archive.is/XISKA
[154] artvilla.com/poet-videos-1/av-vGfQS1yNhaQ.html

As the reader may recall, left-wing counter-protesters in Charlottesville had also utilized flames . . . during their May 14 demonstration against the alt-right. At the time, then-Charlottesville Mayor Mike Signer wrote approvingly that, "These are the kind of 'torches' I like." So, the activity had practically been endorsed by the entire Charlottesville establishment in one form or another.

Nevertheless, as the evening of August 11 arrived, protesters had renewed cause for concern about the safety of proceeding with a torchlit march. We learned through the publication of an article on the left-wing terrorist website "It's Going Down," that our chatroom had been infiltrated by an Antifa spy who was now calling on agitators to attend and disrupt our torchlight parade. Who might be the culprit? Likely there were multiple hostile individuals in the chat. We know for certain Gorcenski and Reverend Seth Wispelwey had been aware of the proposed demonstration "for weeks," according to the Charlottesville Independent Review. We also know *New York Times* technology reporter Kevin Roose was in the chat, since he wrote about it for the *Times*.[155] Another clue: the article was almost immediately publicized on Gorcenski's Twitter account. Gorcenski also claimed that his activities surrounding August 11 prompted a concerned phone call from the FBI, perhaps related to posting pictures of himself with guns[156] and even creating the aforementioned hit list with boxes to check off for every UTR speaker attacked that weekend.[157]

I arrived at McIntire Park around twilight and there were already dozens of activists congregating in the park including Azzmador, Invictus, Cantwell, Evan Thomas, Pierce, and Mosley. Most of the rank-and-file wore the white polos and khaki pants which had become associated with the alt-right and specifically IE. Crucially, there was no one from Nationalist Alliance in attendance. This meant no League, no TWP, no Vanguard, and no NSM, at least as far as I knew. There was no Heimbach, Hill, or Schoep. Until that moment I had no idea

---

[155] web.archive.org/web/20170817144324/https://www.nytimes.com/2017/08/15/technology/discord-chat-app-alt-right.html
[156] web.archive.org/web/20170808170729/https:/twitter.com/EmilyGorcenski/status/888037968816087040
[157] emilygorcenski.com/post/my-fbi-records-from-charlottesville-and-beyond

the Alliance had apparently broken off communication with the other organizers several days before. I demanded Mosley, who I'd been trusting to handle things while I was preoccupied with the ACLU case, tell me why the hell communication had broken down. He shifted attention and refused to directly answer me. He only mumbled, "That happened a while ago. Didn't you know that?" No, I didn't. I tried to call the League press officer Brad Griffin for more information, but he didn't pick up. We were already disunited before UTR had had a chance to happen.

Regardless, the atmosphere was friendly, giddy excitement with an edge of nervous anticipation. The ACLU had argued for our injunction in court earlier that day and the judge's decision was imminent. By this time everyone knew our plans had leaked and we had to make a decision. The group gathered round in a huddle. Cantwell's bodycam was recording, which was important for validating the events that transpired.[158]

"In case some of you guys didn't know already, there was an article up on 'It's Going Down' about the UVA march so we'll have to talk about whether we still want to try and do something with that or whether it's too much a risk at this point," I said.

"The torch thing . . . they're aware of that, the locations and stuff?" asked Cantwell.

"They're aware that it's at UVA. We don't know that they know anything about which statue we're going to. We don't know if they know anything about the field that we're supposed to meet up at. If we were going to move forward with this we would have to choose a different meet-up location and they would be looking for us."

"Is law enforcement already cooperating with us on that? Or is this not something we've involved them in?" asked Cantwell. "I'm gonna tell you from my perspective, if we're going to do it at all I want the cops involved, okay? These guys already turned around and said I drew down on them."

He was referring to an aborted attempt at a *Radical Agenda*

---

[158] bitchute.com/video/KLlfZPoCmF4R

meetup in the parking lot of the Charlottesville Walmart. Gorcenski and several other Antifa who had been obsessively surveilling Cantwell's premium content showed up to crash the meet-up and called the police to falsely accuse Cantwell of aiming his firearm at them. The allegation was later dispelled by parking lot security footage. "They will lie. There's nothing they won't do. They're operating by the rules of warfare and espionage and we need the cops on our side 100% of the time with this." "Ok. I mean I have a contact with the police department. Eli does as well. We can speak to them before we do this, if we do this," I replied. "My suggestion would be . . . and I'll follow your lead no matter what, okay," Cantwell continued. "This is your thing. But my suggestion would be. If they are, for whatever reason unwilling to escort us through this I would suggest calling that portion of it off and we'll just concentrate on making tomorrow go off as smoothly as possible. If these guys fucking attack us we're gonna fucking hurt them. You know what I'm saying?" The crowd murmured in approval. "Hurt them with torches," one member of the crowd said. I did not like that comment at all. I knew I needed to make a strong and unequivocal denunciation of violence. "Not just in terms of tonight but in terms of tomorrow, especially with the legal battle we've had to fight we really want to look like the good guys. We really have to be nonviolent because everything that the media is going to try and do is to try and reattach the stigma of these old groups like the KKK onto us. They're going to try and say that we're terrorists blah, blah, blah. They're already trying to do it just because they don't like what we have to say. So the best thing we can do is act like civilized White people, go and speak our mind and let the rest of Charlottesville: BLM, Antifa chimp the fuck out." With that plan in mind, I exited the huddle and called both Captains Wendy Lewis and Victor Mitchell to inform them about the torch march. They told me that the proposed location of the march, the UVA Rotunda, was in Albemarle County, not Charlottesville, and therefore outside their jurisdiction. I was told that they would call their colleagues at the UVA Police Department and someone would reach out to me shortly. Shortly I received a call from a female police officer identifying herself as Lieutenant Angela Tabler of the UVA Police Department. Earlier in the day, Mosley had identified Nameless Field, a soccer field near the library, as the gathering spot for demonstrators to assemble before marching to the Rotunda. Since he knew more about the plan for marching routes and so forth, I passed the phone to him so he could speak with Tabler directly.

There is some controversy about how this sequence of these events transpired. Following that evening, the University sought to ban me from returning to campus and had Tabler swear out an affidavit under oath claiming that she had already known about the demonstration and had been frantically calling me all day (six times in fact).[159] This is, however, demonstrably false and I have the phone records to prove it. As you can see, the sequence was that I called Lewis first at 7:16 PM and then Mitchell at 7:29 PM. Only then did Tabler call me for the first time at 7:46 PM.[160]

The further validity of my version of events is confirmed by internal emails I obtained through a FOIA request. At 8:12 PM on

Aug 11	6:46 PM	334.695.2197	Charlottes, VA	Incoming, CL	2
Aug 11	6:53 PM	334.695.2197	Charlottes, VA	Eufaula, AL	2
Aug 11	7:11 PM	610.406.2229	Charlottes, VA	Reading, PA	5
Aug 11	7:16 PM	434.566.1431	Charlottes, VA	Charlotsvl, VA	3
Aug 11	7:29 PM	434.566.1458	Charlottes, VA	Charlotsvl, VA	1
Aug 11	7:30 PM	434.566.1431	Charlottes, VA	Charlotsvl, VA	1
Aug 11	7:34 PM	Unavailable	Charlottes, VA	Incoming, CL	4
Aug 11	7:46 PM	434.566.6038	Charlottes, VA	Incoming, CL	5
Aug 11	7:57 PM	404.932.1405	Charlottes, VA	Incoming, CL	7
Aug 11	8:22 PM	434.566.1431	Charlottes, VA	Incoming, CL	11
Aug 11	8:46 PM	804.852.0106	Charlottes, VA	Incoming, CL	3
Aug 11	9:01 PM	586.713.8395	Charlottes, VA	Incoming, CL	4

(Excerpt: Call Logs of Jason Kessler showing Kessler placed OUTGOING calls to Captain Wendy Lewis [434.566.1431] and Captain Mitchell [434.566.1458] about the march and was only then contacted by Lt Tabler [434.566.6038].)

---

[159] jasonkessler.us/wp-content/uploads/2023/12/TablerDeclaration.pdf
[160] jasonkessler.us/wp-content/uploads/2023/11/August-11-Call-Logs.png

August 11, Charlottesville Police Chief Al Thomas sent an email to UVA Police Chief Michael Gibson: "Captain Mitchell spoke with Kessler who asked for police protection tonight. He forwarded him to Angela."[161] Chief Gibson responded: "One of my folks has been in contact with Kessler. I think we're good for right now. My folks are watching this closely."[162]

The fact the anti-UTR side controlled the reins of power so totally that they could make even the cops lie under oath about what happened is one of the frighteningly Orwellian aspects of trying to overcome the mythology and disinformation around the rally. Our multifarious enemies hated us enough to justify lying in order to entrap us. Like Cantwell said, "They will lie. There's nothing they won't do. They're operating by the rules of warfare and espionage . . ." This wouldn't be the last egregious example of scandalously false lies told about the alt-right's activities that night.

After Mosley got off the phone, he informed me Tabler had promised to send officers to secure the protest and create separation from the counter-protesters or militants who might be looking to do harm. I made an announcement to this effect and a cheer of exhilaration went through the crowd. Soon there would be even bigger cause for celebration.

Before we departed McIntire, I received a telephone call from Captain Lewis informing me that around 8 PM, the ACLU had prevailed in securing an injunction reinstating our permit for the next day! She told me the police were now going back to their original security plan. I was ecstatic because I believed this meant we would have police protection to prevent violence at the rally. When I made the announcement, the crowd was even louder and more thrilled than before. The moment felt historic and exhilarating.

The decisive factors for U.S. District Judge Glen Conrad, a George W. Bush appointee, were the disparate treatment of UTR compared with the counter-demonstrations in Jackson and McGuffey Parks

---

[161] jasonkessler.us/wp-content/uploads/2020/05/Highlighted-Kessler-asks-for-protection.png
[162] jasonkessler.us/wp-content/uploads/2020/05/Highlight-UVa-Chief-in-touch-with-Kessler.png

which had not been canceled or relocated, and the biased social media posts I had collected from Signer, Bellamy, and others in the Charlottesville government. In his decision, Conrad wrote:

> Based on the current record, the court concludes that Kessler has shown that he will likely prove that the decision to revoke his permit was based on the content of his speech. Kessler's assertion in this regard is supported by the fact that the City solely revoked his permit, but left in place the permits issued to counter-protestors. The disparity in treatment between the two groups with opposing views suggests that the defendants' decision to revoke Kessler's permit was based on the content of his speech rather than other neutral factors that would be equally applicable to Kessler and those protesting against him. This conclusion is bolstered by other evidence, including communications on social media indicating that members of City Council oppose Kessler's political viewpoint. At this stage of the proceedings, the evidence cited by Kessler supports the conclusion that the City's decision constitutes a content-based restriction of speech.[163]

I did a livestream on Periscope where I gloated unceremoniously about the victory. By 8:34 PM, Lewis had sent me three texts confirming some details of the police department's alleged re-commitment to protecting UTR: "Working on enlarging your area now," "Water and power will be unlocked and on by 7am," and "All security teams talked with and original plan with escorts for vip/speakers in place."

I drove to UVA and, anticipating the potential for vandalism, parked my personal vehicle well away from the Rotunda in a monitored downtown parking lot. This turned out to be a smart move since vehicles identified with the protesters were found with tires slashed and windows smashed out later that night. I walked up Main Street,

---

[163] casetext.com/case/kessler-v-city-of-charlottesville

the main strip on the UVA corner, towards Nameless Field. There was clearly a gathering energy, with a small but consistent flow of demonstrators walking in the same direction. On my right, I passed by St. Paul's Memorial Church. I looked up and saw several angry-looking men with semi-automatic rifles overlooking the top of the steps going to the church. According to the Charlottesville Independent Review, these men were members of the anarchist gun club Redneck Revolt, who had been firearm training using alt-right targets that summer and were invited by Congregate Charlottesville to act as their personal militia.[164] In fact, Congregate Charlottesville was formed just a few weeks before UTR, to invite upwards of 1,000 "faith leaders" to physically challenge UTR participants with their bodies and be willing to go to jail in doing so. According to Heaphy: "The security team scouted the external perimeter, posted guards at ingress and egress points, and monitored the social media communications of Spencer, Kessler, and other supporters of the Unite The Right event." At the time neither I, nor anyone else associated with UTR, had any idea about the church service and counter-protester training that was transpiring at St. Paul's at the same time as our demonstration. But we came to find out after the fact how important this assembly was. The service was the culmination of a series of counter-protester trainings led by radical left-wing queer liberation pastor Wispelwey and his Congregate Charlottesville. This group believed in "confrontation" with UTR protesters and had split from a larger group, the Charlottesville Clergy Collective, over its unwillingness to escalate hostilities with protesters. The service was attended by national celebrities like Black activist Cornel West and left-wing Jewish journalist Katie Couric, who was there filming a documentary for NatGeo.[165] Many of the most politically powerful and influential figures in Charlottesville were also in attendance including Signer, Bellamy, and Black Virginia District Court Judge Claude V. Worrell II.

The church service was a mix of violent, apocalyptic rhetoric and

---

[164] Heaphy pp. 114, 123
[165] youtube.com/watch?v=FDIfPhx-Fm0

unhinged, delusional paranoia. Cornel West told the crowd: "We have to take a stand. That's why some of us came to fight and get arrested if necessary."[166] A Black female preacher named Traci Blackmon compared the crowd of the most politically powerful figures in Charlottesville to the biblical David squaring off against the alleged Goliath of the alt-right. She implored the crowd to take "preparation for the battleground" and consider that David didn't just kill Goliath, he unsheathed his sword and cut Goliath's head off. "David doesn't just knock him down and kill him. But David takes his head off. Every time a stone knocks a giant down we'll be celebrating but we won't get relief until we CUT THE HEAD OFF!"[167]

Despite the fact the alt-right didn't even know that anything was going on at St. Paul's, a completely fictional persecution yarn had been spun by the congregants, who apparently thought they were the center of our universe. According to the Heaphy Report: "At 8:21 p.m., [Signer] sent a text message to City Manager Jones and Chief Thomas, informing them that 'four alt right' were inside the church and appeared to be dangerous." Obviously, this was a delusional fiction and (surprise, surprise) no evidence of these men or how Signer knew they were "dangerous" "alt-right" has ever materialized. Perhaps he had mistaken Redneck Revolt for the alt-right, since he might not have known that leftists also carry guns? Judge Worrell also called Lieutenant Mooney of CPD to request police protection.[168] By far, the biggest whopper of a lie came from Wispelwey, West, and others who claimed the church was "surrounded" by "torch-wielding Nazis" who "held [them] hostage in the church."[169] In reality the proximity of the torch demonstration to St. Paul's was captured by Couric's documentary crew, which surely would have released footage of this alleged encirclement had it really taken place. From the steps of St. Paul's Church where Couric and NatGeo filmed, the torches were only visible as pinpoints of light far in the distance.

---

[166] bitchute.com/video/mONw5cjq1g6Q
[167] facebook.com/SojournersMagazine/videos/10154913829892794
[168] Heaphy p. 115
[169] democracynow.org/2017/8/14/cornel_west_rev_toni_blackmon_clergy

Katie Couric points to the UVA torch demonstration in the distance

The torch demonstration as seen from the steps of St Paul's Church (which was allegedly "surrounded")

Meanwhile, hundreds of protesters were gathered in the wide-open expanse of Nameless Field along with a smattering of left and far-left "independent journalists" like Ford Fischer of News2Share and the Antifa-aligned Unicorn Riot. What we didn't see were any police. Apparently, they were in hiding, shaking in their boots with the same level of delusional paranoia effecting the left-wing activists. According to the Heaphy Report: "The two senior VSP officials saw the torches for the first time while driving up University Avenue, and Colonel Flaherty pulled his VSP vehicle into the parking lot of the University President's home at Carrs [sic] Hill. When Flaherty saw hundreds of torches emerge from behind the Rotunda, he recalled instructing Daniels to give him a sidearm, as he anticipated trouble and he had no intention of 'wading into white supremacists unarmed.'" Before, during, and after the event, the police assumption was that we were dangerous and illegitimate as protesters so they refused protection and de-escalation, ensuring they could blame us for the fights that transpired in a self-fulfilling prophecy. As for the UVA Police Department, they were waiting across the street from the Rotunda. In spite of their promises to us over the phone, they'd apparently been ordered to take a hands-off approach.

Although I was an "organizer," I had zero control over the crowd. Mosley, on the other hand, had come prepared with a bullhorn and was shouting orders like a military commander. He ordered the demonstrators into a single file line and on cue, each began to light their tikis. The smell of citronella hung over the cool night air. At one point I tried to step off and lead the crowd, but without a megaphone it was impossible. This seemed to be an IE operation first and foremost with a hierarchy of adjutants reporting under Mosley's authority and helping to keep stragglers in line. While we were waiting for the marching orders, I was approached by the journalist Fischer. He asked me what our intention was in using the tiki torches.[170] I answered: "The torches are to commemorate the fallen dead of our European brothers and sisters: like Robert E. Lee, like Thomas Jefferson, like

---

[170] youtube.com/watch?v=tYnxf5VHu80

George Washington who are under attack by these Leftist Cultural Marxists who hate White people, who hate White people's history and want to blame them for things that happened in the past that every race on Earth did but only White people are being persecuted for. So this is to honor the fallen dead." "Do you think Thomas Jefferson would have participated in something like this?" Fischer asked, perhaps with a note of disapproval in his voice. "Oh, absolutely!" I answered. "He was a revolutionary. We are too." Despite the controversial nature of our protest, I was secure in the belief Jefferson would welcome it. About his beloved university Jefferson stated: "This institution will be based on the illimitable freedom of the human mind." This sentiment is sharply at odds with the woke anti-speech, anti-White zealots running UVA today and their reaction to the torch protest. "What kind of revolution do you seek? A revolution that replaces what we have with something else?" Fischer asked. "Right now we are in a civil rights struggle," I replied. "A civil rights struggle to save White people from an ethnic cleansing which is happening across the Western world. Our monuments are being torn down. They are being removed and replaced and our people are being torn down and replaced through immigration policies. It's very symbolic with the way they're trying to remove White people from the history of the United States and Europe that they're trying to remove White people from the ground that they walk on as well." "Last thing: it seems like the left and right have gotten to this point where it seems like there is warfare rhetoric between the two. Is this a war for you?" "This is political discourse. And as long as we have organizations and lawyers who are willing to fight for us in court perhaps we can have a peaceful solution. If the ACLU was not successful today and the Charlottesville City government was allowed to deny us our Constitutional First Amendment rights we might be in a different situation than we are today . . . As of today the Constitution was upheld and the people who founded this country have a fighting chance to take it back."

Eventually Mosley shouted through his bullhorn for the march to begin, and the line, which now numbered at perhaps 200, most of which were carrying tikis, began to snake its way out of Nameless Field in the direction of the Rotunda. As the line began to move, the crowd let loose a whooping cry. It had to be the loudest rebel yell heard in America since the days of the Civil War. To observers it must have been a truly impressive and awe-inspiring sight. Dave Reilly was flying a drone overhead that captured an amazing view of the massive illuminated procession.[171] Being a part of it was surreal. You knew you were doing something historic and using such an ancient source of natural light made it feel like we were living like people of another era. I thought about Martin Luther King Jr. and the Black civil rights movement. I thought, "Now we have our own civil rights movement." It was time for us to have one. We need robust representation like other groups in America have. "You will not replace us! You will not replace us!" the marchers started to chant. I was proud to be part of this brave group of White people.

---

[171] bitchute.com/video/yHqtc230vr08

All at once someone with a camera, possibly from Unicorn Riot, swung around to my left and started filming me. Somewhere in the distance the chant started to change. Although the majority stuck to the original, approved chant, a small but vocal minority were chanting "Jews will not replace us!" I was incredibly embarrassed. This was beyond the scope of what this basic, pro-White demonstration was supposed to be about. And with the camera on me I felt like I had no choice but to carry on, silently marching as if nothing untoward was happening. Years later I heard Damigo refer to what had happened as the "troll's veto." In other words, a subset of trolls hijacking the event and messaging for their own agenda. A similar, but even louder, unapproved chant was "Blood and soil." I didn't like that because I strongly disapproved of the individuals trying to associate my rally with Third Reich sloganeering and imagery. I was a White civil rights guy.

Suddenly Spencer burst out of the shadows into line beside me. He'd been hiding in wait somewhere on the UVA Lawn with a couple of bodyguards. I said hello but, like usual, he seemed to be in a foul mood. He started complaining about the route Mosley was directing the march. It did seem Mosley was a bit lost, which would have been understandable considering that he was in a completely strange town at night. I walked up and pointed him back in the right direction.

Cantwell was marching nearby. Despite having a good, cautious perspective during the McIntire Park meeting, his behavior was raising some eyebrows during the march. He kept making unnecessary, aggressive contact with the hostile media marching alongside us, including Unicorn Riot. One of my bodyguards leaned in and asked me if he was okay and if anybody was watching him. In his mind, Cantwell probably thought he was protecting the group, but we were worried he might expose himself and others to unnecessary legal jeopardy. Later, Cantwell would be one of only a handful of marchers who got in a fight with Antifa, and months later, would become a media poster child for our side's alleged violent conduct.

At that point none of us had any idea we were going anywhere except an empty plaza. We thought if there was going to be a confrontation it would've happened during the march. We were in for one nasty surprise.

ANTIFA'S NASTY SURPRISE

Unbeknownst to us at the time, some of the most violent Antifa freaks in the country were at UVA under the command of Communications Director Luis Oyola, a self-identified member of the extremist group Anarchist People of Color (APOC), and Gorcenski. On the "It's Going Down" podcast, *Ex-Worker*, Oyola described how a rift had broken out between the less confrontational activists at St. Paul and their more militant and violent friends in Antifa. This led them to split off in search of confrontation at the Thomas Jefferson statue.[172] "We organized to, in whatever ways we could, disrupt the torchlit rally," Oyola said on the podcast. "We knew this was an opportunity for the Charlottesville community to stand up to them and let them know that we weren't going to allow them to organize again." There were a small number of UVA student allies already at the statue and the Antifa, like Oyola, claimed to be going there to "protect" them. In reality, the approximately dozen Antifa militants included convicted felons and at least one domestic terrorist. They came armed and prepared to start a riot in order to prevent the alt-right from being able to speak and peaceably assemble as intended. They'd been preparing for this confrontation for a long time, ever since the "torch march was revealed through leaks and anonymous hearsay even weeks before August 12." Oyola said Antifa were using a "diversity of tactics [including] open carry, anti-fascist blocs, blockading . . . any tactic that would go towards the goal of defending Charlottesville from fascism." What this moron

---

[172] bitchute.com/video/OOUmgpJCUsqy

was calling "fascism" was our American right to speak and assemble without permission from his violent thugs.

Antifa Militants Identified at the Thomas Jefferson Monument

Liter (center) holds a canister of mace; Zoller (center-right) came strapped with a handgun; anti-speech zealots lock arms to block the Jefferson statue

Holly McGlawn Zoller is the blonde in the black top at the center of the above picture. Against UVA firearm policy, she had a handgun holstered at the hip. In the center of the photograph in the grey long-sleeved shirt and jeans is her boyfriend, Sean Liter. He's holding some kind of weapon, likely mace or pepper spray, in his right hand. Together they are the founders of Louisville's Antifa chapter, Louisville Anti-Racist Action.[173]

Also along for the ride were two big Toms from Philly: Tom Massey and Tom Keenan from Philly's Antifa chapter Philly Anti-Racist Action. Massey was mentioned earlier for his participation at the Trump inauguration riots and his hope there would be more opportunities for violence in the future and more opportunities to "punch Nazis."

---

[173] leoweekly.com/2017/08/story-two-louisville-antifa-charlottesville

Thomas Jackson Massey Philly ARA

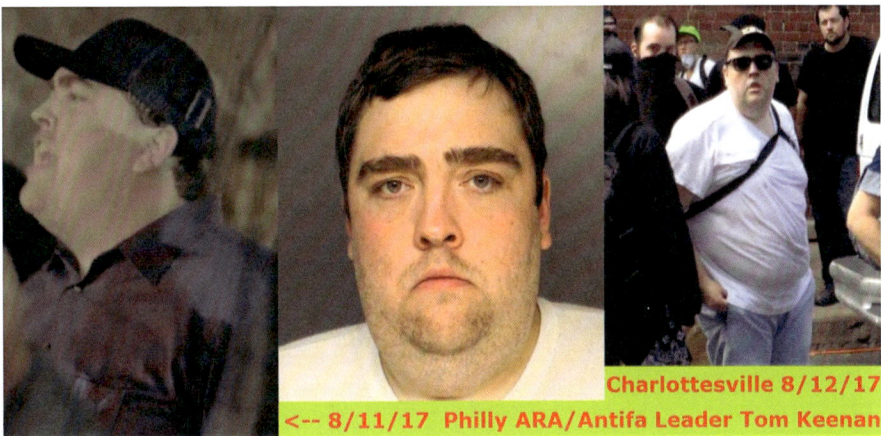

Charlottesville 8/12/17
<-- 8/11/17 Philly ARA/Antifa Leader Tom Keenan

On August 11 he wore a long-sleeved orange shirt under a blue t-shirt.

Perhaps by wearing UVA school colors he thought he could blend in as a student. But he and Keenan were too old to be typical UVA students, and their massive frames were far from the images of the "helpless, frail students" depicted by the media. In the near future they would be charged with assault for a violent, racially motivated attack on Hispanic U.S. Marines they mistook for "Proud Boys."[174]

Also from Philly Antifa was Paul Minton, a felon convicted of "conspiracy to tamper with evidence" and "abuse of a corpse" for

---

[174] dailymail.co.uk/news/article-6503495/Two-innocent-marines-beaten-antifa-protesters-MACE.html

Violent felon Paul Minton, a proud Antifa, helped dispose of the corpse of a murder victim

Paul Minton, in the crowd at the UVA Rotunda on August 11

hiding the dead body of a murder victim.[175] The macabre incident happened in Minton's old skinhead days. That's right, Minton used to be a "Hollywood Nazi," slang for guys who acted like characters from *American History X*. While watching TV with two skinhead friends, Yohan Lee and Keith Pierce Jr., Minton observed Pierce drive a two-pound hammer into Lee's head 30 times and then helped dispose of the dead body.

Brent Betterly of Chicago Antifa or Southside ARA, along with two accomplices, was charged and convicted for crimes related to plotting to firebomb Chicago Mayor Rahm Emanuel's home during a North Atlantic Treaty Organization summit.[176] According to NBC News: "Other alleged targets included police stations and the Prudential Building campaign headquarters of President Barack Obama."[177]

Known Chicago and South Florida Antifa Terrorist
Brent Vincent Betterly

Lindsey Moers was another Philly-based militant waiting for us at the Rotunda. She came equipped with an expandable baton which she used to full effect. This baton was later recovered by the FBI and disclosed in a search warrant application the FBI submitted for Moers in federal district court.[178]

---

[175] newspapers.com/article/the-philadelphia-inquirer/18337045
[176] cbsnews.com/chicago/news/sentencing-for-nato-3-set-for-april-25
[177] nbcnews.com/news/world/nato-3-plead-not-guilty-alleged-firebomb-plot-flna858671
[178] s3.documentcloud.org/documents/20698671/amazon-facebook-google-provide-data-on-unite-the-right-rioter.pdf

Lindsey Moers (left) with an unidentified "trans" Antifa

Mikey Longo Jr. spits onto protesters, looking to provoke violence

Mikey Longo Jr. is another Philly Antifa caught engaging in violence throughout the UTR weekend. He's pictured above spitting on UTR protesters during the August 11 protest.

The leader of the group was likely Emily Gorcenski. In October 2017, Gorcenski stated about his role on August 11 and 12 that, "Maybe the wrong person to accuse of having no experience is one of the

Violent "trans" Antifa activist Edward "Emily" Gorcenski

people who helped organize an event that led to 70 WH [White House] resignations."[179] Gorcenski, like Holly Zoller, was likely strapped with a firearm on the night of August 11. He has mentioned carrying firearms during the weekend protest events several times including in September 2017: "You know I'm not an ideological non-violent advocate, right? I literally *pulled a fucking gun* on August 12,"[180] and May 2018 when he said, "You all have *no idea* how goddam [sic] close Charlottesville got to an open shootout. No goddamn idea."[181]

Additionally, there were about a dozen young people, at least some of which have in fact been confirmed as UVA students. They held up a banner reading VA STUDENTS ACT AGAINST WHITE SUPREMACY and were chanting "black lives matter." One of the youths sat in a wheelchair, although I was familiar with this woman from Charlottesville City Council, where she would walk around freely without assistance. The wheelchair was for effect, to make herself look like a vulnerable, disabled girl being picked on by "white supremacists." Looking like a victim for the media is a key component of left-wing activist training

---

[179] web.archive.org/web/20200531093043/https:/twitter.com/EmilyGorcenski/status/915646316570701825
[180] web.archive.org/web/20190501163137/https:/twitter.com/EmilyGorcenski/status/907006080529694720
[181] archive.is/Z2rIk

and has been since the time of Martin Luther King Jr. and probably earlier. They had an agenda to harm me and UTR, which has its roots in the activism of the New Left and King. The mainstream public education version of King's activism is filled with scary pictures of firehoses and dogs. But in reality, King sought out conflict. He purposefully looked for towns with police chiefs who would overreact, and recruited women and children to stand up front and look like victims. This might sound like heresy to those taught a sanitized hagiography of King's life, but these facts have been reported even by Black journalists writing for *The Washington Post*.[182] This was all a stage play for the media to twist into propaganda about heroic victims and villainous "white supremacists." The difference between then and now is that the radical, racial activists also run the city councils, universities, and police departments. They can stage themselves to look like victims and then have their lackeys in the police departments arrest their political rivals, to be tried by leftist prosecutors and judges. Of course, the media ate that up and have consistently reported that we "surrounded a group of peaceful UVA students," which is a huge inaccuracy by omission. Not once was it ever mentioned the majority of those in attendance were violent Antifa. This is how the media and left-wing activists framed us for something we didn't do: including willful omission, error, and spite. We were guilty first, with a story made up to justify it later.

Back in the alt-right march, we'd made our way up the back entrance to the Rotunda, with its large, white marble stairs winding around to the front of the building. When we got to the top of the front steps, we could see down into the plaza with the Thomas Jefferson statue for the first time. The fact there were counter-protesters, likely armed, and no police caused a shiver of panic up my spine. As we made our way down the Rotunda steps, into the trap laid for us, the Antifa Torch Network tweeted a video of us coming down the stairs where they announced: "Here come the Nazis.

---

[182] washingtonpost.com/posteverything/wp/2015/10/01/dont-criticize-black-lives-matter-for-provoking-violence-the-civil-rights-movement-did-too

They're coming for the statue right now. They will not be allowed to take the statue," with one of their followers labeling us "Like lambs to the slaughter."[183] I remember looking back seeing the crowd marching inexorably towards the plaza and wanting to stop them, but it was too late. "Hold on!" I shouted but no one could hear me. Mosley was still jabbering away on the megaphone. Why wasn't he trying to stop the march?

The night of August 11 was the first time I understood the crowd as a force of nature: one which, in a state of excitement, can become as uncontrollable as a gale wind or a bolt of lightning. In his *Psychology of Crowds* (1895), French sociologist Gustave Le Bon wrote that:

> By the mere fact that he forms part of an organised crowd, a man descends several rungs in the ladder of civilisation. Isolated, he may be a cultivated individual; in a crowd, he is a barbarian—that is, a creature acting by instinct. He possesses the spontaneity, the violence, the ferocity, and also the enthusiasm and heroism of primitive beings, whom he further tends to resemble by the facility with which he allows himself to be impressed by words and images—which would be entirely without action on each of the isolated individuals composing the crowd—and to be induced to commit acts contrary to his most obvious interests and his best-known habits. An individual in a crowd is a grain of sand amid other grains of sand, which the wind stirs up at will.

Le Bon didn't think it was hopeless to control the crowd, but they need authority and structure. The structure that I tried to implement required robust police intervention. When they denied that to us, we were left with nothing but the wild, untrammeled, primitivism of aimless masses.

I had four movement friends watching my back that night to

---

[183] twitter.com/torchantifa/status/896371721795772416

make sure I was safe. Once we realized there was no stopping the crowd, we walked to the perimeter of the plaza, far away from the Antifa counter-protesters. As more and more UTR demonstrators filed into the plaza, the entire area was filled in, leaving protesters and counter-protesters within striking distance of one another. This was the exact thing we were trying to avoid by calling the police. Where the hell were they?! Answer: they were waiting across the street hoping for violence to break out so they could disband the protest as an unlawful assembly.

I didn't actually see much of what occurred next. At the time I saw the backs of the rows of torch-bearing protesters in front of me and participated in a "White Lives Matter!" chant. At some point, I saw liquid mist shooting out, like from a small cannon, in both directions. My informal security grabbed me by the shoulders and whisked me even further away from the violence we assumed was taking place.

In retrospect, I have studied more videos, photos, and other evidence than anyone else alive and can reconstruct a pretty accurate picture of what went down. With none of the expected and requested separation from police, UTR and Antifa protesters were smack-talking

Despite assurances from police they would separate hostile groups, UVA police waited across the street, allowing violence to unfold

one another hard. As if that wasn't enough, Antifa were doing their best to "disrupt the torchlit rally" by baiting the demonstrators into a violent conflict. Big Tom Massey was lunging into the crowd and slapping at protesters.[184] Mikey Longo Jr. was spitting into the crowd.[185]

At some point the bait worked and the two sides began engaging in mutual combat. Massey got into a bone-crushing brawl with an apparent skinhead whom I've never seen before or since. Cantwell ended up deploying pepper spray as he was being charged by an anonymous man referred to in our community as Beanie Man (for the choice of head-wear he wore that night). In the midst of the fighting, Lindsey Moers took out her baton and started clubbing guys over the head with it.[186]

Only then in the immediate aftermath of the fighting did UVA police finally come in and break things up. They arrested one IE member named Ian Hoffman, whose charges where subsequently dropped. For many years, the only individual successfully prosecuted

Lindsey Moers (right) in shades and baseball cap raises a metal baton to strike protesters on August 11

---

[184] bitchute.com/video/Ey5kfWImNgf0
[185] facebook.com/N2Sreports/videos/1489732477801303 (41:40)
[186] facebook.com/SamperFi/videos/10154975627623251 (8-9 seconds in)

from this incident was Cantwell, who was charged with felony "malicious use of gas" for deploying pepper spray. Gorcenski and an accomplice named Kristopher Goad from ASH Antifa in Richmond, Virginia, claimed they'd been burned by overspray from Cantwell's deployment of mace. The evidence was inconclusive, owing to the fact there were multiple deployments of spray from both sides that night. However, Cantwell jumped at the opportunity to take a misdemeanor plea deal which would allow him to retain his firearm rights.

We walked back orderly to Nameless Field in order to dispose of the tikis. When we got back, I stood on a picnic table and thanked everyone for attending. There was a chant of "Kessler! Kessler! Kessler!" which I was largely embarrassed by. Sadly, the alt-right would soon turn on me, so it would be the first and last time a crowd of them chanted my name.

I left UVA, now bathed in the red and blue lights of police cars and fire engines. It was like a climactic scene from a movie with the pulse-pounding resolution a mere morning away. The night of August 11, I stayed at the home of a nearby relative out of an abundance of caution for my personal safety. At the time, I was treating my lifelong insomnia with Ambien, an extremely effective sedative with potentially severe hallucinogenic side-effects. The proper way to take the medication was to immediately close your eyes and drift off to sleep. However, when I'd stay up clacking away on my laptop keyboard, after taking the pill, I'd find reality warping around me like I'd taken a hit of acid. The next morning there'd be things that I'd written, sometimes wildly out of character, which I did not remember writing. Or I'd sleepwalk into the kitchen and devour food left and right without any cognition of what I was doing. Thankfully, none of this happened on August 11. However, I drifted off into a deep, prolonged slumber and allowed myself to sleep in a bit the next morning, sort of in self-congratulation for what had been accomplished so far with the ACLU and the permit. Big, huge, colossal mistake. I should have been up early demanding scouting reports, checking in with allies on the ground, etc. I had way too much faith in everything: my putative allies, the judicial system, and the police. It was time for my rude awakening.

ANTIFA'S NASTY SURPRISE

One of two original posters for UTR

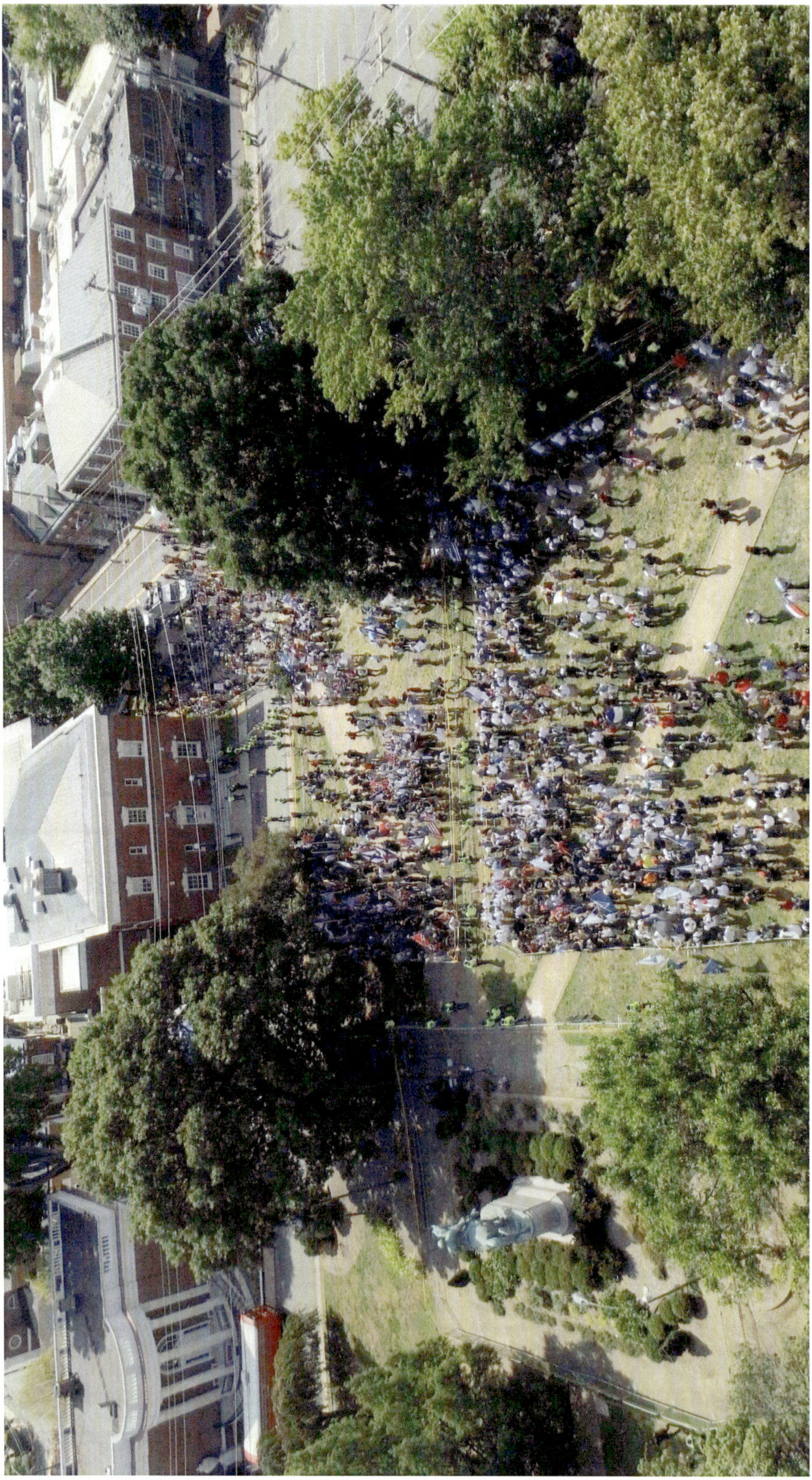

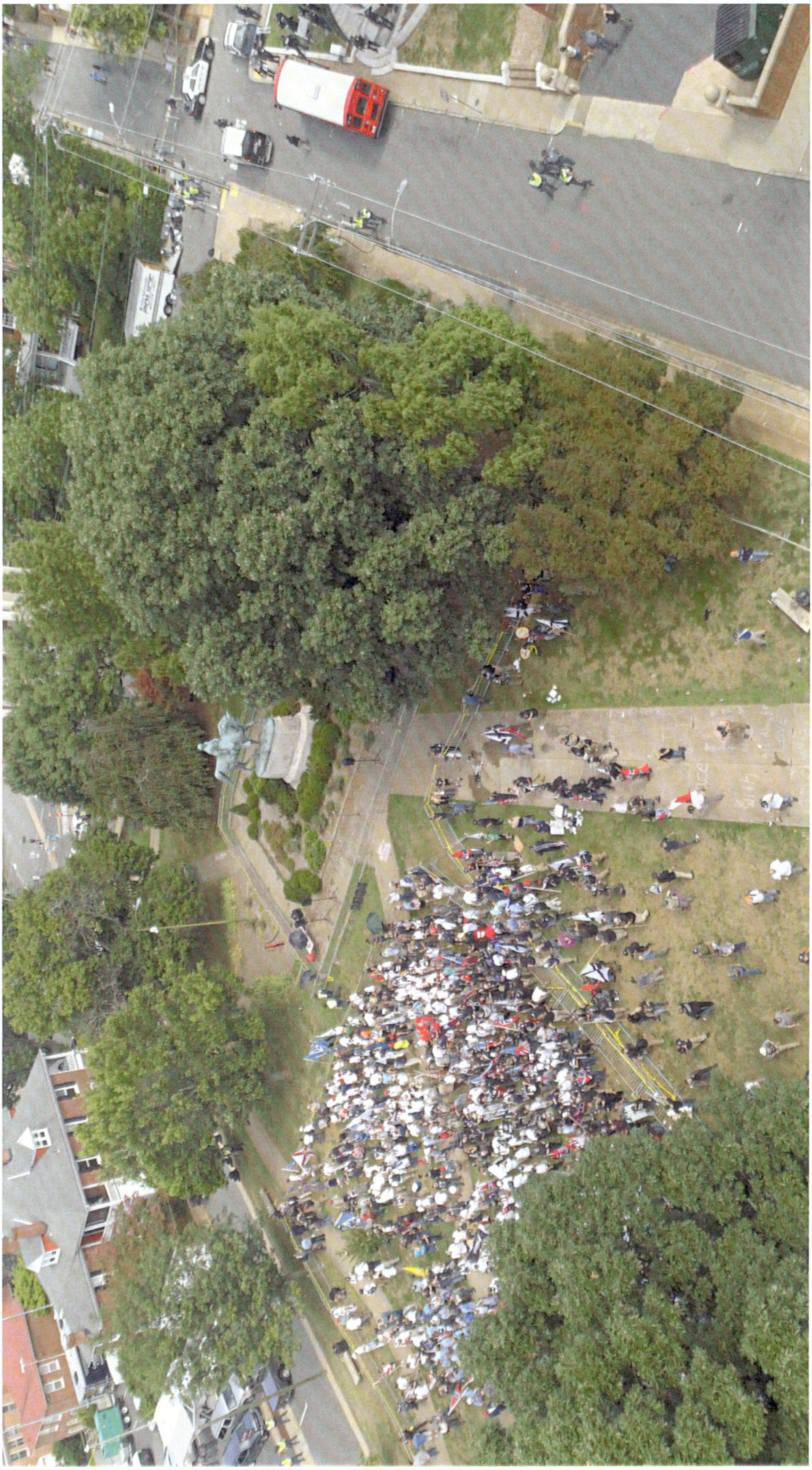

AUGUST 12, 2017: UNITE THE RIGHT

The next morning, I was met by my security crew, four guys in white polos and khakis who never used their real names but watched my back like brothers the whole weekend. They were led by a military veteran using the pseudonym Tyson Belisaurius, the same sobriquet he used as host of the *Godcast* podcast on *TRS*. We piled into someone's four-door sedan and booked for McIntire Park, the meeting point for rally-goers where they could catch a shuttle to Lee Park. The mood at McIntire was jubilant. There were hundreds of men and women from all over the country, carrying American and Dixie flags, banners, and all the other accoutrements of a vibrant protest scene. Some wore helmets and carried shields, as protection from the projectiles and other weapons we expected to be deployed against us by the anarchists. The press has repeatedly slandered the protesters who wore helmets and carried shields, for allegedly "looking for a fight," an argument later picked up by opportunistic members of the Charlottesville City government. In addition to being necessary tools to protect against potentially lethal projectiles being hurled by the counter-protesters, I received explicit permission from Captain Lewis in the weeks before the rally, for protesters to utilize helmets and shields during the rally.

There were some hilarious shenanigans ensuing due to the once-in-a-lifetime mish mash of several generations of White Nationalist celebrities. For example, this the first and perhaps only time *America First with Nicholas J. Fuentes* host Nicholas Fuentes met former Louisiana

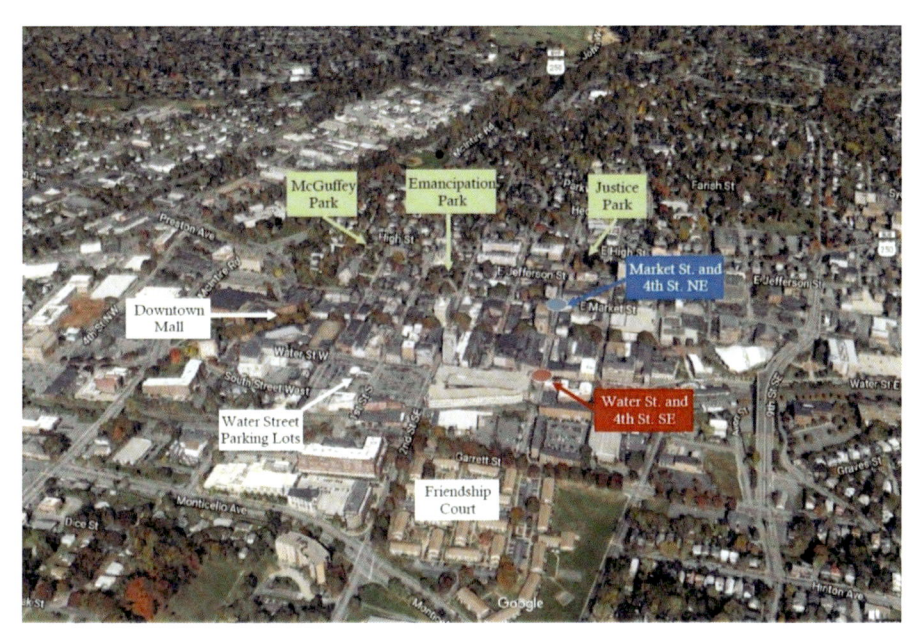

An overhead view of the Charlottesville downtown area where UTR was to take place

State Representative David Duke, with amusing results.[187] At the time, Fuentes was co-hosting a program called *Nationalist Review* with James Allsup, the White Nationalist personality who'd been interviewing Spencer when I met him the day before Trump's inauguration. Since then, Fuentes has gone on to be one of the most controversial and censored personalities in the dissident right. At the time of UTR though, he was apparently still clinging to hopes of mainstream acceptance. "Did you see Dr. Duke?" Allsup asked. "I didn't!" Fuentes exclaimed, obviously excited. "Was he here?! The Duke?" "The Dukester himself," Allsup nonchalantly repeated. Suddenly, realizing he was being recorded and not wanting to have "bad optics" for associating with Duke, Fuentes became serious as the grave. "I disavow." There was an awkward moment of silence before Allsup started backpedaling as well. "Uh, yeah. Of course! Of course . . . Disavow . . . Of course." The amusing thing about Fuentes' fearful

---

[187] bitchute.com/video/NOomKAZsBtDR

disavowal over Duke's "bad optics" is that he would later go on to livestream himself liberally using ethnic slurs like "kike" and "nigger," violently massacring Orthodox Jews in *Grand Theft Auto*[188] and urging protesters to storm the U.S. Capitol on January 6, 2021,[189] all before complaining that mainstream conservatives like Kyle Rittenhouse had the temerity to disavow *him*. Such is the right-wing circle jerk of "optics" and "disavowals." Perhaps the right-wing version of "the revolution eating its own" is "live by the disavowal, die by the disavowal." The loquacious Duke, on the other hand, spent the afternoon confidently strutting between admiring fans and inquisitive news media. When a journalist from NBC News asked, "What does today represent to you?" Duke answered: "This represents a turning point for the people of this country. We are determined to take our country back. We're gonna fulfill the promises of Donald Trump. That's what we believed in. That's why we voted for Donald Trump. Because he said he's going to take our country back and that's what we gotta do."[190]

I was already picking up signs of ominous dark clouds on the horizon. Why were there no police at McIntire Park to help escort the speakers? I asked "Kurt," one of Mosley's lieutenants, but he didn't seem to know the answer. Even more threateningly, the park had dozens of long, white prison buses parked throughout the lot, as if there were preparations for mass arrests at McIntire. Worse, neither "Kurt" or any of Mosley's other lieutenants in the park seemed to have any idea how I was being shuttled to the event. It hadn't dawned on me yet, but I'd been the victim of a hostile takeover, with Mosley and Spencer now firmly in control of the alt-right faction of the rally and the Hard Right (LoS, TWP, NSM, and Vanguard) off doing God knows what on their own.

The Charlottesville Independent Review quotes a CPD Sergeant Tony Newberry blaming Spencer's entourage for the lack of a police escort. According to Heaphy: "Newberry suggested the speakers load into one of two passenger vans and join a convoy of unmarked police

---

[188] bitchute.com/video/OmOaYMu7MhHl
[189] bitchute.com/video/ab3MJBhbd5Ba
[190] youtube.com/watch?v=fULPlGwjJMA

vehicles. The vans would be waved through barricaded streets and park on Jefferson Street . . . Pierce was in agreement with the plan" but then Pierce disagreed with Newberry's suggestion to bring in the speakers at 7:30 to 8 AM because it would leave the VIPs as sitting ducks in the park for too long before the scheduled start to the event.[191] According to Heaphy, this disagreement still hadn't been resolved by the morning of August 12. Just after 9 AM:

> Newberry called Pierce's cell phone and told him, "There's never going to be a better time than right now." Pierce said he understood and responded that he would get everyone together and call Newberry back. A few minutes later, Pierce called back and told Newberry that the speakers had changed their minds about coming in separately because they wanted to "walk in with their audiences." There would be no police escort from McIntire Park. Newberry told us that he had a hunch that Pierce had been tricked into working with him and that the rally organizers had never planned to be brought in through the back of the park. After the call ended, Newberry turned to his partner in the van and told him, "They do not plan on this going well."[192]

While Heaphy's investigation is an indispensable font of information about UTR, and he generally did an admirable job presenting a significantly unbiased report, Heaphy makes the mistake of considering Newberry's account as the unassailable truth when he should have been as skeptical of the police officers as anyone else. As we covered earlier with Lieutenant Tabler, law enforcement was willing to lie about what happened. How do we know? Unbeknownst to Newberry or Heaphy, Jack Pierce was recording his phone conversations, and so we can account for what really happened with scientific accuracy.[193]

---

[191] Heaphy p. 97
[192] Heaphy p. 124
[193] bitchute.com/video/749EtIiKTp9X

"Here's the deal, Jack." Newberry started. "So if the speakers want to go in with all the attendees and all that there's nothing I can do to help get 'em in there. You guys want to stop it at McIntire and unload with everybody else and walk up you can do it. But we're not breaking down barricades and all that. They'll just have to come in with the audience. They just need to let me know that's what they're doing. If you want the speakers to have an escort in, we can do that. It looks like the backside of the park is still going to be good for that. What I would recommend is that you get them in a couple of vehicles, follow us in our van up to, and we can come to the park, but follow us up McIntyre. We would turn onto East High Street. We would unload at 2nd Street the one way. We will walk you down, and then once you're in the barricades, we will retreat, and you'll have all the police protection there. So, let them know. That's where we're standing with it, but *if you guys want to come in with the audience, it's just like a general admission concert. You just walk in.*" [Emphasis added]

"When that happens," Pierce responded, *"that's honestly probably what's going to happen is we're going to walk in with the general population. If and when we do that, I will contact you when we're about to unload."* [Emphasis added]

There are two points we can draw from this conversation: number one, Newberry was exaggerating the level of noncooperation with Pierce. There is a serious gap between telling Heaphy, "They do not plan on this going well" and agreeing, fully informed of Pierce's plan, that "if you guys want to come in with the audience, it's just like a general admission concert. You just walk in." Second, it's unclear why Pierce was representing himself as the decision-maker on police escorts for all speakers rather than just Spencer. We can infer that this was another consequence of the Mosley/Spencer mutiny. I had been led to believe the police escorts for speakers were always going to be at McIntire and I wasn't consulted in any way about these proposed changes. Spencer's team was apparently making decisions of critical importance to the safety of the other speakers without consulting or informing them in any way. This turned out to be of critical importance as we will see speakers such as Baked Alaska, Cantwell, Monoxide, and Spencer himself, were violently assaulted on the way into the venue sans police protection. It's important not to overstate the significance of Pierce calling off police escorts for speakers. This decision does not explain the general police stand-down, the lack of separation between protesters and counter-protesters, and the unwillingness to make arrests of violent hecklers. It may, however, have given police a mulligan for the four speakers who were assaulted.

My security team, kept out of the loop by Spencer, Mosley, and Pierce, had no idea any of this was going on and determined to get me to Lee Park by whatever means necessary. We didn't waste another minute waiting around for the slow-running shuttles. We piled back into the four-door sedan, with the intention of driving as close to the maw of the protest zone as possible. This was an incredibly dangerous plan considering Antifa and BLM were attacking any vehicles they suspected of carrying protesters for the rally. One such incident, captured during the livestream of BuzzFeed media personality Blake Montgomery, depicted rioters using sticks to beat on the windows of a white van (likely transporting sound equipment for Lee Park).[194] Another even more shocking incident occurred on Water Street (opposite side of the Downtown Mall from Lee Park) as a gray sedan containing protesters trying to leave a commercial parking lot was surrounded by a crowd of angry Black rioters. The men struck the vehicle multiple times with punches, kicks, rocks, and sticks. "Motherfucker! Get the fuck outta here," yelled a Black man in a white tank top with dreadlocks. When the vehicle finally made it out of the lot and was able to attempt to speed away the crowd began sprinting after it. "We matter!" screamed a woman in pursuit of the vehicle, an apparent allusion to the BLM slogan.

The closest my crew was able to get to Lee Park by car was High Street, about a block behind Lee Park and a block and a half down from Jackson Park where one of Heinecke's counter-demonstrations

---

[194] bitchute.com/video/Q0DGiR0PWMmE

was happening. At that point, traffic came to a standstill due to throngs of protesters blocking cars in front of us, leading to a traffic jam. Everyone except for the driver exited the sedan. Wading through the crowd we tried to enter the park through the rear, but our path was blocked by metal barricades. We walked the long way around the block towards the public library, tracing the perimeter of the barricades until we came to an opening on the right-hand side guarded by a VSP trooper.

"Hi, I'm the permit holder for the event. Can you let me into the park?" I asked.

"No one is allowed entrance here. You have to go around to the front," said the trooper. He pointed towards Main Street, where the front entrances to the park were hidden behind hundreds of armed and angry-looking counter-demonstrators. I squared my jaw, breathed a deep sigh and headed in the direction of the mob.

THE UNIFIED COMMAND CENTER

We've established several ways the police were supposed to be maintaining order at the event but weren't, and we hadn't even seen a Charlottesville police officer. This begs the question: where were they? According to Heaphy, leadership from CPD and VSP, with members of the Charlottesville government and FBI, had set up what they were calling a Unified Command Center inside the Wells Fargo building a block away on the Downtown Mall.[195] The leading officials from the Charlottesville government in attendance were Captain Thomas and City Manager Jones. There were also a number of staff members on hand like Thomas' assistant Emily Lantz and Captain Lewis. What they were talking about in there seems like a bunch of confused drivel from irresponsible people in way over their heads. "Mitchell's original plan called for the Unite The Right demonstrators to occupy the eastern protest zone, but CPD now understood that those individuals would be arriving from the west . . . Captain Mitchell switched the designated areas for demonstrators and counter-protesters, placing the former in the southwest quadrant and the latter in the southeast quadrant. That information was then conveyed to Jason Kessler by Captain Lewis late on August 11."

As the reader will recall, the recordings of my meetings with Mitchell and Lewis had promised that the park would only be split between protesters and counter-protesters if I didn't have a permit.

---

[195] Heaphy p. 96

We were to have the entire park if the court granted us an injunction. The fact they never seem to remember their broken promises to me, shows the bad faith of the police officers I was trying to work with. This is important because they later tried to blame protesters for "coming in from the wrong direction."

Throughout the morning, before my arrival, police in the Unified Command Center passively watched swelling counter-protester violence. At first, a few merely tested the waters, by throwing rocks and other projectiles at the protesters in Lee Park. But they did so with head on swivel for any cops who might be assertive in arresting violent agitators. But to their surprise, nothing happened. There were no cops anywhere in sight. So, they upped the ante. Cautiously throwing rocks turned into throwing punches and beating protesters with picket signs, or rushing into Lee Park with sticks and attacking demonstrators. Still the police sat on their hands. In response to the growing chorus of law enforcement who wanted to step in and prevent violence, Thomas gave the order, "Let them fight, it will make it easier to declare an unlawful assembly." Thomas' order was witnessed and conveyed to Heaphy by both Lantz and Lewis.

One individual who was conspicuously not invited to the Unified Command Center was Mayor Mike Signer, whose harebrained scheme to relocate the event at the last minute was arguably most responsible for the developing chaos. In his UTR memoir, *Cry Havoc*, he depicts himself as a tragic hero, trying valiantly to gain access to the Command Center so he could right the wrongs he saw around him. "Councilors were receiving updates via email from Maurice Jones about increasing violence at the park," Signer wrote. "At 11:19 a.m., I sent Jones a text saying, 'I need to come up to Wells Fargo. Won't be in your way but I need to be here.'[196] He responded, 'I'm concerned about your safety getting here . . . At 11:40 a.m., I responded to Maurice Jones: 'Al works for you. You have barred me from the center. We are not together. I don't know what's happening. We are not unified. We can't say no comment or it has to wait. I'm at city hall.' Jones responded,

---

[196] *Cry Havoc* p. 198

'It has to wait. We have to let this play out for a bit before going in front of the cameras."

These text exchanges revealed in Signer's book are critical because they offer a glimpse at communications between Charlottesville decision makers that were illegally destroyed after the rally. The Charlottesville Independent Review revealed Thomas destroyed his text message history in apparent violation of the Virginia Public Records Act. In response to a FOIA lawsuit I filed against the Charlottesville government, Communications Officer Brian Wheeler confirmed that Maurice Jones' phone was also wiped when he hastily left employment with the Charlottesville government after the rally.[197] According to the Virginia Public Records Act, by law, correspondence of city managers is required to be retained "permanent[ly] in agency."[198] After the rally, Signer texted Jones and Thomas: "Why were people allowed to beat each other in the streets?" Signer alleges that Jones justified this policy citing "concern that he and the police shared about 'images' of police using batons, or even weapons, against the violence."[199]

No further knowledge has emerged about the FBI's involvement in the Unified Command Center: who was there, why they were there, and what, if any, reaction they had to Police Chief Al Thomas ordering his officers to "let them fight." Did they have any objection to this order? *Why did Al Thomas feel so comfortable giving that order in their presence if they weren't in on it?* What has emerged is the political prejudice animating members of the Charlottesville FBI, a very small field office subordinate to the larger office in Richmond. W.Wade Douthit, one of only three FBI agents I ever interacted with from the Charlottesville Field Office, was the FBI's investigating officer in the James Fields homicide case, and therefore a high-ranking member of the team likely in attendance at the Unified Command Center. I caught

---

[197] jasonkessler.us/wp-content/uploads/2023/12/Wheeler-Letter-Phone-Wiped.pdf
[198] Va Code Ann. 42.1-82(a)(2) and Library of Virginia, Records Retention and Disposition Schedule, General Schedule No. GS-19. County and Municipal Governments, Administrative Records, Series 010038 and 010006
[199] *Cry Havoc* p. 230

him on LinkedIn reposting an article encouraging others to throw pictures of Robert E. Lee, the focus of our demonstration, in the trash because Lee "communicates ideas about race and equality with which I seek no association."[200] Finally, it should be pointed out that the FBI (specifically Douthit) sought and obtained search warrants related to acts of violence by Antifa rioters including Lindsey Moers and another Antifa woman named Rachel Myles, but chose not to prosecute even a single assault committed against the permitted protest.[201]

---

[200] i.imgur.com/0EMowQi.png
[201] thedailybeast.com/fbi-got-warrants-for-unite-the-right-organizer-jason-kessler-antifa-activists

Staging "The Resistance"

All of the August 11 Antifa, including Betterly, Gorcenski, Liter, and Zoller, returned for August 12 armed and with backup from even more of their militant comrades. One photograph from that day captured Zoller strolling to the rally with a baseball bat in hand, ready for some "mostly peaceful protesting." Notable additions were trained combat fighters from the Elevate MMA dojo in Durham, North Carolina. These agitators included James Neil-Ritchie, Sam Carey, Elizabeth Schroder, Josh Masharka, and Anderson Sweetser: allies from the Carolina Anti-Racist collective. Neal-Ritchie, Carey, and Sweetser were actually on UVA campus together on August 11, but came just a little too late to "punch nazis" with their comrades.[202]

The Antifa had three primary staging points: 1) Jackson (aka Justice) Park, 2) McGuffey Park, and 3) churches affiliated with the militant-left Congregate Cville. Let's begin with the two "demonstrations" permitted to UVA Professor Heinecke. As known by CPD all along, the purpose of these parks was not for protest activity. Jackson Park was patrolled by the anarchist militias Socialist Rifle Association and Redneck Revolt, led by University of North Carolina-Chapel Hill Professor of Asian and Middle Eastern Studies Dwayne Dixon. The groups brandished semi-automatic rifles like the ones used in the desert training video where they fired on alt-right targets. According to the Independent Review, a witness "spoke with a Redneck Revolt member and learned that they intended to prevent Unite The Right

---

[202] youtu.be/JEpDiM0M610 (4:50)

Holly Zoller (left) walks to UTR with baseball bat in hand

demonstrators from coming to Justice Park." Dixon and his comrades seem to have mistaken a public park, open to everyone regardless of ideology, for the DMZ into North Korea. Nevertheless, this stated objective was carried out with brio. When two Confederate flag-bearing demonstrators passed through Jackson Park on the way to Lee, they were accosted and assaulted by a mob, led by two of the extremists surrounding the Thomas Jefferson statue on August 11. When one of them was knocked to the ground by the crowd, Kristopher Goad of ASH Antifa leaped on top of the defenseless man and began pummeling him in the face.[203] Lindsey Moers seized this opportunity to pull out her baton, hit one of the men in the head from behind, and then crack the skull of the other man already being beaten on the ground. This event was captured by the ACLU of Virginia in a tweet caption: "Both sides were hitting each other at Justice Park before police arrived."[204] Despite this mob violence, the police made no attempt to declare an unlawful assembly or curtail

---

[203] youtube.com/watch?v=j6iQGoE2ynE
[204] twitter.com/acluva/status/896410932355751937y

Heinecke's violent assembly in any way. By all accounts, a left-wing army was allowed to set up operations there with no oversight whatsoever from law enforcement.

The other staging ground was in the parking lots of churches affiliated with Congregate Cville, where armed militants wearing red bandannas (a fashion accessory associated with anarchists and communists) freely patrolled and coordinated. However, there were some restrictions on the mostly White male Antifa, but only because of their race, not ideology or commitment to violence. According to Deborah Porras, a visiting minister, First United Methodist Church (FUMC) "installed metal detectors and required white males to have a 'sponsor' to enter the building."[205] In a shocking series of photographs, FUMC Pastor Phil Woodson is seen coordinating with unidentified

First United Methodist Church Pastor Phil Woodson was one of many church leaders who used their property as staging grounds for violent Antifa on August 12

---

[205] Heaphy p. 123

CHARLOTTESVILLE AND THE DEATH OF FREE SPEECH

Antifa who left his staging area to commit wanton acts of violence against the permitted demonstration.

A livestream video captured the men, who had been using United Methodist as their staging ground, pummeling a man with an American flag after he'd been knocked helplessly to the ground.[206] The men began kicking him and bludgeoning him with the Refuse Fascism picket signs reading, No! The Trump/Pence Regime Must Go! The clergy groups themselves were aware of the Antifa's violent intentions, and despite their "nonviolent trainings," participated in the violence themselves. Clergy Collective leader and BLM Charlottesville founder Don Gathers marched to Lee Park with a mob of robe-wearing far-left priests carrying a "walking stick." For reference, I've never before or since seen Gathers use a "walking stick" in public (although I had seen him bring an electric cattle prod to City Council meetings).

Antifa photographed earlier in the FUMC grounds with Pastor Phil Woodson would go on to brutally attack protesters outside Lee Park

---

[206] bitchute.com/video/oUAiU1KuCEz9

Gathers used this stick to bludgeon protesters marching to the demonstration,[207] then complained, like all the other hypocrites about the "violent Unite the Right protesters." Congregate Charlottesville leader Wispelwey, a batshit, crazy-eyed left-wing zealot, refused to denounce Antifa's violent tactics at a symposium on UTR: "They [Antifa] have their tools to achieve their purposes, and they are not ones I will personally use, but let me stress that our purposes were the same."[208]

He has also endorsed the antifascist concept of "diversity of tactics," a thinly veiled euphemism for employing a mixture of violent and nonviolent strategies. "A 'diversity of tactics,' well organized and committed to 'unified' outcomes, is always welcome," he wrote.[209] The "Socialist Worker" website explains: "The 'diversity of tactics' idea emerged in the global justice movement after the 1999 Battle of Seattle against the meeting of the World Trade Organization. It was

Reverend Seth Wispelwey used churches in Congregate Charlottesville to stage Antifa rioters during UTR

---

[207] bitchute.com/video/aRpCw5H3Hqqi
[208] slate.com/articles/news_and_politics/politics/2017/08/what_the_alt_left_was_actually_doing_in_charlottesville.html
[209] twitter.com/RevSethDub/status/1071396564109852673

an attempt to bridge the gap between the black bloc; those who wanted to engage in 'nonviolent direct action,' like sitting in to block entrances; and those who wanted to engage in peaceful protests and marches."[210] To summarize, the permitted demonstrations in McGuffey and Jackson, as well as the parking lots of the communist clergy, were used as staging grounds for the most violent agitators. Many of them left these staging grounds heading for Market Street where they could physically assault protesters. Just as I'd tried to warn Captain Lewis, Chief Thomas, and Maurice Jones, it unnecessarily clogged the route to the demonstration with dangerous hostiles. Very strange tactical choice for a city allegedly concerned about "overcrowding" in the downtown area.

---

[210] socialistworker.org/2012/03/26/diversity-of-tactics

THE ANTIFA ASSAULT ON UNITE THE RIGHT

Using the church parking lots and Heinecke's permitted parks as staging grounds, Antifa, predictably, launched a coordinated assault to shut down the Lee Park demonstration. Antifa Communications Director and APOC leader Luis Oyola described their coordination on the *Ex-Worker* podcast: "Closer to 11am was when the antifascist contingent mobilized from Justice Park. They were in the numbers of a hundred to a hundred and twenty. They came with shields. They came with flags. They came with poles. They came with reinforced banners . . . They came with everything that was necessary to stop this rally from happening."

Oyola reveals much in his description of unambiguously offensive weapons like poles and the clear intention, without euphemisms about "defending Charlottesville," to "stop the rally from happening." However, he doesn't give a full account of the more dangerous weapons employed by his squadron, which included pepper spray, balloons filled with biohazards like urine and feces, tear gas, batons, brass knuckles, semi-automatic rifles, handguns, and even improvised flamethrowers. Counter-protester DeAndre Harris later testified in Charlottesville Circuit Court that black-clad White men (read: Antifa) were walking around with bags filled with weapons and handing them out to Black people in the crowd like himself. Harris, who was also caught on camera hurling Coke cans at protesters,[211] says that he

---

[211] vdare.com/wp-content/uploads/2018/02/frozencoke.jpg

Antifa Communications Director Luis Oyola coordinated counter-protester violence on August 11-12, 2017

picked out a steel Maglite for "his protection." More on that later. Statements from Oyola and others make it clear that their strategy, besides simply beating people on the way into the venue, was to run into the park, attack, and then retreat into the safety of the anarchist mob on Market Street. From there, the victims would be outnumbered and perfect targets for a mob assault. "As it got closer to noon, the antifascist bloc was successful in drawing away the most heavily shielded contingent of Nazis. They were successful in drawing them away from the park and making them more vulnerable. As that happened many people were in the line of fire of projectiles, of pepper spray, of tear gas, and a lot of people were hurt and beaten on both sides." In the company of his fellow extremists, Oyola entirely drops the pretext that they were acting in "self-defense." "From what I observed on my street it was mostly Nazis who were getting beat..."

There are at least two vivid examples of this strategy captured on video: one involving Louisville Antifa Liter[212] and another with the

---
[212] bitchute.com/video/BltgPCHe5Ddl

Durham MMA fighter Neil-Ritchie.[213] In the first video, Liter, clad in a black motorcycle helmet, protective padding, and wielding a kendo stick in each hand, runs up to the barricades just inside the park and drives the sticks into the back and ass of a protester with his back turned. This is unambiguously an assault, not self-defense. Liter then cowardly retreats from the park before the victim has an opportunity to fight back. The other attack involved Ritchie, poorly disguised in baseball cap and sunglasses, darting into the park and clubbing a defenseless, unaware victim with a thick, wooden dowel rod then running away into the mob outside the park. After the rally, at a left-wing protest on the UNC-Durham Campus, Ritchie gloated: "Antifascists . . . expelled them from the park with sticks and fists and paint balloons and shields and just their bodies. The reason that's important is we know we can do that, right?" With police and their political bosses refusing to prosecute attacks against the permitted rally-goers, apparently Ritchie and his extremist radical cadre could "do that" without consequences.

Convicted terrorist Brent Vincent Betterly was up to his violent tricks again. Like other Antifa, he was constantly changing his clothes throughout the weekend in order to aid disguise and prevent identification. At the time of his most violent assault, against a U.S. Army veteran and foster care reform advocate named Harold Sloke, Betterly was disguised in a black Pabst Blue Ribbon t-shirt, gray jean shorts, a red motorcycle helmet, aviator sunglasses, and a black medical mask. Keep in mind that this was pre-COVID and Virginia had anti-masking laws which were strictly enforced against the Klan on July 8. However, cops gave Antifa free rein to mask up during violent assaults on August 12. Despite his disguise, Betterly was identifiable through his various uncovered tattoos, including one on his right inner forearm reading, REAL EYES, REALIZE, REAL LIES, and another on his left outer forearm reading, NO MAD, ISAIAH.[214]

---

[213] bitchute.com/video/5Le0HUn2EXbL
[214] arrestfacts.com/Brent-Betterly-0c5S31

THE ANTIFA ASSAULT ON UNITE THE RIGHT

James Neil-Ritchie, an MMA fighter with Elevate MMA, attacks protesters in Lee Park using a kendo stick

Convicted domestic terrorist Brent Betterly (right) attacks a defenseless protester

Just prior to the altercation, a mob of counter-protesters was trying to rob Sloke's black DON'T TREAD ON ME flag. A physical struggle for the flag ended with Sloke bent over, his head in a lowered, defenseless position as he attempted to retrieve it off the Market Street blacktop. Sensing an opportunity, Betterly rushed in with a jag of metal pipe and swung in a downward slope towards his head and face.[215] One of Betterly's Antifa conspirators, William Cory Lovell, rushed in to follow up the pipe attack by bashing Sloke over the head and gut with his bike helmet. On a separate occasion, Betterly was photographed recklessly firing pepper spray into a crowd of UTR protesters.

One of the most deranged and sociopathic Antifa in attendance that day was Corey Lemley of Nashville. Lemley looked like a shorter, slovenlier version of comedian Russell Brand, with his long hair tucked into a gray beanie, scraggly beard, and bohemian fashion sense. He wore a black t-shirt with white cartoon characters depicting a man with a raised baseball bat about to club an anthropomorphic swastika. Like the character on his shirt, he wielded a metal baseball bat festooned with red, black, and white Antifa stickers.

Lemley is a particularly noxious left-wing authoritarian who has called to "Gulag all Trump supporters"[216] and promised that "Trump supporters gonna get that ass whipped" at protests.[217] However on August 12, one of his victims was a harmless cameraman. Antifa are notoriously hostile to being filmed by members of the media who, typically and ironically, share their political agenda. Assaults occurred on multiple left-wing journalists that day including urine and mud being thrown on Katie Couric's NatGeo team[218] and *The Hill*'s Taylor Lorenz being punched in the face by Louisa, Virginia, Antifa, Jacob L. Smith.[219] The Lemley incident involved a cameraman standing on the Market Street sidewalk outside the Jefferson-Madison Regional

---

[215] bitchute.com/video/szExC3AAx33l
[216] jasonkessler.us/wp-content/uploads/2023/12/Corey-Lemley-Gulag-All-Trump-Supporters.pdf
[217] jasonkessler.us/wp-content/uploads/2023/12/Corey-Lemley-Trump-Supporters-Gonna-Get-That-Ass-Whipped.pdf
[218] dailymail.co.uk/news/article-4806282/Katie-Couric-producers-sprayed-urine-Charlottesville.html
[219] bitchute.com/video/ZNcOUeySFeCly

Nashville Antifa Corey Lemley carrying an aluminum baseball bat

Library surrounded by a group of black-clad extremists who'd taken issue with his neutral filming of the scene outside Lee Park, where the Antifa assaults were occurring. Among the group was Paul Minton, the corpse-disposing felon who was at the torchlit protest the night before. Lemley was there livestreaming with his cell phone as the men first covered the news camera lens with a black hoodie and then tried to grapple the device out of the reporter's hands. Minton repeatedly punched the reporter as they struggled for the camera. "Yeah, break that shit!" Lemley screamed enthusiastically near the top of his lungs. "BREAK THAT SHIT, YEAH!" Now surrounded and afraid, the reporter turned as Lemley screamed, "Get the fuck out of here, punk ass!" Although the cameraman was no longer filming and the camera was slung inert over his shoulder, Lemley rushed in and struck it with his bat. Lemley turned away, brandishing the baseball bat for viewers of his livestream to see and boasted: "I whooped that motherfucker's shit camera with this motherfucker right here."[220]

As expected, once CPD withdrew police escorts without ever once contacting me, several of the planned UTR speakers were assaulted making their way into the venue. Cantwell was maced by Mikey Longo Jr., the loogie-spitting Antifa from August 11, now donning a waist-length black wig. The chemical attack on Cantwell, the second in two days, caused him excruciating pain and required his eyes to be flushed out with milk.[221] Baked Alaska was sprayed with what has been described as hydrochloric acid.[222] The damage to his eyes was so severe that he required hospitalization and allegedly received permanent loss of function to his eyesight. Johnny Monoxide told me he has "acid burn scars from being attacked on August 12." There appeared to have been multiple mace attacks on Spencer, one when he entered the park and another as he stood dangerously close to the barricades facing the counter-protesters.

---

[220] bitchute.com/video/pA8YsaTtPNTD
[221] youtube.com/watch?v=3S1plV2-Cqw
[222] bitchute.com/video/lUvQF7QEB5qD

MY ENTRANCE INTO LEE PARK

My small crew went unnoticed as we nervously strolled down Market Street towards the easternmost front entrance to the park. We'd picked an auspicious moment to try our luck. When I gazed east, in the direction of Charlottesville City Hall, there was an absolutely massive and impressive marching column of the heretofore MIA Nationalist Alliance. They were far in the distance but making a beeline for Lee Park. Out front were League leaders Tubbs and Hill, along with TWP leader Heimbach. All of the armed and dangerous counter-protesters looked right through me like I was a ghost. Their immediate safety depended on reckoning with the tidal wave of Nationalist fury heading straight in their direction. Apparently, the Nationalist Alliance had split off from the planning done by Spencer and IE due to trust issues. There also appeared to be some kind of paranoia about me. During a speech pumping up Nationalist Alliance activists inside the Market Street Garage where they parked, ranking League member Ike Baker barked: "Kessler said he wasn't going to allow us into the park. Well how about we decide whether we're going to let him into the park?!"[223] This was followed by some raucous cheering. It's very odd he would have said this since I never claimed that I didn't want anyone to come. It was an event open to the general public. However, I had asked the NSM to tone it down when I realized they were a neo-Nazi group. Obviously,

---

[223] jasonkessler.us/wp-content/uploads/2023/12/Ike-Baker-Speech.mp4

I believed everyone had a right to demonstrate, but I did not want my rally to be associated with Third Reich imagery. That would have been hijacking the message of the demonstration and would be used in guilt-by-association attacks on the more moderate attendees of the rally. Nevertheless, however we ended up there, I was glad to see the League and the others on August 12. Using their distraction as cover, my team first slipped into the park on the easternmost corner closest to us. At the time, there was a line of radical left-wing clergy, including Wispelwey and West, standing at the entrance. From media depictions published after the fact, I learned their intention was to affect the "nonviolent" portion of the diversity of tactics strategy by chaining together to block entrance to the park. However, by the time my squad approached, their line had been broken and they were standing, like everyone else, mouths agape in awe at the Nationalist Alliance column marching in their direction. Cornel West revealed he and his entourage were there to get locked up by impeding the Constitutional right of my group to free assembly and speech. He also revealed something even more sinister. "We were there to get arrested," West told an interviewer two days after the rally. *"We couldn't get arrested because the police had pulled back and were just allowing fellow citizens to go at each other."*

As opposed to the raucous, violent counter-protester assembly in the streets below, Lee Park was tranquil. I didn't see any fighting. I definitely didn't see swastikas, Klan robes, or any of the other incendiary imagery the media has tried to paint the event with.[224] It was normal looking people, standing around with placards, flags, and other protest paraphernalia patiently milling around waiting for the speeches to begin.[225] However, we needed to speak with a police officer and one

---

[224] News articles associating men in Klan robes with UTR came from deceitfully recycled images of the July 8 Klan rally.
[225] When the topic of Nazi flags comes up, a common talking point online revolves around one individual who actually brought a Nazi swastika flag to the protest. It is often stated this individual must have been a fed plant to make the other protesters look bad. Observers often comment it looked like the flag still had crease marks from where it had recently been unfolded from its packaging. The photo of this young man carrying the swastika flag is often the header image for left-wing media articles. Although he is the only individual I am aware of carrying such a flag, his prominent placement in so many media articles about the event gives the general

of the other speakers to find out what the hell was going on. There were a number of VSP officers hidden far away behind barricades in the speaker area which encompassed the entire back half of the park. I only saw one lone VSP officer near the barricades . . . on the other side of the park. There was a barricade running down the middle of Lee Park, ensuring that we would have to exit back onto Market Street to enter on the other side. This was in direct contradiction to the assurances Chief Thomas had given me about us having both sides of the park if we secured the injunction in federal court. The only reason there would be barricades in the center of the park was if they were enforcing the cockamamie idea about dividing the park between counter-protesters and protesters facing off in dangerous proximity to one another, neither of which had a permit. Even more significantly, the 200 CPD officers promised for the back of Lee Park were missing, as were officers stationed at the entrances and eight squadrons of police in and around Lee Park to keep the peace. We were on our own in this deliberate set-up.

My crew slipped out and back in again on the westernmost side of Lee Park on Market Street. Several speakers and other notables, like Spencer, were clustered around towards the barricade splitting the front side of the park from the rear. Spencer and I greeted each other but it was too loud to hold a conversation. On top of that, the park was uncomfortably crowded and the set-up for the park was all wrong. Besides the unnecessary barricade running down the middle of the park, there was another splitting the front half of the park from the back, which had nothing but the Lee monument, our inert sound

---

public the false impression there were many people with such flags at the event. This does seem suspicious. However, I am reasonably certain this individual was not a "fed," but a socially awkward guy without an understanding of how inappropriate his behavior would look to others.

In 2018, I attended a Nationalist Solutions conference at Montgomery Bell State Park in Tennessee. During an intermission between speeches, I was approached by a friendly husband and wife couple who claimed to have been at Charlottesville. At some point in the conversation, I mentioned the young man with the swastika and how he must have been a plant to make everyone look bad. "Oh no! That's our son!" they exclaimed. "He lives with us and we brought him to the protest." Subsequent to that conversation I have occasionally come across photos over the years where I have seen that same couple at Charlottesville. In a few of the photos they are even marching near the man with the swastika flag. While this is not definitive, I am inclined to believe this couple at their word and do not believe the young man was a "fed."

equipment, and a handful of shiftless VSP officers. Besides the truncated size of the park allotted to us, which apparently Charlottesville wanted to be half-filled with counter-protesters, the dozens of speakers, VIPs, security, and other staff who were supposed to be in the speakers' area were stuck up front, monopolizing critical space for attendees. Outside on Market Street, the anarchists and communists grouped up into a human barricade with shields, reinforced banners, and flag poles at ready to attempt to prevent the Nationalist Alliance from getting through to the park. The human barricade was several rows deep with militants like Massey, Keenan, Betterly, and others skulking behind the front row with Singapore canes, cans of mace, and other dangerous weapons.

Then the collision occurred: the unstoppable force met the immovable object . . . and the object moved. The Antifa stuck out their chests, squeezed their Soviet hammer and sickle flags, and pulled in tight to prevent passage. At first, the League front line, including Tubbs, tried to push through without violence. But several counter-protesters began throwing punches and it was on. The League threw down and gave even better than they got in the ensuing brawl, this despite insane acts of violence from the leftists, including a nut in the front wildly swinging a hammer at them.[226] Hill was forced to use a walking cane to fight back Nic Smith of the left-wing People's Power Network who lunged at him with a haymaker of an attempted punch.[227] The end result, after about 30 seconds of knockdown, drag out fighting, was that the path was cleared.

The air was thick with the stench of tear gas and sweat. Lee Park had become a holding pen with hundreds of protesters crammed shoulder to shoulder like cattle. I'd been assured by Police Chief Thomas that we would have use of the full park, but now we were being corralled into two small barricaded squares occupying less than half the park. I couldn't even enter the speakers' area. "I'm the permit holder!" I exhorted the lone VSP officer near the barricade. "We can't let you in there," a VSP officer responded. "Who can?"

---

[226] bitchute.com/video/0VW40lKQW7XB
[227] bitchute.com/video/462dROGDd6Em

"City of Charlottesville Police." But they were nowhere to be seen. Projectiles were flying overhead like artillery shells: balloons filled with urine and feces, rocks, bricks, paint, and whatever other detritus the anarchist mob surrounding the park could weaponize. Outside the park, a Black supremacist was screaming racial abuse. We were nothing but "fucking animals" and "inbred pieces of shit," according to the shouts of the hate-filled Black man with veins protruding from his neck. Ahead of me a tall, lanky man stumbled wounded through a small opening in the barricades at the entrance to the park. He had a gas mask pulled back to reveal horrible purple bruises across his face and his right eye swollen shut. To my left, Spencer was doubled over in agony from being pepper sprayed. A small group of his friends was trying to offer medical assistance by pouring a bottle of water into his burning eyes.

I started to sound the alarm to the public on a livestream from my cellphone:, "If anyone gets hurt because of this situation then it's 100% on the heads of the Charlottesville Police Department." Something I was saying got their attention. Towards the barricades waddled Lieutenant Jim Mooney, a mustachioed man, about 5′ 8″ with a corpulent gut stretching the fabric of his dark blue police uniform. "We finally have an officer with the Charlottesville Police Department," I told the livestream viewers. "Why aren't the speakers being allowed into the speaking area?" Mooney made a somewhat theatrical show of looking at his wristwatch as if it afforded him some devastatingly clever rejoinder. "In 28 minutes they will be allowed . . ." It was about 11:32 AM. I understood Mooney was falsely implying our permitted time had not yet begun. "No! We had a permit from 10 AM to 5 PM!" Mooney pretended like he hadn't heard what I said. Charlottesville police were playing cute. They had no intention of ever allowing anyone to speak. "The event's scheduled from 12 to 5," Mooney monotonously droned with cruel satisfaction. "No! It's on the permit. I made a change to that permit," I firmly reiterated. Mooney repeated: "In 28 minutes we will let you in."

A new wave of tear gas enveloped the protest grounds, seething from a canister chucked onto the lawn by the anarchist rioters. "Look we're being gassed now! The Charlottesville Police Department is allowing people to come in here and gas us. They won't allow us into the event even though we had a permit from 10 AM and I can show that document.[228] We made an amendment to the petition."

The Charlottesville Independent Review states that CPD Captain David Shifflett recommended a declaration of unlawful assembly at 10:59 AM, and that the actual unlawful assembly declaration was declared at 11:31 AM,[229] exactly the same time as Mooney approached me in Lee Park. This confirms he was not speaking with me in good faith and had no intention to allow speeches "in 28 minutes." He knew his gang in blue would have us forced out of the park by then.

CPD finally marched into the park in a single-file line clad in helmets, body armor, and carrying riot shields. We thought they had finally come to bring order. A cop at the front of the line raised an electric megaphone to his lips: "This has been declared an unlawful assembly! You are ordered to disperse." Instead of bringing order, they formed a tight line across the width of the park, raised their shields, and began to inch forward. Certain protesters like TWP's Matt Parrott and *TRS*-affiliated activist Joseph Jordan (aka Eric Striker) tried to offer up civil disobedience by refusing to budge, but only ended up under arrest for their troubles. As the cop shield wall inched forward, hundreds of protesters, mostly unarmed, were driven into the waiting arms of the mob baying for their blood in the street below. I tried to get my people out of there as quickly and safely as possible: "To McIntire!" I shouted, trying to give the confused crowd some direction. But as we made our way down the stairs exiting the park, liters of pepper spray were deployed on our helpless crowd. Militants like Massey were waiting with an extendable cane to beat protesters on their way out. Worst of all, a Black thug named Corey Long, who had been assaulting protesters and burning their Confederate flags all day, created an improvised flamethrower by holding a Bic lighter up to an aerosol spray canister and shooting a billowing plume of fire towards our crowd as they descended the stairs.

---

[228] jasonkessler.us/wp-content/uploads/2023/11/Unite-the-Right-Permit-Application.pdf
[229] Heaphy p. 192

Corey Long (right) shoots an improvised flamethrower at UTR attendees trying to exit Lee Park following the unlawful assembly declaration

Although this was clearly attempted murder, Long was charged with a measly disorderly conduct by Charlottesville's Commonwealth Attorney Joe Platania. It was an insult, especially considering that Long was one of only two convictions for the assaults done to our people that day and the severity of the charges pressed against our side for far, far less. Incredibly, a UTR attendee named Richard Preston who fired a single warning shot into the dirt near Long's feet, during the flamethrower attack, using his legally purchased firearm, was severely punished with a felony and four-year prison sentence.[230] His charge was "discharging a firearm within 1,000 feet (300 meters) of a school," an obscure law contorted to prosecute Preston for an entirely reasonable response in defense of others.

According to Antifa's Communications Director Oyola: "We were able to communicate that Kessler planned to go to McIntire as a backup. It was during the dispersal that some of the more violent . . . the more violent hand-to-hand clashes happened and as groups of Nazis were leaving the area and Charlottesville residents alongside antifascists from all over the US demonstrated to them that they were

---

[230] apnews.com/general-news-national-national-21d3b28146644d45930763e29efb9c1a

not welcome. They were chased to their parking lots. They were chased to McIntire Park." Oyola was right. A lot of the most violent and chaotic episodes happened after the declaration of unlawful assembly. The demonstrators tried to orderly leave the area but were subjected to outrageous displays of violence. No effort was made by police to try and prevent attacks on demonstrators as they attempted to comply with the dispersal order. This is when many of the most dangerous previously discussed acts of violence occurred, like the flamethrower attack on the crowd and the mob assaults on cars attempting to leave the downtown area.

Among the most prominent flare-ups of violence focused on by the media is the alleged assault on a Black "protester" named DeAndre Shakur Harris. "Protester" in this case should be in scare quotes because Harris spent the entire protest, not chanting or giving speeches, but flagrantly assaulting demonstrators: by throwing Coke cans at their heads and helping his friend Corey Long (the flamethrower guy) mug protesters and rob them of their flags. After the unlawful assembly was declared, a group of League activists, including Harold Crews of Walkertown, North Carolina, and League Tennessee State Chairman Richard Hamblen, were walking east up Market Street towards the parking garage where they had parked their cars. The two men were stalked by a mob including several White Antifa, like Rachel Myles of Washington, D.C., and several trash talking Black men from Virginia including Harris and Long. Around 12:05 PM, Harris and Long were repeatedly taunting the men, calling them (ironically) "niggers," "bitch ass niggers," and challenging them to "do something" very threateningly. A third Black man, Donald Blakney, followed along, ominously twirling a massive dowel rod in his hands like Babe Ruth in the batter's circle. Blakney would end up clobbering Eric Mattson, a White protester from Arkansas, in the back of the head while he was trying to leave the area, giving him a concussion. Blakney would later plead guilty to the assault in one of the sweetheart deals offered only to the handful of counter-protesters charged after the rally.[231]

---

[231] c-ville.com/blakney-accepts-plea-deal

When taunts failed to achieve the desired reaction, Long began lunging towards the protesters to grab a flag. In front of the parking garage, he succeeded in grasping the fabric of Crews' Confederate flag, beginning a violent struggle for control. Sensing an opportunity, Harris swung the steel Maglite he'd been carrying in an arc down on top of Crews' head. At this point Crews' head began gushing blood and he stumbled back. All hell broke loose. A group of men including Daniel Borden, Jacob Scott Goodwin, Alex Michael Ramos, and Tyler Watkins Davis rushed forward to defend Crews by knocking Harris to the ground and pummeling him. Ramos allegedly hit him only once with his fist but others used sticks and shields. The violence was all over in a matter of seconds, but by then Harris' head had sustained wounds requiring stitches. Around the same time this was going on, Rachel Myles led a peripheral assault on Crews and his friend Hamblen, an elderly man with a snowy white beard.[232] After his assault at the hands of Harris, Crews was standing, in shock, in the middle of Market Street, blood gushing from a wound on the side of his face. An unidentified White man wearing black, snuck in from behind and attacked Crews a second time with a blow to the back of his head from a steel pipe. Myles entered the fray by grappling Hamblen, yanking him to the ground and repeatedly punching him in the side of the face. These assaults were known to the FBI, whose search warrant application describes in detail law enforcement's knowledge of the attacks and who had committed them.[233] To date, none of these crimes perpetrated against the permitted demonstrators have been prosecuted in federal court. There was an intentionally sabotaged effort to hold Harris accountable for the assault in Charlottesville District Court. Neither the police nor prosecutors showed any interest in seeking justice for Harris' victim, Crews. Finally, tired of being ignored, Crews went to the Albemarle-Charlottesville Regional Jail and had the magistrate swear out a warrant for Harris' arrest based on the video and photographic evidence. The charge

---

[232] bitchute.com/video/tH6VTz7G8Vop
[233] jasonkessler.us/wp-content/uploads/2023/12/Rachel-Myles-Search-Warrant.pdf

was for felony malicious wounding. The Charlottesville "justice system" sabotaged the prosecution in two ways: First, Commonwealth Attorney David Chapman reduced the charge to misdemeanor assault, based on purely political considerations. Second, his successor Joseph Platania intentionally blew the case so Harris would be found not guilty. I spoke to an attorney who witnessed the trial, and noted Platania's failure to play crucial video evidence of the attack before the trial judge. He told me: "Platania is a competent attorney and I've never seen him perform so badly. He threw that case."[234]

After the rally was disbanded, most UTR demonstrators made their way back to McIntire Park to regroup from a safe distance. Here, a smattering of journalists conducted interviews while Enoch and Duke gave impromptu speeches to their supporters. A major focus of the Discord had been planning for "afterparties," but the difficulty of renting a space, like a VFW hall, without cancellation, made it impossible to have one unified meetup for everyone. So, in actuality, there were several afterparties that split up the demonstrators after they left McIntire. There were separate gatherings for Nationalist Alliance activists and another *TRS* event attended by Duke and Enoch. I joined a party at a house in the countryside outside Charlottesville that was attended by Spencer, Mosley, and some right-leaning journalists like Faith Goldy of *Rebel News*.

Despite the disappointment of not being able to hold our demonstration, there was still a joyful comradery in being surrounded by so many like-minded activists from around the country. There was beer in Dixie cups and excited socializing all around. A large-screen TV in the living room was set to national news, which was, unsurprisingly, wall-to-wall coverage of the Charlottesville aftermath.

At some point, a small meeting was held in an upstairs bedroom attended by myself, Spencer, Mosley, IE member Dave Reilly, and IE leader Damigo. For reasons known only to him, Reilly was once again surreptitiously recording events[235] as he had been in May when

---

[234] nbcnews.com/news/nbcblk/man-attacked-charlottesville-charged-assault-unexpected-turn-n809576
[235] bitchute.com/video/LrkdjArp3oCx

Spencer and IE members were throwing up Roman salutes. I was hoping the meeting might be about legal and public relations strategies for fighting back against what the Charlottesville government had done to violate our civil liberties. But Spencer had other ideas. He sat on the corner of the bed seething like an overstuffed balloon about to pop. Then he began the most extraordinary rant I have ever personally witnessed in my life.

"I am so mad. I am so fucking mad at these people. They don't do this to fucking me." As he started to speak, Damigo backed him up with soft little affirmations of "Yes" and "That's right." Spencer couldn't hear anything else though. He was in a rage trance like I have never seen. "We're going to fucking ritualistically humiliate them. I am coming back here every fucking weekend if I have to. Like this is never over. I win. They fucking lose. That's how the world fucking works. Little fucking kikes. They get ruled by people like me. Little fucking octoroons. My ancestors fucking enslaved those little pieces of fucking shit. I rule the fucking world." Mosley began to cackle in approval like Salacious Crumb in Jabba the Hutt's palace. "Those pieces of shit get ruled by people like me," Spencer continued. "They look up and see a face like mine looking down at them. That's how the fucking world works. We are going to destroy this fucking town."

The whole thing was surreal, and once I realized what was going on, I sat there in silence, horrified. I wanted to leave. This wasn't about Whites defending themselves and their history. Spencer was a sociopath, a narcissist, and a megalomaniac. Unbeknownst to us, there was still a major shoe left to drop in the story of the rally, perhaps the biggest one of all, with dire consequences for the survival of the nascent alt-right movement and the direction of all our lives. I heard shouting from downstairs. Something huge was just announced on the news. I used the excuse to leave the room and Spencer behind.

According to the Heaphy Report, at 1:41 PM, that's 2 hours and 10 minutes after the unlawful assembly declaration, a gray Dodge Challenger, driven by a protester from Ohio named James Alex Fields Jr., drove into a crowd of counter-protesters on 4th Street and Water Street, killing one and injuring dozens more. I remember first being informed of this, miles away from the protest grounds, and being in shock. How do you process something like that? It was the most surreal moment of my life.

JAMES FIELDS, HEATHER HEYER, & THE CRASH THAT CHANGED EVERYTHING

By the time James Fields pulled his battered Dodge Challenger over to the side of the road to be placed under arrest for the murder of Heather Heyer, the rally had been over for hours and most of us had left the scene. What happened there was more about how police managed the aftermath of the disaster they'd created than a consequence of the rally itself. Nevertheless, because powerful political interests wanted an excuse to "get" us for the rally, we have taken the lion's share of the blame. The sentiment within the general public is that James Fields committed an intentional, premeditated, first degree homicide. The perception within the dissident right, and a minority of the right-wing in general, is that Fields' car was attacked by a mob of rioters and he had no choice but to drive through them in order to potentially save his own life. I'll cover both of these perspectives.

As I have covered, the rioters were attacking cars during and after the rally, including mob attacks on Water Street near where the crash occurred. 4th Street, where the incident occurred, crosses through the red brick walkway of the Charlottesville Downtown Mall. Normally, traffic stops at a stop sign before crossing through the Mall, because it's a pedestrian footpath. On August 12, 2017, this short stretch of 4th Street crossing the Downtown Mall was supposed to be closed off to vehicle traffic. A wooden sawhorse had been placed in the middle of the street at Market and 4th Streets to prevent vehicle entry. Additionally, a school resource officer named Tammy Shiflett was assigned to guard the entrance to the street and her squad car was parked to obstruct entry to 4th Street. However, after the unlawful assembly declaration, Shiflett became frightened by the surge of protesters and counter-protesters headed in her direction. She radioed for help and was relieved of duty, taking her squad car with her and leaving only the lone wooden sawhorse covering perhaps a third of the street.[236] Finally, the sawhorse itself was eventually removed by "unknown persons."[237] Several automobiles, including a maroon Honda Odyssey minivan and a white Toyota Camry, turned onto 4th Street and ended up trapped on the Downtown Mall. There was both an unlawful assembly in effect from the Charlottesville government and a state of emergency which had been declared by Virginia Governor Terry McAuliffe at 12:06 PM. Despite this, there were bands of heavily armed leftist protesters marching through the streets "celebrating" that the police had stopped the UTR rally before it could begin. In spite of the state of emergency, there was no attempt to enforce the order by keeping the left-wing marchers off of the streets. They simply walked around picking out and assaulting isolated stragglers from the protest like Daniel Ferguson, a Virginian who was beaten by a mob on the Downtown Mall near the site of the crash.[238] These lawless crowds were what backed up traffic throughout the downtown Charlottesville area, including at 4th and Water.

On the Discord, I had warned attendees about how dangerous it would be to park near the Charlottesville Downtown Mall. But James Fields was not in the Discord. He parked at the McDonald's just past the end of the Mall on Ridge McIntire Road. He came by himself and marched into Lee Park haphazardly beside Enoch and his *TRS* crew.

Once in the park, Fields stood in front near the barrier between Lee Park and Market Street. There was a line of men standing beside him and the Nationalist Alliance group Vanguard America handed

---

[236] Heaphy p. 139
[237] Heaphy p. 163
[238] youtube.com/watch?v=oVz6kns8HRM

James Fields (right) marching towards Lee Park with Mike Enoch (left)

all of the men standing in front a shield with the Vanguard logo. Yet there is no evidence Fields was a Vanguard member. Nigel Krofta, the man who stood beside Fields in Lee Park and testified to handing him the shield was not a Vanguard member either, but participated in passing them down the line. By the time of Fields' arrest later that day, officers found his white polo shirt stained yellow and smelling of urine.[239] Likely he'd been attacked with a piss-filled water balloon during the rally.

During his homicide trial, prosecutors brought up a text exchange with his mother to insinuate he'd arrived in Charlottesville with the

---

[239] dailyprogress.com/news/fieldstrial/day-7-shes-the-enemy-fields-told-his-mother-by-phone/article_7b6f44e4-f7d7-11e8-aff5-675e69d1bced.html

premeditated intent to kill. Three days before Fields left Ohio for Charlottesville, he texted his mother: "I got the weekend off, so I'll be able to go to the rally." She replied, "Be careful." Fields responded with a picture of Adolf Hitler and the message: "We're not the ones who need to be careful."[240] Also, in May 2017, Fields had reposted a meme showing a car driving into a crowd of people with the caption: "You have the right to protest but I'm late for work."[241] As discussed earlier, these memes were not unusual at the time or indicative of a plan to murder people. They were so ubiquitous in social media posts from conservatives that the meme was celebrated by *The Daily Caller* and Fox News. It beggars belief that he, or anyone else, could have predicted the outrageous sequence of events leading to the police stand-down, the tacit government approval of roving rioters during a state of emergency, and Officer Shiflett's abandonment of her post at 4th and Water. Further, after being forced out of Lee Park with the other protesters, Fields introduced himself to three other UTR protesters named Sarah Bolstad, Hayden Calhoun, and Joshua Matthews. At the time, his mood appeared to be calm, not the anxiety-ridden demeanor of a man about to commit an act of terror. "He didn't seem like the kind of person who would do that—or who was about to do something like that," Bolstad said. The group accepted an offer from Fields to drive them to their vehicles, but he declined an invitation to lunch "because he wanted to leave Charlottesville." Fields bought a Powerade and returned with his new friends in tow to the McDonald's where he'd parked his car. After dropping off the couple at the Jefferson School and then Matthews at a downtown parking garage, he programmed his Ohio home address into his smartphone GPS. This was around 1:39 PM, less than five minutes before the fateful crash. There was no reason for him to program that GPS with his Ohio home address if he had any other intention besides returning home. We can safely say James Fields had no premeditated designs on murder at this point.

---

[240] wtop.com/virginia/2018/12/prosecutors-seek-to-use-hitler-image-texted-to-mother-in-james-alex-fields-murder-trial
[241] wtop.com/virginia/2018/11/judge-car-crash-meme-admissible-in-charlottesville-murder-trial

After that, Fields circled the perimeter of the Downtown Mall twice, perhaps lost or trapped from exit by the lawless crowds. The route suggested by his GPS was unavailable due to road closures. It was during this time that he was spotted by militia leader Dwayne Dixon of Redneck Revolt who claims to have brandished his rifle at Fields while he was driving past. In January 2018, Dixon posted a photo of his AR semi-automatic rifle with the boast: "I used this rifle to chase off James Fields from our block of 4th St before he attacked the marchers to the south."[242] Dixon elaborated during an invited speaking engagement at Harvard University: "James Fields, driving his Charger, slow-rolled our Western perimeter, so that was Fourth Street, several times. One time he paused right in front of me and I waved him off with my rifle. In his last pass, he accelerated and a block away he killed Heather."[243] On that second pass, Fields turned onto 4th Street where his escape was blocked by the maroon Odyssey and the white Camry. Instead of inching her way through the crowd, a rotund, mulatto woman driving the Odyssey had gotten out to livestream protesters. Fields tried to back up but it's unclear why he didn't back out all the way. There is no video to show what may or may not have been blocking his way to the rear or any altercations that may have occurred. The punitive interpretation is that this is where Fields decided to intentionally ram his car into a crowd of people, backing up to get enough runway for acceleration. Most people in the general public think premeditated, or first-degree murder requires cold, calculated intent to murder over a day or more. As bizarre as it may sound to laymen, legal premeditation only requires a second or more of forethought. So perhaps this momentary pause after backing up is where Fields conceived of his murderous plot. On the other hand, perhaps his path was blocked. Maybe there were rioters armed with bats (as we will see later there absolutely were) or, like Dwayne Dixon, semi-automatic rifles. Fields later told a magistrate judge: "I didn't know what to do" when he saw rioters circling around the cars in front of him.

---

[242] jasonkessler.us/2018/01/13/james-fields-was-chased-with-a-semi-automatic-rifle-before-crash
[243] bitchute.com/video/KLITXiqL0OE

Around the time Fields was retrieving his car from the McDonald's parking lot, another group of counter-protesters was gathering in one of the Water Street parking lots including Heather Heyer, a morbidly obese White woman chain smoking Newport menthol cigarettes. Like other woke White radicals, she was supporting her Black friends that day: a local activist named Courtney Commander, and Marcus Martin, a career criminal and convicted armed robber.[244]

They joined a marching column, including many black-clad Antifa carrying anarchist and communist flags, while boisterously chanting, "Antifascista!" The mob was heavily armed and included rioters with baseball bats and firearms, among them Gorcenski who, as the reader will recall, boasted: "I literally *pulled a fucking gun* on August 12."[245] The crowd marched up Water Street and turned onto 4th moments before Fields hit the accelerator. At this point, Fields accelerated towards the crowd driving at approximately 23 to 28 miles per hour.[246]

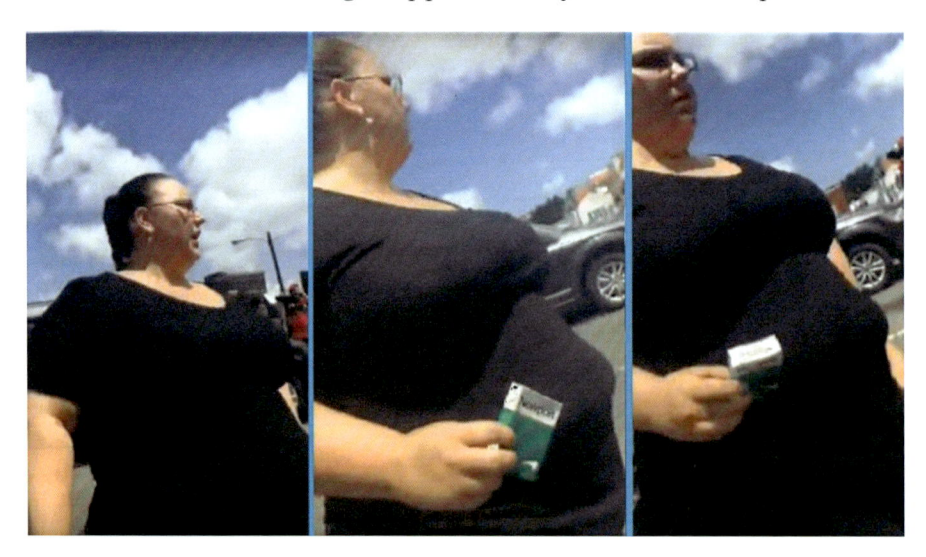

Heather Heyer from an August 12 livestream on Water Street

---

[244] dailyprogress.com/news/nelson-man-sentenced-to-five-years-in-armed-robbery/article_4707526a-41d3-11e3-9e1b-001a4bcf6878.html
[245] web.archive.org/web/20190501163137/https:/twitter.com/EmilyGorcenski/status/907006080529694720
[246] dailyprogress.com/news/fieldstrial/day-8-fields-drove-at-28-mph-before-hitting-crowd-police-say/article_427ea78c-f8c3-11e8-8686-3f477078b96c.html

His vehicle is struck at least twice before he drives into the crowd: first by a long-haired ginger male bashing the rear driver's side bumper with a wooden flag pole. The impact makes a loud sound (like a gunshot from Dwayne Dixon's rifle perhaps).[247] The second strike came to the front passenger side from a White male rioter wearing a white t-shirt who attacked with a club or other blunt object. The video is not especially high quality, and very pixelated further away from the camera, but it appears there may have been a third attacker, a Black male in a black t-shirt attacking with his fists, also from the front right-hand side.

At this point, Fields enters the crowd hitting dozens of protesters, including Heyer, before crashing into the back of the Toyota Camry. Notably, he drove straight forward, not onto the sidewalk where there were many more people for him to hit. Since Fields never testified in his own defense and we are missing video of what transpired behind Fields when he backed up, we have less definitive knowledge of what danger may have been lurking behind him or if he was attacked during that period. What we can say for certain is that as he accelerated forward

A counter-protester strikes James Fields' Dodge Challenger before the crash

---

[247] bitchute.com/video/LNFaZQaQVlf7

CHARLOTTESVILLE AND THE DEATH OF FREE SPEECH

the second time, at speeds comparable to the legal limit in a school safety zone, his Challenger was struck from behind by a rioter with a stick. Pictures from just before the crash show the illuminated red brake lights of Fields' car. There are really only two interpretations of this fact: 1) Fields was trying to slow down before driving into the crowd, and, 2) The brake lights were a result of the lights automatically signaling when the car bottomed out on a speed bump.[248] The answer seems to be unknowable and therefore in the eye of the beholder. However, I would posit that Occam's Razor implies Fields purposely hit the brakes, because that is what normally causes the brake lights to illuminate. The burden of proof should be on critics who argue that it was some other rare alternative.

Heather Heyer (circled in center) was hit dead-on by the Challenger

---

[248] *Summer of Hate* p. 16

Although there is a lot of skepticism online about whether Heyer was actually hit by the car or simply died of a heart attack, it is clear from video analysis as well as the coroner's report that Heyer received blunt force injury to her torso and rolled off the hood of Fields' Challenger. About 35 other people were also injured in the crash. A significant amount of the confusion may be due to popular videos from a YouTuber named "DanTheOracle," who created a three-part series on the crash. He initially shared his conclusion Heyer wasn't hit at all, before reversing himself in a subsequent video.[249] However, by then the theory had been shared by other massive alt-right outlets like *The Daily Stormer*.

Following the impact, Heyer was treated by Antifa "street medics" who, perhaps a little too aggressively, beat on her chest in order to revive her. She ultimately succumbed to cardiac arrest on the scene as a result of "blunt force injury to the torso."[250] This is technically a heart stoppage, although a crucial precipitating factor was impact with a car traveling between 23 and 28 miles per hour. That being said, we should also consider how fast her heart was already beating, at a sustained rate, on that hot summer day, walking around with a dangerous amount of excess fat and chain-smoking mentholated death sticks. This would not provide a suitable legal defense for Fields, but it should be put into perspective there is a reason Heyer, and only Heyer, died from impact with a car driving at school safety zone speeds. In the video there are several people impacted in shocking ways who did not die, including a woman flung like a rock from a slingshot on top of the Toyota Camry and a man beating Fields' windshield with a stick whose hip was crushed when Fields backed his rear bumper, carrying the attacker, into a parked car. Also injured in the crash was Heyer's friend, the convicted armed robber Marcus Martin. He was flung head over heels and suffered a broken ankle, twisted tibia bone, and destroyed ligaments.[251] Presumably, his days

---

[249] odysee.com/@DanTheOracle:d/Charlottesville-Making-a-Murderer-3
[250] richmond.com/heather-heyer-autopsy-report/pdf_452e3703-c19c-5f4c-9bea-2e2bd0db8883.html
[251] nbcnews.com/news/nbcblk/charlottesville-survivor-marcus-martin-still-healing-after-deadly-rally-n828466

as an armed home invader are through, not only because of his injury, but like all of the Black activists injured that day he was gifted a windfall of GoFundMe cash totaling $61,480, endorsements from celebrities like Ellen DeGeneres (who gifted him an additional $25,000), and an all-expenses paid wedding by Love Wins Bella Giornata Events to fellow protester Marissa Blair. The couple are now divorced so it is possible he has fallen back on hard times.[252]

After colliding with the Toyota Camry, about a dozen Antifa rioters who had been behind him on 4th Street came rushing in with aluminum baseball bats and other weapons to begin smashing out his back windshield. We can infer that these same armed militants were behind him, or at least around him on 4th Street, when he was initially attempting to back up before driving forward through the crowd. Fields backed up again, this time all the way back out onto Market Street. He drove east, with his front bumper hanging off, windows smashed out, and a VSP helicopter monitoring his flight from the skies overhead. Fields made a right onto Avon Street near the amphitheater at the end of the Downtown Mall. Police cruisers were in pursuit looking out for his license plate number and the ostentatiously hanging bumper. Four minutes after the collision, Fields pulled over to the shoulder of Monticello Avenue, fed his keys through the driver's side window and waited to be arrested.[253] He was apprehended by Officer Steve Young, who would go on to lead Fields' homicide investigation. Bodycam footage from the arrest depicted Fields sobbing "I'm sorry that—I don't know. I didn't want to hurt people, but I thought they were attacking me."[254] According to WTOP: "Later in a police headquarters interview room, Fields was read his Miranda rights and he declined to speak. When told several people were severely injured and one had died . . . Fields hyperventilated for several minutes." Taylor Lorenz, a left-wing journalist on scene for *The Hill* witnessed the crash. She reported: ". . . several police officers at the station here think the guy running people down wasn't malicious.

---

[252] DeAndre Harris raised $166,045, which he spent on things like rap music videos and tennis shoes.
[253] Heaphy p. 144
[254] wtop.com/virginia/2018/12/james-alex-fields-shows-remorse-scorn-after-fatal-charlottesville-car-crash

They said the driver was scared."[255] Lorenz later deleted the tweet after an online struggle session with keyboard warriors outraged she had substantiated Fields' prospective legal arguments.

As if all of this wasn't horrendous enough, at 4:40 PM, nearly five hours after the unlawful assembly declaration, the VSP helicopter which had been monitoring the Fields crash from the skies overhead mysteriously crashed near the Farmington Country Club. The two officers inside, Lieutenant H. Jay Cullen and Trooper-Pilot Berke M.M. Bates, were both killed on impact. Obviously, like the Fields incident, this crash happened long after the rally was over and had nothing to do with the conduct of the rally organizers, but rather the haphazard operation of police. A final report from the National Transportation Safety Board found the crash occurred due to pilot "loss of control and a lack of recent and recurrent pilot training."[256]

In December 2018, Fields was tried in Charlottesville Circuit Court and convicted of first-degree murder, multiple counts of aggravated malicious wounding, leaving the scene of an accident, and malicious wounding. He was sentenced to a life term plus 419 years and $480,000 in fines. Following his initial conviction, he also pled guilty to 49 federal hate crimes in order to avoid the death penalty.[257] The courthouse where his federal trial would have been located is also in Charlottesville. As someone who lived in the Charlottesville area during this time and saw the unrelenting tearjerking emotional propaganda from local news, I don't believe there was any way Fields could get a fair trial in that area under those circumstances, especially with the heightened community prejudice around his irrelevant but much-publicized neo-Nazi beliefs. As a VDARE commentator using the pen name "Charlottesville Survivor" wrote: "It's was akin to Camus' novel *The Stranger*, where the defendant's socially disturbing behavior leads to his conviction rather than anything germane."[258]

---

[255] archive.is/7KFS8
[256] wric.com/news/virginia-news/final-report-lack-of-training-likely-cause-in-copter-crash-during-2017-unite-the-right-rally-in-charlottesville
[257] npr.org/2019/07/15/741756615/virginia-court-sentences-neo-nazi-james-fields-jr-to-life-in-prison
[258] vdare.com/articles/unequal-justice-in-fields-charlottesville-trial-and-increasingly-throughout-the-left-s-americay

We can partially assess whether Fields received a fair trial from an unbiased jury of his peers by comparing his sentence with other similar incidents. Those who say Fields received a fair trial might point to Black mass murderer Darrell Brooks Jr., who drove his vehicle into a 2021 Christmas parade in Waukesha, Wisconsin. He had previously expressed murderous hatred towards White people and his victims were all White. Brooks received six consecutive life sentences and an additional 762 years in prison.[259] This sentence is not dissimilar to Fields' although we should note that Brooks killed six and Fields only one. In most cases however, it is abundantly true that leftists and anti-Whites are charged and sentenced more leniently. For example, in December 2020, Vancouver Police declined to press charges against an Antifa militant, Charles R. Holliday-Smith, after he used his pickup truck to run over and severely wound a Proud Boys activist named Shane Moon.[260] Shannon Brandt received only five years in prison for running over and killing an 18-year-old North Dakota man named Cayler Ellingson because he thought the victim was a "Republican extremist." According to CBS News: "Brandt initially claimed he ran Ellingson over after a political argument and that the teen had threatened him and was part of a radical group."[261] On September 26, 2020, a BLM protester named Tatiana Turner rammed her vehicle into a crowd of counter-protesters wearing pro-Trump clothing and holding American flags following her own rally. She was initially charged with one felony count of attempted murder with premeditation and deliberation, six felony counts of assault with a deadly weapon, including one causing great bodily injury, one felony count of mayhem, and two felony counts of the use of pepper spray by a felon. Protesters supported her outside the courtroom with signs reading, Self Defense Is Not A Crime. In September 2021, a judge dismissed the lesser counts against her and then dismissed the

---

[259] spectrumnews1.com/wi/milwaukee/news/2022/11/21/nov-21-marks-one-year-anniversary-of-waukesha-parade-tragedy
[260] thegatewaypundit.com/2020/12/prosecutors-decline-charge-black-lives-matter-militant-ran-proud-boy-washington
[261] cbsnews.com/news/shannon-brandt-5-years-prison-death-cayler-ellingson-north-dakota

attempted murder charge in December 2022.[262] A Seattle resident named Dawit Kelete received only five and a half years after absolutely plowing into a BLM highway protest at a stunning rate of speed, killing protester Summer Taylor and severely wounding her friend Diaz Love. This may seem like quite a discrepancy with the James Fields' case but then Kelete is a Somali immigrant, not a Neo-Nazi.[263] These "car attacks" seem to be prosecuted differently based on politics, yet another way First Amendment-protected political beliefs of the political right are punished through alternative backdoor means in American courts.

One of the worst mistakes of my nascent political career involved an incendiary tweet about the death of Heather Heyer. Six days after the rally, I was in a dark place mentally and emotionally. I was still reeling from the trauma of being attacked by a mob on August 13 and the absolute deluge of threats, harassment, and betrayal I'd been subjected to since the rally. My personal phone number had been doxed and I had been receiving threats and the vilest anti-White murder and rape fantasies for days. The media was refusing to hear our side of the conflict and I was agitated by their ridiculous Heather Heyer propaganda depicting her as an angel and a martyr. Like the media always does when creating a leftist martyr, they used a cherry-picked photo depicting her like an innocent, chubby cherub rather than the accurate photo of her appearance on August 12: as a grotesquely obese, black-clad radical, chain-smoking Newport cigarettes, with a Black convicted felon in a heavily armed mob defying a state of emergency order.

I've had a problem with recurrent insomnia since childhood, and as stated earlier, in 2017 I was treating it with Ambien, a drug with potentially dangerous side-effects. The FDA (U.S. Food and Drug Administration) warns "complex sleep behaviors—such as sleepwalking, sleep-driving, sleep-cooking, and engaging in other activities while not

---

[262] ocregister.com/2022/12/12/blm-activist-from-long-beach-no-longer-facing-attempted-murder-for-yorba-linda-collision
[263] seattletimes.com/seattle-news/law-justice/driver-who-killed-blm-protester-on-i-5-in-seattle-sentenced-to-over-6-years

fully awake may occur" while on the drug, particularly when paired with alcohol consumption.[264] On the night of Friday, August 18, I was suffering from extreme anxiety and depression. I was consuming alcohol and took the sleeping pill. Instead of going straight to bed, I stayed up on my bed posting on social media. At some point I lost consciousness but was still typing. When I woke up the next morning, I was under attack. I'd posted: "Heather Heyer was a fat, disgusting Communist. Communists have killed 94 million. Looks like it was payback time." Some of the worst abuse I suffered for this mistake was from private messages from my "friends" like Mosley and Spencer, who quickly capitalized on my human weakness by issuing a public statement denouncing me for the comment. "Payback is a morally reprehensible idea," Spencer wrote on Twitter.

From my perspective, part of the reason I was in such a horrendous mental state was that, since the rally, I'd had to suffer the abuse of the world mostly alone. The alt-right completely fell apart into internecine squabbling and every-man-for-himself cowardice. We should have been supporting one another like the 300 Spartans holding off the Persian hordes. But of course, as I demonstrated earlier, the right was never "united" at UTR, and the slightest bit of pressure would have exposed those divisions, let alone the cavalcade of attacks we faced from the entire world after August 12. I apologized publicly but there was no acceptance or forgiveness to be had from any quarter. The responses fell into two camps: those who would forever hold it against me and those who agreed with it. Almost no one gave a damn about the technical truth that it was an out-of-character statement from me brought on by extreme anxiety, sleep deprivation, and drugs. On a side note, I am proud to state that I have not taken Ambien since 2018, and gradually learned to induce drowsiness by other methods, such as reading at bedtime.

What that tweet was *not*, was any kind of admission that I or anyone else associated with the protest knew about or condoned any plans to illegally hurt protesters. Both CPD and the FBI searched for

---

[264] americanaddictioncenters.org/ambien-treatment/side-effects

and failed to find any plans or communication between Fields and the protest organizers. He wasn't even in the Discord. Officer Steve Young, the lead CPD investigator in the James Fields homicide case was deposed under oath on July 15, 2020.[265] Officer Young testified that not only did he not find any coordination between Fields and the protest organizers (including myself) but no hint of communication whatsoever. Fields was a loner and a complete stranger to everyone else involved. Further, the FBI conducted their own investigation and came to the same conclusion. "The FBI I think headquartered out of Louisville, Kentucky conducted a search of his residence and laptops," Young testified. My attorney at the time, James Kolenich of Ohio, asked the crucial follow-up: "Did they recover any information indicating that he had conspired with any persons regarding the murder of Heather Heyer?" Young responded simply, "No."

---

[265] jasonkessler.us/wp-content/uploads/2023/12/Steve-Young-Deposition.pdf

THE PRESS CONFERENCE ASSAULT

By the evening of August 12, I was greatly disturbed by the early signs of the monolithic false mythology developing in the media about what had transpired during the rally. All of the blame was being placed on the protesters, with some of the offensive, but constitutionally protected, speech being used to convict the protesters for the violence in the court of public opinion. Even "conservative" outlets like Fox News were running a narrative that the permitted protesters were to blame and cherry picking incidents, like selective elements of the DeAndre Harris fight, to make us look bad. None of the copious evidence of Antifa and BLM violence I have chronicled in this book was seeing the light of day. There was some tepid, but insufficient, criticism of the Charlottesville government and police for the stand-down. I needed to break the media embargo on the UTR perspective by speaking directly to journalists. I first contacted Fox News reporter Doug McKelway who was on assignment in Charlottesville. He declined, citing potential blowback from "platforming" the UTR organizer (some journalistic standards acceding to the mob, eh?). I then suggested he offer an interview with me to rising network star Tucker Carlson, who could do an adversarial interview where he asked me tough questions in order to blunt criticism. Unlike future controversial cases such as J6 and Douglass Mackey, Carlson demurred, leaving us completely voiceless and defenseless. I determined that the only option I had to bypass the media embargo was to call a press conference in front of City Hall before all of the national media left town. It was a risky gamble but would be too much of a spectacle for them to ignore. I notified Spencer of this plan with the intention that he and his crew would join me. At first, he agreed to join me, so I sent out an email blast to all of my media contacts announcing the press conference that afternoon of August 13. I chose to hold the conference in front of City Hall, thinking that its proximity to the police station would make the event safer from attacks. Unfortunately, after I'd already staked my reputation in announcing my intention to do this conference, Spencer backed out, thinking only of himself as usual. "I'm sorry," he said, "but I won't attend the press conference today. You're not listening to leadership."

With mere hours until the scheduled conference, I did not have time to find others to back me up. I tried emailing a few contacts, but everyone had already left town. If this thing was happening, I'd have to march into Mordor alone, in the heart of the orcs stronghold of power, to deliver my message. At the appointed time, I parked on an inconspicuous street a block or two from the Downtown Mall to avoid notice and walked to City Hall, my heart pounding nervously in my chest. In my head I thought of the popular expression about the thin line between bravery and stupidity as I passed by the street where Heather Heyer died. If I was recognized here, before I came into view of the police, the mob would likely tear me apart. When I climbed to the top of a flight of stairs and stepped onto the red brick of the Downtown Mall there were perhaps a hundred people crowded in the plaza in front of City Hall and, ironically, next to Charlottesville's "Free Speech Wall." I came in unnoticed from behind while everyone was staring forward at a cluster of microphones set in front of City Hall bearing the names of various prestigious news organizations. Above me to the right I saw a police sniper crouched on top of the building that housed the Charlottesville Welcome Center and a bus stop. His gun was aimed where I was to be speaking. There was a line of VSP in the back but no sign of CPD anywhere. I told a VSP officer that I had arrived for the speech, thinking he would escort me through the crowd to prevent violence from breaking out, but like all of the cops on both August 11 and 12, he reacted as if his own personal well-being was all that mattered. So, I cautiously, and nervously, made my way through the crowd to the microphones. A murmur went through the crowd, then some shouting. They called me a "murderer" although I'd had nothing at all to do with Heyer's death. It was a few minutes until the top of the hour when I planned to give the speech. I pulled a leaf of paper from my pocket with notes scribbled with the high points of what I wanted to address. My intention was to disavow the violence that happened during the rally and then try to blow the whistle on how CPD had caused the chaos by breaking all their promises to me and standing down. I barely got out the first part, and it was hard, if not impossible, to hear me over the boos and cursing. In some videos the national media bleeped out the cursing in such a way that it covered up my words. Two local men, Jeff Winder of Afton, Virginia, and Brandon Collins, former leader of the Charlottesville Socialist Party, rushed the stage. Winder started screaming "Indict for murder now!" The men gradually inched forward at first. Like the violent protesters the day before, they seemed to be testing the water before escalation, looking over to see if any police were going to stop them. They weren't. Winder was aggressively screaming in my face closer and closer as the violent mob closed in around me. Scared, I tried to back away and leave. Winder followed and took a swing, connecting with the back of my head. Collins started shoving me hard trying to make me lose my balance. The crowd was now rushing in towards me and a woman surged ahead of the rest and tackled the back of my knee causing me to lose my balance and fall to the ground. Incredibly, after a police investigation I would come to find out this woman was Phoebe Stevens, my most recent ex-girlfriend and the woman who had originally given me Spencer's phone number. At that point, after allowing me to be brutalized and nearly killed by the crowd, CPD *finally* intervened and took me back into the safety of the police station. Along the way I was cursed, threatened, and spat on, all before the eyes of the national media which, so concerned about "political violence" for the last 24 hours, suddenly erupted into celebration.

CHIEF THOMAS LIES TO THE NATIONAL PRESS

B
esides deleting incriminating text messages he sent on the day of the rally, Chief Al Thomas manufactured false documents and called a press conference on August 14 where he lied in an attempt to shift blame onto the permitted protesters.[266] In front of the national media, Thomas repeatedly said blame for violence was on protesters because they were allegedly supposed to have entered from the back of Lee Park. "We had a plan to bring them in at the rear of the park. They had agreed to cooperate with the plan. Unfortunately, uh, they did not, um, follow the plan." This narrative was uncritically parroted by the lying press with nary a fact check.

In reality, they were only a handful of protesters who police had discussed with one another about coming in through the back, and never directly with me. According to internal documents, the rear was discussed, but only as point of entry for the scheduled speakers of the event and their security staff. It is outrageous to imply that about a dozen individuals walking into the venue from the general admission entrances on Market Street were to blame. The speakers were in fact the ones who'd been attacked. Clearly, Thomas was trying to deceive the public into thinking counter-protesters were supposed to be on Market Street and UTR attendees had entered from Market Street in defiance of police orders spoiling for a fight.

As with so many of the facts related to Charlottesville, you don't

---

[266] bitchute.com/embed/rCkOtPzf47y1

have to trust my word for it. You can look at the primary source documents I was able to acquire through FOIA requests. After Thomas' misleading and downright deceitful press conference, Captain Wendy Lewis sent him an email admonishing him for distorting the truth.[267] "One minor issue, it was the speakers and their security staff that were supposed to enter through the back of the park," Lewis wrote in an August 16 email. Although she may have been trying to find a way of gently and politely criticizing her superior it was clearly not a "minor issue." It was the crux of Thomas' defense to the international media about the police conduct at the rally and it was a lie.

If there was any doubt whatsoever the Charlottesville government was knowingly misleading the public, Thomas and Charlottesville Communications Director Miriam Dickler continued spreading the disinformation about the supposed entry routes for protesters days after Lewis' email. By August 18, I had publicly criticized Thomas' statements as inaccurate. In response to a journalist email, Dickler stated: "No, Chief Thomas did not lie to the public at his press conference. As the chief has said in previous statements to the press, 'In preparing the park, we established three areas, one for the demonstrators, one for counter demonstrators and an area between the two for police officers. The security plan called for the demonstrators to enter through the rear of the park, and we also staged law enforcement in that area to facilitate that entrance. Rather than doing so, the demonstrators entered from the front of the park.'"

Besides the deceitful implication that our protesters were not supposed to enter on Market Street, there is the additional lie that we were entering into a side of the park designated for counter-protesters, once again making us look like the aggressors. As you'll no doubt remember from my meeting with Chief Thomas on August 7, he told me the plan to split the park was only for if we lost in federal court. He assured us we would have both sides if we received an injunction. Interestingly, without knowing about this alleged plan to bring speakers in from the back of the park, I had accidentally attempted entry from

---

[267] jasonkessler.us/wp-content/uploads/2020/05/Highlight-Wendy-Lewis-1.png

the rear on August 12 and could find no accessible point of entry. When I had spoken to an officer at the side of the park, he did not direct me to enter from the back. Thomas saw the phony statement from Dickler and forwarded it to Captain Lewis as if it was an example of a narrative she should emulate. She replied with a second email reiterating her criticism of how misleading his blame-shifting narrative was. "Did anyone correct Miriam's statement? It gives the impression that the rear of the park was entry point for all the alt-right demonstrators?"[268] No correction from Thomas or Dickler was ever given, either to the public or to the journalist.

---

[268] jasonkessler.us/wp-content/uploads/2020/05/Highlight-Wendy-Lewis.png

TRUMP'S CHARLOTTESVILLE PRESS CONFERENCE

On August 15, President Donald Trump held a press conference addressing the events in Charlottesville from New York City's Trump Tower where he reiterated many of the core themes behind my rally, thus proving their broad appeal.

> I'm not putting anybody on a moral plane. What I'm saying is this: You had a group on one side and you had a

Donald Trump press conference in Trump Tower (August 15, 2017)

group on the other and they came at each other with clubs and it was vicious and it was horrible and it was a horrible thing to watch. But there is another side. There was a group on this side—you can call them the left, you've just called them the left—that came, violently attacking the other group. So you can say what you want, but that's the way it is.

I think there's blame on both sides. And I have no doubt about it, and you don't have any doubt about it either. And if you reported it accurately, you would say it.

George Washington was a slave owner. So will George Washington now lose his status? Are we gonna take down statues to George Washington? How about Thomas Jefferson? What do you think of Thomas Jefferson? You like him? OK, good. Are we gonna take down the statue—'cause he was a major slave owner—now are we gonna take down his statue?

So you know what, it's fine. You're changing history, you're changing culture, and you had people—and I'm not talking about the neo-Nazis and the white nationalists—because they should be condemned totally, but you had many people in that group, other than neo-Nazis and white nationalists, OK, and the press has treated them absolutely unfairly. In the other group also, you had some fine people, but you also had troublemakers. And you see them come with the black outfits, and with the helmets and with the baseball bats. You had a lot of bad people in the other group, too.

"Were you saying the press has treated white nationalists unfairly?" pestered a fake news media "reporter."

You had a lot of people in that group that were there to innocently protest—and very legally protest—because, I don't know if you know, they had a permit; the other group didn't have a permit. There are two sides to a story.

When I heard that, I was so excited I pumped my fist and shouted for joy. Alas, that was the closest we would ever get to having the public hear the real truth behind what happened at the rally.

Aftermath

Charlottesville's Unite the Right rally was a seminal moment in American history and a defining moment of the Trump era in American politics. So much has happened since then that is affected by UTR and its fallout. It has become part of the tapestry of American history. Yet there are a few moments of particularly important significance for both the people who went to UTR and the nation at large.

Several weeks after the rally, then-Mayor Signer was chastised for overstepping his authority. After a three-hour meeting on August 30, Signer read a prepared statement but took no questions from the press. At this "public apology press conference," Signer agreed to stop making public pronouncements without the council's consensus and agreed to cease meeting with senior City Hall staffers unless accompanied by another councilor: "I have taken several actions as mayor and made several communications that have been inconsistent with the collaboration required by our system of governance and that overstepped the bounds of my role as mayor. These actions included an ill-advised Facebook post which impugned the reputations of our city manager Maurice Jones and our chief of police Al Thomas for which I sincerely apologize."

A week before Signer's apology, a leaked email memo putatively from City Council to Jones, but predominantly composed by Signer alone, showed how far the mayor was overstepping his bounds. As Jones wrote: "On two separate occasions during the height of the crisis, the mayor threatened my job and that of the police chief because of our concerns about allowing him to be part of the command center. He said, 'You work for me,' and I replied that 'I worked for the City Council.'"

I was completely unaware of the turf wars, duplicity, and dysfunction that was endemic in Charlottesville's city government, which could only hurt my chances of expecting fair treatment from tainted public officials. Things continued spinning out of control for Signer at City Council meetings, which became a pot boiler of violent explosive tension after the rally.

An indication of just how out of control and off the wall City Council meetings had become, is summed up perfectly in *Summer of Hate*. As Hawes Spencer explains in Chapter 7 of his book under the subheading COUNCIL MEETING TURNS CHAOTIC, at the first City Council meeting since the rally, on August 21, "the interruptions began almost as soon as Mayor Signer opened" it. Unable to even deliver his prepared remarks, he warned the more aggressive in the audience that they could be removed, and he was forced to order police to remove three belligerents. While the unhinged continued shouting and screaming, "two women suddenly climbed atop the dais to unfurl a banner reading BLOOD ON YOUR HANDS to applause and chants of 'resign, resign, resign.'" Signer announced the end of the meeting, "and all five counselors departed under police escort." When they returned, Signer handed control of the meeting over to Bellamy, but the unhinged behavior continued, and a man began yelling at Signer: "I see the fucking smile on your goddamn face. You should go outside and kick yourself in the ass." Signer replied: "That's a threat. We have kids watching." It continued to careen out of control, when many from the audience surrounded the dais. Signer again departed, and Councilor "Szakos banged the mayor's gavel." "Fuck your gavel," someone shouted.[269]

None of the Antifa and only a few of the violent Blacks were prosecuted for their actions on August 12. So emboldened was Socialist Rifle Association, for actions which amounted to a terrorist attack on Americans right to speak and assemble, that they posted a celebratory

---

[269] *Summer of Hate* p. 100

picture of the weaponry they employed against the rally along with the boast: "For eight hours we held off Nazis and kept cops out of the park while BLM, queer activists, anarchists of color, antifa contingents, and IWW[270] columns all staged successful actions to fuck shit up and put blood in the mouths of white supremacists. This is historical: the armed left held streets in an American city once again."

Socialist Rifle Association Backup
August 15, 2017

We are so incredibly proud of the SRA and Redneck Revolt heroes who held the line against Nazi scum this past weekend in Charlottesville.

This is from a comrade who stood with our Socialist Rifle Association contingent:

"How to fight fascism: tools from Redneck Revolt's A12 deployment to Justice Park. For eight hours we held off Nazis and kept cops out of the park while BLM, queer activists, anarchists of color, antifa contingents, and IWW columns all staged successful actions to fuck shit up and put blood in the mouths of white supremacists. This is historical: the armed left held streets in an American city once again."

202   7 Comments 50 Shares

---

[270] iww.org

Recall that Redneck Revolt leader Dwayne Dixon was invited to speak at Harvard as a guest of honor. He celebrated his actions that day along with a coterie of radical professors and students at the nation's most elite university: "[We were] physically fighting: kicking, striking, bloodying, cracking heads. I mean bloody, ugly things that I would never wish but we need people with this moral clarity and determination."[271]

Several lawsuits were filed against the protesters; the only one that went to trial was *Sines v. Kessler*. This was a professional political hit job by some of the most powerful, politically connected Jewish attorneys and activists in the country such as Karen Dunn, an Obama administration advisor, and Roberta Kaplan, a lesbian friend of Hillary Clinton who argued the case legalizing same sex marriage before SCOTUS.

Kaplan was invited to Charlottesville by her friend Dahlia Lithwick, whom I previously mentioned was a panelist at the free speech symposium I attended in 2016. Lithwick had hand selected a number of plaintiffs whom she felt would elicit sympathy as women, racial minorities, students, and left-wing political activists. Kaplan told them that they might be thinking about suing the police for their conduct at the rally but that "if you do that you can't be in our case." She informed them, "if you're in our case, you're probably not gonna get a lot of money at the end," but that her lawsuit was their best shot at getting revenge against the UTR organizers. Asked by a reporter what the ideal outcome of the lawsuit would be, Kaplan crowed: *"We absolutely can and will bankrupt these groups. And then we will chase these people around for the rest of their lives. So if they try to buy a new home, we will put a lien on the home. If they get a new job, we will garnish their wages."*[272]

The trial was an absolutely crooked and corrupt display of how the civil courts are biased in favor of moneyed interest, non-White ethnic lobbies, and against conservatives and Whites. The campaign

---

[271] youtube.com/watch?v=U0dgg9dXLm0
[272] momentmag.com/roberta-kaplan-takes-white-supremacy-to-court

Amy Spitalnick (left) with attorney Roberta Kaplan (right) conducting their multi-million-dollar fundraising campaign at a San Francisco synagogue (November 13, 2019)

to persecute UTR organizers for exercising their First Amendment rights was financed by the Jewish-centric nonprofit, Integrity First for America, whose Executive Director Amy Spitalnick, allegedly the granddaughter of Holocaust survivors, has received the usual fawning publicity. Spitalnick was formerly spokesperson for disgraced New York Attorney General Eric Schneiderman, who suspended an investigation into the Harvey Weinstein rape allegations after Weinstein's attorneys at Boies Schiller sent $10,000 to Manhattan District Attorney Cy Vance and $25,000 to New York Governor Andrew Cuomo.

According to Internal Revenue Service (IRS) financial disclosures, IFA raised $22,717,744 for the *Sines* lawsuit between 2017 and 2022![273] It hasn't been publicly stated who has been funding litigation since then, during appeals, or how much it costs. If the purpose of the litigation was to compensate those injured by Fields, it seems like spending at least $23 million to receive a $2 million verdict was a

---

[273] charitiesnys.com/RegistrySearch/show_details.jsp?id={3086C288-0000-C318-8442-B755D378D55B}

massive waste of money. They very well could have just given that money directly to their clients, but it was first and foremost a vindictive political hit job motivated by race hatred towards Whites. They spent a fortune to overwhelm defendants who didn't have the same financial resources to hire whole teams of lawyers, expert witnesses, private investigators, and all the assets of a multi-milliondollar legal team. Most of the defendants couldn't even afford to pay attorneys. This was not "justice." This was the rich and politically connected brutalizing the poor in a broken system where "justice" goes to the highest bidder.

Much of the funding was provided by Jewish Silicon Valley billionaires like LinkedIn founder Reid Hoffman and Craig Newmark of Craigslist, Jewish actors like Topher Grace of *That 70's Show*, hedge fund managers, the ADL, and SPLC.

IFA is connected to other infamous members of the Jewish community. For instance, Hoffman ran public relations for infamous Jewish pedophile and sex criminal Jeffrey Epstein after his first round of prostitution charges.[274] Kaplan, the lead attorney paid by IFA in *Sines v. Kessler*, formerly represented the prolific Jewish rapist and media mogul Weinstein.[275] IFA paid Boies Schiller attorneys to assist Kaplan in the anti-UTR lawfare. Founding partner David Boies famously took over representation of Weinstein after Kaplan and was a vicious attack dog against Weinstein's rape victims. Boies Schiller acted as the liaison between Weinstein and Black Cube, a firm run by former Mossad spies.[276]

IFA was also connected to other shady, dishonest political shenanigans. For instance, IFA claimed funds donated by supporters would only go towards the *Sines v. Kessler* litigation, yet surreptitiously donated $620,000 to the firm Bean, LLC on behalf of Fusion GPS, the shady firm that released the phony "piss dossier" which helped jumpstart the debunked Trump-Russia collusion hoax.[277]

---

[274] businessinsider.com/linkedin-founder-reid-hoffman-apologizes-helping-jeffrey-epstein-2019-9
[275] variety.com/2019/biz/news/harvey-weinstein-she-said-1203329374
[276] theguardian.com/film/2020/jan/30/harvey-weinstein-black-cube-new-york-times
[277] dailycaller.com/2020/12/21/fusion-gps-reid-hoffman-dossier

In contrast, many of the defendants like Cantwell and Spencer were forced to represent themselves due to lack of funds. The powerhouse Jewish attorneys had a cutthroat strategy to win rather than get to the bottom of the truth about what happened at Charlottesville. They somehow got the judge to bar testimony from Detective Young about how there was no conspiracy between organizers and Fields, and bar admission of Heaphy's Independent Review finding fault for the violence in missteps by the Charlottesville government. The court excluded all of my evidence, which I had painstakingly collected over four years, because Kaplan and Dunn claimed they had not received it from my attorney in time. The trial took place during COVID hysteria and they were able to have the judge exclude all jurors who did not want to wear a mask during the entirety of the trial, which necessarily prejudiced jury selection against conservatives. The judge granted them *outrageous* jury instructions that there can be a "conspiracy" even between two people *who have never met*, agreed on any shared purpose, or even communicated with one another at all! Finally, when it looked like we might win the trial outright despite all these systemic disadvantages, a potentially favorable juror who spoke about anti-White discrimination he received during his childhood in Hawaii was removed . . . not because he had COVID, or because his child had COVID, but because *someone* at his child's school allegedly had COVID! Instead of allowing the jury plenty of time to deliberate, Kaplan's case went way past the allotted time for both the defense and plaintiffs, forcing the jury to make a rush decision or risk being sequestered during the upcoming Thanksgiving holiday. Despite all this, the jury was deadlocked on Kaplan and Dunn's signature federal conspiracy count and only ruled in their favor on some lesser state violations. Nevertheless, the cynical liars then received an HBO documentary about their "successful" lawsuit as well as fawning national coverage on programs like MSNBC's *Morning Joe* where Dunn claimed the jury returned a finding of "complete liability," which is clearly not true. But who is going to challenge them on it? We might as well be Galileo or Socrates expecting a fair trial or an admission of tyranny from the government and judiciary. They are in power and we are not. It's as simple as that.

The initial judgement in *Sines* was for $26 million split between all defendants. However, the majority of this was ruled illegal under Virginia law and reduced to a mere $2.35 million. The key to understanding this is knowing the difference between compensatory and punitive damages. Compensatory damages are the value of the actual injury done to plaintiffs. Punitive damages are when a jury wants to send a message based on what they see as offensive or outrageous conduct of the defendants. Almost all of the judgment, $24 million, was in punitive damages. However, state and constitutional law restricts the ability of jurors to award outsized punitive damage awards that are vastly out of proportion to the actual harm done to plaintiffs, as measured by the compensatory award. Thus, the $24 million in punitive damages was reduced to the Virginia cap of $350,000. These numbers are mostly for show, as few of the defendants had assets or savings which could be seized under law. To my knowledge nothing has been collected as of the writing of this book.[278]

I held a follow-up rally on August 12, 2018, in Washington, D.C. I did it because I perceived Charlottesville was being used to intimidate us from speaking in the public square. Despite enormous pressure, the event was largely a success, although much smaller than the original UTR. This was in part due to another betrayal by law enforcement. Our plan was to gather supporters at a Vienna, Virginia metro station for about an hour before departing on the metro for a march to Lafayette Square. When I arrived, a Black cop informed me we would have to leave right away or not at all, stranding all of my supporters who hadn't already arrived 45 minutes before the scheduled departure. Nevertheless, the media was shocked to see we were completely nonviolent when the police did their jobs and Antifa looked absolutely horrid beating up cops and journalists in frustration. When we came out of the metro near Lafayette, there were tens of thousands of furious counter-protesters. The cops formed a line like some ancient phalanx and pushed through the hordes of barbarians with we few

---

[278] washingtonpost.com/dc-md-va/2023/01/03/charlottesville-unite-the-right-damages

protesters like Caesars marching in triumph. Perhaps the most awe-inspiring moment of my life so far.

On January 6, 2021, Trump supporters experienced their own Charlottesville. In what was supposed to be a protest over what many Americans viewed as a stolen election, political leaders, Capitol Police, and the FBI allowed a right-wing protest to spin out of control, and then used it to attack Donald Trump politically and mass incarcerate his followers. Democrat and former House Speaker Nancy Pelosi refused to send in the National Guard in time to maintain order. Many of the activists who went to Charlottesville stayed away from J6 because they suspected it was a trap. Nevertheless a few Charlottesville attendees like Fuentes and Baked Alaska were in attendance.

During the summer of 2020, following the death of Black Minnesota career criminal George Floyd while in police custody, left-wing protests and riots broke out all over the country resulting in at least 25 deaths[279] as well as countless injuries, rampant looting of businesses, and firebombing of police stations and vehicles. The financial cost of the 2020 "Summer of Love" riots is estimated to be between $1 billion and $2 billion, according to the Insurance Information Institute and Property Claim Services, making it the most expensive civil disorder in U.S. history.[280] What happened next showed the nerve UTR struck was still being felt by the radical left even three years later. Anti-White racists began tearing down hundreds of historical monuments, at first only to Confederate leaders, before moving on to U.S. presidents, explorers, European writers, and even abolitionists. It appeared the rage was merely focused on White men and toppling the last vestiges of their civilization.

---

[279] theguardian.com/world/2020/oct/31/americans-killed-protests-political-unrest-acled
[280] axios.com/2020/09/16/riots-cost-property-damage

THE MOCK EXECUTION OF THE LEE MONUMENT

Following a years-long legal fight, City of Charlottesville removed the Robert E. Lee monument and handed it over to Swords into Plowshares, a nonprofit created by Jalane Schmidt, the radical UVA professor and UTR counter-protest organizer who also founded Cville Black Lives Matter. In October 2023, the monument was defaced and then destroyed at a leftist-owned foundry in a kind of mock execution. There was something ominously sadistic about the demolition, as celebrated by *The Washington Post* in a series of graphic videos and pictures framed like a pornographic snuff film for anti-Whites.[281]

From the beginning headline, *Charlottesville's Lee statue meets its end, in a 2,250-degree furnace*, the *Post* article was clearly intended to rub salt in the wounds of our sharply divided country and culture by celebrating the vandalism as a sadistic and ritualistic murder—as if done to the conservative White men that the Woke Left so loathes, rather than a monument of bronze. As Elon Musk succinctly put it after viewing the video, "They absolutely want your extinction."[282]

Post readers were subjected to a video loop created by breaking news video editor Hadley Green depicting the head of Robert E. Lee, laying prostrate and helpless, as a goon from the foundry cuts through the metal, lacerating his visage like one of the face masks collected by

---

[281] washingtonpost.com/dc-md-va/interactive/2023/civil-war-monument-melting-robert-e-lee-confederate
[282] x.com/elonmusk/status/1717917760166993982

Charlottesville's Lee monument was superheated and melted into metal ingots

serial killer "Buffalo Bill" in *The Silence of the Lambs*. The piece by Green and co-author Teo Armus revels in horror novel prose, describing the act as a "celebration" of a "grim act."

"Counter-Currents" columnist and author Jim Goad offered this vividly brutal description of the video's climax: Lee's visage

> ... super-heated to the point where it glowed, offering the stark and ghastly image of a military leader — who by multiple accounts was a gracious and noble man — suffering amid hellfire for all eternity.[283]

Unlike most videos placed onto news sites in 2023, there were no inconvenient ads placed either before or after the *Post*'s video that might delay anyone from being immediately confronted with the violent act. Nor did the video player shuffle to other content, as most do these days, so any readers who revere Lee's memory would experience the maximum trauma from the deliberately gratuitous sadism of Green's video.

---

[283] counter-currents.com/2023/10/the-worst-week-yet-149

Mock execution of Charlottesville's Robert E. Lee statue at an undisclosed foundry in the South (October 21, 2023)

Since race plays such a large part in the controversy over the Robert E. Lee statue and the UTR rally, it is worth asking Green's racial background. The surname Green has Saxon, Old English origins, but in modern times, often denotes Ashkenazi Jewish ancestry. Many Ashkenazim have anglicized names. In the case of Green as a Jewish surname it comes from "grin" or "Gryn," the Yiddish words for "green." I asked her about this directly, but she declined to comment.

I also asked the Black-presenting Schmidt if she is part-Jewish, as her name might suggest—no answer either.

It's worth noting that Lee's method of "execution" was being burned in an oven, perhaps a deliberate reference to the Holocaust, since in my experience Jewish activists have been exceptionally passionate about inflicting retribution towards anything associated with the UTR rally.

The Washington Post team took the extremely unusual and arguably unprofessional step of "agree(ing) not to name" the foundry where the destruction of the Lee statue took place "because of participants'

THE MOCK EXECUTION OF THE LEE MONUMENT

≡Q   The Washington Post   Sign in

Hadley Green
Washington, D.C.

Breaking news video editor

Education: Tufts University, BA in international relations; UNC-Chapel Hill Hussman School of Journalism and Media, MA in visual communication

Hadley Green is a breaking news video editor for The Washington Post. She produces original video stories and helps coordinate The Post's live video coverage. She joined The Post in 2021 and previously worked as a visual journalist with the Salem News and WBUR.

Edit Profile   •••

Jalane Schmidt

fears of violence." But behind that protective shield of anonymity the foundry workers were trash-talking tough guys. "It's a better sculpture now than it's ever been," one of them said according to Green and Armus. The owner of the foundry, whom the *Post* writers described as a Black man, reportedly said: "When you're approached with such an honor, especially to destroy hate, you have to do it."

Schmidt's Swords into Plowshares group was apparently in attendance: hooting, hollering, and getting drunk on champagne and bourbon like some bloodthirsty medieval crowd at a public execution. That's exactly what this was to them.

The execution of Hugh Despenser the Younger, as depicted in the Froissart of Louis of Gruuthuse

The morbid, implicitly homicidal, language surrounding Regime Media depictions of this vandalism is not limited to *The Washington Post*. Significantly, NPR anthropomorphized the statue, describing the dismemberment of its face into a "death mask" which "falls to the floor with a loud clank." Then, reveling in the grisly melting of the statue into molded metal ingots, Schmidt reportedly laughed that it was like knocking "meatloaf" out of a pan—yet another telling reference to flesh.[284]

Erin Thompson, writing in *The New York Times*, gleefully described how the "plasma torch sliced into the face of Robert E Lee." The gratuitous title of her piece taunted that the statue "surrenders to the furnace." Thompson described how after dismembering and incinerating the statue, "Drops of molten red metal cascaded to the ground," vividly depicting something akin to the red blood of a murder victim pouring from his body.[285]

The clear intention of all of this masturbatory celebration was to demoralize the contingent of White America who have not forgotten or disinherited the heroes of Western civilization.

---

[284] npr.org/2023/10/26/1208603609/confederate-general-robert-e-lee-monument-melted-down-charlottesville-virginia

[285] archive.ph/CyFLa

TORCH MARCH PROSECUTIONS... SIX YEARS LATER

In February 2023, a grand jury convened in Albemarle County at the behest of Soros-funded Commonwealth Attorney Jim Hingeley. The purpose was to fulfill Hingeley's campaign promise of prosecuting the nonviolent protesters who carried torches during the August 11, 2017 demonstration nearly six years earlier. The prosecutions had been advocated for years, particularly within the far-left UVA Law community, which included many prominent Antifa-aligned organizers of the counter-protest, like Anne Coughlin and Ben Doherty. In 2018, these individuals had nearly fomented a riot when I tried to use the UVA Law library to study for defense in my UTR-linked civil cases and then had me banned so that I could no longer use those resources.

Despite pressure from activists like Coughlin, Doherty, and other Antifa, prosecutors in both Charlottesville and Albemarle County, where UVA campus is located, resisted calls to prosecute protesters under Virginia Statute § 18.2-423.01B, which states "Any person who, with the intent of intimidating any person or group of persons, burns an object on a highway or other public place in a manner having a direct tendency to place another person in reasonable fear or apprehension of death or bodily injury is guilty of a Class 6 felony." Applying the law to nonviolent protesters carrying lit objects as part of the message of their demonstration would have been a novel interpretation of the law—a massive expansion of its intended purpose—and run afoul of First Amendment considerations. Hingeley was not dissuaded by these free speech concerns from both Democrats and Republicans alike. He hired a new assistant prosecutor named Lawton Tufts to spearhead the prosecutions and they were off to the races.

An indeterminate number of secretive, sealed indictments were issued, which have resulted in 12 arrests as of this publication. Despite the unusual length of time, which might typically be considered a due process violation, Virginia has no statute of limitations on felonies.

In October 2023, I was contacted by one of the individuals connected to the defense for the accused. He had some concerns about potential bias on the court, specifically Judge Claude Worrell II, whom we've already mentioned was a witness at St. Paul's Church on August 11. Worrell was now the Chief Justice for the 16th Judicial Circuit of Virginia and had been denying bond in hearings for all the torch defendants who came before him, including men who had completely clean criminal records. As a result of this, a couple of defendants had pled guilty rather than be away from their jobs and families during the extensive pre-trial period.

I was no stranger to investigating this kind of courtroom bias. During the *Sines* trial I uncovered evidence that friends of plaintiff Elizabeth Sines—Hutton Marshall and Joshua Lefebvre—were clerks in presiding Clinton-appointed federal Judge Norman K. Moon's court and had improperly dismissed my lawsuit against the City for First Amendment violations, without recusing themselves for the appearance of bias. Sines had even shouted out to Lefebvre during the livestream of her Water Street march with Heather Heyer and went to Lefebvre's home to mentally convalesce after the crash, making him a key witness to her mental state.[286]

Following this, the now-defunct website "National Justice"[287] had uncovered evidence that one of the law clerks—Dascher Pasco—who ruled against our motions to dismiss the civil case, was a

---

[286] bitchute.com/video/mvSXYkxTsLYz
[287] unz.com/estriker/bombshell-staff-writing-legal-opinions-for-charlottesville-judge-norman-moon-hold-egregious-conflicts-of-interest

former president of the Jewish Law Student Association who had made hostile statements on her Facebook page against defendants and the UTR rally during a trip to Jerusalem, funded, in-part, by the Israeli government:

> As I sat in Jerusalem discussing antisemitism, I learned about the atrocities happening at home.
>
> Words cannot adequately capture my feelings, but to know that people are chanting "Jew [sic] will not replace us," among other horrendous phrases, steps away from my house in Charlottesville disgusts me.
>
> To know that friends and loved ones are willing to stand up against hatred gives me hope.[288]

In another rambling Facebook screed, Pasco implored her followers to, "Fight all racism as strongly as you fight anti-Semitism and fight it regardless of the speaker."[289] This was a totally inappropriate person to have been making key decisions in that case, which could have and should have been dismissed without her surreptitious invasion of the court and intrusion into what should have been an unbiased legal process.[290]

When I began to look into Worrell, I realized his wife, a White woman named Kathryn Laughon, was a radical self-identified Antifa activist who had been posting anti-White tweets ("Honestly I do kind of hate white people.")[291] and calling for the prosecution of the torch marchers under the controversial left-wing interpretation of the burning objects statute.[292] She had also taken part in a podcast called *The Pledge*, with her anti-White, America-hating, mixed-race daughter Althea Laughon-Worrell.[293] In the podcast, Laughon and her daughter describe being central witnesses to the events along with Judge Worrell.

---

[288] archive.is/aJsi4
[289] archive.is/OxAzv
[290] jasonkessler.us/blog/2020/03/24/motions-filed-for-recusal-of-charlottesville-rally-clerks
[291] counter-currents.com/wp-content/uploads/2023/11/Laughon3.png
[292] jasonkessler.us/wp-content/uploads/2023/09/word-image-2530-7.png
[293] audacy.com/podcasts/the-pledge-podcast-25222/my-whole-world-shifted-168242930

According to Laughon-Worrell:

> After it was over, we had to stay inside the church, and we had to leave quietly and in small groups. And it was terrifying. I present very white to the world. I'm mixed. I'm black and I'm white, and I'm also gay. And you may not know these things from looking at me. But it was still terrifying because my large black father was in that church with us. We had to run to our cars to try and stay away from these people because they were going to attack us.[294]

Despite apparently running in fear from defendants during the events central to the torch protest cases, Worrell did not recuse himself or acknowledge his conflict until attorneys for the defense brought the matter before the court. At this point he recused himself, too late to help the men who pled guilty due to Worrell's bond denial.

Following this revelation, the entire 16th Judicial Circuit was recused and then recusal hearings were held for Assistant Commonwealth Attorney Tufts. Tufts was friends with Laughon, including on Facebook, and had been a central liaison between counter-protest groups like BLM and SURJ, and CPD during UTR. Tufts was recused against his will by Judge H. Thomas Padrick Jr., who had been brought in to replace Worrell. In his ruling Padrick stated: "Looking at the totality of the evidence that's been presented, there is an appearance of a conflict, and the Commonwealth's Attorney's Office should recuse."

When I first began my investigation of the court corruption in these cases, there was very little interest within the pro-White movement for covering the conflict or helping the defendants out. What I have found, unfortunately, is that guys without a social media following or platform are essentially non-entities in politics, since helping them doesn't confer any resource or status benefits. The most shocking example of this was when I called Cantwell, whom I had supported during his incarceration, offered him a job upon his release,

---

[294] jasonkessler.us/blog/2023/10/02/the-night-the-lights-went-out-in-charlottesville-judicial-prejudice-in-a-southern-towny

and did my best to promote when he restarted his livestreaming career. In a private conversation, Cantwell was very rude, constantly interrupting me and dismissively claiming that, "No one cares about what is happening in Charlottesville. Everyone already knows the courts are corrupt." He kept trying to change the subject to a peripheral detail I had mentioned about Invictus, now charged with a crime, being unable to talk about his case publicly due to a gag order. Bizarrely, Cantwell called me a liar and demanded evidence of the gag order, and tried to diminish me by telling me I could "call into his program" like anyone else, but that he would not allow me to talk about the cases as a guest. Clearly, he wanted to put me in a subservient position from which he could humiliate me. I had been holding my tongue for several minutes of abuse and finally told him: "Fuck off."

This one insult led Cantwell into a psychotic rage comparable to the feud with movement rivals which sent him to prison in 2021 for threats and extortion. He went back and started reading depositions where I was grilled by Jewish attorneys like Kaplan and amplifying their desperate and unwarranted claims against me, for instance, that I had "tipped off" Antifa. This was not something related to UTR; it had to do with the months *before* UTR when Antifa were following my supporters to bars and restaurants and demanding management ban us. On one occasion, we set a trap where we went to a conservative biker bar with friendly management and pretended we were having a meeting with Richard Spencer to draw Antifa into an embarrassing rebuff. Cantwell started insinuating this had something to do with the August rally, and telling his audience I was to blame for his arrest! It was a totally dishonest, scummy, and emotionally unstable reaction. To make matters worse, when Invictus had his gag order lifted, Cantwell had him on to discuss the torch cases and pretended as if he was in the defendants' corner all along. From that point, I reflected on how wrong I had been to have overlooked Cantwell's instability in the past and his collaboration with the FBI, repeated arrests, and engagement with child protective services to attack the children of movement rivals. I was done with him.

SKOKIE TO CHARLOTTESVILLE: HISTORICAL ANALYSIS

The premise of the UTR rally on August 11 and 12, 2017, would be inconceivable without the landmark 1977 SCOTUS case *National Socialist Party of America v. Village of Skokie* brought by attorneys from the ACLU, and a comparison between the two landmark cases is as good a place to conclude this volume as any. For one, we never would have conceived of UTR unless we believed we had an unalienable right to demonstrate, even in a hostile community which believed us to be "Nazis." Second, our right to protest was affirmed in our own landmark ACLU case, *Kessler v. City of Charlottesville*, which relied on *Skokie* for precedent. Therefore, this book on Charlottesville would be incomplete without comparing and contrasting the resulting Skokie and Charlottesville demonstrations to draw some conclusions about why only one of them turned out so horribly wrong. As you will see, the left-wing argument that Skokie was different than Charlottesville because only one involved the prospect of violence is pure lies and sophistry. Both rallies existed in an era of extreme threat of counter-protester violence. By the laws of both the United States and God Almighty, a man has a right to defend himself from violent aggression while he is exercising his free speech civil liberties. The difference in outcomes between 1978 and 2017 relied exclusively on whether police were committed to defending controversial speech from mob violence.

In 1977, the National Socialist Party of America (NSPA) was headquartered in the Marquette Park area of Chicago, Illinois, and led by Frank Collin. Collin was a former member of George Lincoln Rockwell's American Nazi Party who had been excommunicated for Jewish ancestry, a fact which he denied at the time but was undoubtedly true (Collin's father Max Collin, born Max Cohn, was a Jewish immigrant from Munich, Germany). The group regularly held demonstrations in Marquette Park, a hotbed for controversial protests, including a demonstration by Martin Luther King Jr.[295] which had devolved into violence. The City of Chicago eventually imposed what would now be considered a prohibitively expensive and illegal insurance requirement of $250,000 to obtain a permit for Marquette Park, which led the NSPA to seek alternative sites in Chicago suburbs like Cicero, Berwyn, and (fatefully) the heavy Jewish suburb of Skokie.[296] Collin and the NSPA were represented by Jewish ACLU attorney David Goldberger, who successfully upheld their rights before SCOTUS. However, once NSPA had been vindicated of their rights, they returned, not to Skokie, but to their originally intended protest ground in Chicago's Marquette Park. With a clear mandate from judicial authorities, the Chicago Police Department understood their obligations and carried out the difficult task of protecting the NSPA rally. Around 2,000 people milled around

---

[295] time.com/5096937/martin-luther-king-jr-picture-chicago
[296] interactive.wbez.org/curiouscity/chicagonazineighborhood

Marquette Park during the NSPA's celebratory rally on July 9, 1978. It has been estimated that about 66% were anti-Nazi while 33% were sympathetic. There were scuffles, but **at least 400 riot-helmeted police officers separated the hostile elements of the crowd from 25 NSPA demonstrators** clad in their brown shirts and swastika armbands, conducting 72 arrests.[297] Muscular intervention of Chicago Police at the post-SCOTUS rally was the only thing that allowed the NSPA to exercise their free speech without the event turning into a large brawl, or a riot, like in Charlottesville. The wide separation of protesters from counter-protesters at the July 9 Marquette Park rally mirrored the successful police cordon of nationalist protesters by Washington, D.C. Police at the UTR 2 event on August 12, 2018.[298]

Critics of the Charlottesville rally, like Kaplan, feign respect for the First Amendment by claiming 2017 was about violence, not free speech. However, when you isolate the statements from organizers expressing concern over counter-protester violence and recommending "you bring picket sign posts, shields, and other self-defense implements which can be turned from a free speech tool to a self-defense weapon should things turn ugly," this is no different than the situation which existed in 1978. It is a fallacy that the NSPA marches were somehow more "pure" and untainted by the specter of violence or violent rhetoric. "The Nazis will not march in Skokie . . . Should the Nazis appear we will break their heads. There will be violence in the streets," threatened Rabbi Meir Kahane, co-founder of the Jewish Defense League (JDL). NSPA leader Collin responded with threats of his own: "I can promise you this: that come hell or high water, Supreme Court or no Supreme Court, arrest or no arrest, violence or no violence, Rabbi Kahane or no Rabbi Kahane, we are going into Skokie, by God this year. And we don't care how much violence they're gonna bring on our heads. We'll give it back to them three times as much." Prior to the SCOTUS case, brawls had broken out between the NSPA and the angry counter-protesters at marches. A

---

[297] nytimes.com/1978/07/10/archives/72-seized-at-rally-of-nazis-in-chicago-police-keep-2000-under.html
[298] wusa9.com/article/news/local/2-arrests-made-during-unite-the-right-rally-no-injuries-reported/65-583369069

man was choked at a Berwyn march in 1972. At least three Nazis ran in to punch on a Jewish man who was grappling with a fourth member of their group. Riot police were brought in but not before Collin's face was covered in a crimson mask of blood.[299]

Another occasion on July 8, 1972, turned into a violent clash between the National Socialists and the JDL. According to the *Chicago Tribune*: "Members of the American Nazi Party and the Jewish Defense League had a brief but lively fist fight in front of the Berwyn Municipal Building yesterday before being separated by police garbed in riot gear. Frank Collin, head of the Nazi group, emerged from the fight with blood trickling down his neck, and two others of his band nursed bruises." The demonstration was to protest Berwyn's

Buzz Alpert (left), a member of the Jewish Defense League sought physical confrontations with Collin's National Socialist Party during protests in the 1970s

[299] bitchute.com/video/KF9qtL00WPzA

refusal to permit the neo-Nazi group to hold a public meeting in the suburb.[300]

On November 14, 1977, anti-racists brawled with NSPA while they were picketing a speech by "Nazi hunter" Simon Wiesenthal at Triton Junior College. Collin and two other men were placed under arrest.

In 2017, the alt-right was under the assumption their protests would be subject to the same level of violence from rabid counter-demonstrators and that self-defensive violence might be necessary. A planned speech by conservative Milo Yiannopolous at the UC Berkeley campus on February 1 had turned into a riot thanks to the appearance of at least 150 black bloc Antifa militants. According to Wikipedia:[301]

Frank Collin, center, pulls the shirt of a Jewish Defense League member during a Nazi Party demonstration at Berwyn City Hall (July 8, 1972)

---

[300] chicagotribune.com/visuals/vintage/ct-skokie-swastika-war-nazi-party-chicago-photos-20170308-photogallery.html
[301] en.wikipedia.org/wiki/2017_Berkeley_protests

The group of interrupting protestors set fires, damaged property, threw fireworks, attacked members of the crowd, and threw rocks at the police. Within twenty minutes of the start of the violence, the Yiannopoulos event was officially canceled by the university police department due to security concerns, and protesters were ordered to disperse. The interrupting protesters continued for several hours afterwards, with some protesters moving into downtown Berkeley to break windows at several banks, a Starbucks, a Target, a Sprint store, and a T-Mobile store. Among those assaulted were a Syrian Muslim, who was pepper sprayed and hit with a rod by an interrupting protester who said "You look like a Nazi," and Kiara Robles, who was pepper sprayed while being interviewed by a TV reporter. One person was arrested for failure to disperse, and there was an estimated $100,000 in damage.[302]

The aforementioned April 15, pro-Trump free speech event held in Berkeley's Martin Luther King Jr. Civic Center Park turned into an all-out riot, with counter-protesters exploding fireworks, smoke bombs, deploying pepper spray, and turning everything in the found environment into weapons. Eleven people were injured, six of whom were hospitalized, including one person who was stabbed. Police "seized a handful of cans of peppers [sic] spray, some knives, and dozens of sign and flag poles, skateboards, and other blunt objects" from members of the crowd. Twenty people were arrested.[303]

On that day, the Berkeley Police had engaged in a "stand down" policy. That is the defining variable in why a free speech event turned into a riot. It was the same at UTR on August 12. City officials had been briefed to expect violence from counter-demonstrators seeking to shut down the permitted event.[304] Not only that, they were counting on it.

---

[302] archive.is/HhHTh
[303] latimes.com/local/lanowy/la-me-ln-berkeley-trump-rally-20170415-story.html
[304] Heaphy p. 187

An independent review commissioned by the City after August 12[305] found that, "rather than engage the crowd and prevent fights, the [CPD] plan was to declare the event unlawful and disperse the crowd." Charlottesville officers told third party investigators they had been ordered not to engage over "every little thing"; not to "go in and break up fights"; not to interrupt "mutual combat"; and officers were not to be sent out among the crowd where they might get hurt.

During the August 12, 2017, event, Chief Thomas and City Manager Maurice Jones purposely sabotaged the rally by allowing hundreds of violent, armed counter-protesters to attack the permitted UTR rally so they could use the ensuing violence as legal justification to shut down the event. Again, Thomas' assistant Emily Lantz and Captain Lewis, who were with him in the Unified Command Center that day, upon being advised violence had broken out the Chief stated: "Let them fight, it will make it easier to declare an unlawful assembly."

Remember the verdict of Heaphy Report investigators: "City of Charlottesville protected neither free expression nor public safety on August 12. The City was unable to protect the right of free expression and facilitate the permit holder's offensive speech." As a result of the Charlottesville government's reckless decisions, many were injured, some grievously, and one person had died. Further it was clear from recent judicial precedent that Charlottesville had an affirmative duty to protect the permitted demonstration from counter-protester violence. In 2015, an *en banc*—when all judges of a court sit to hear a case—decision from the U.S. Court of Appeals for the Sixth Circuit case called *Bible Believers v. Wayne County* dealt with police removing a group of Christian evangelicals, known as the Bible Believers, from a Dearborn, Michigan, Arab International Festival. The Bible Believers demonstrated carrying signs critical of Islam and artificial pigs' heads on pikes. When Muslims started throwing rocks at them, police ended the Bible Believers demonstration prematurely. The Sixth Circuit held that: "If the officers allow a hostile audience to silence a

---

[305] policinginstitute.org/wp-content/uploads/2017/12/Charlottesville-Critical-Incident-Review-2017.pdf

speaker, the officers themselves effectively silence a speaker and effectuate a heckler's veto." *Bible Believers* was the most strongly worded enunciation of the legal principle that police have an affirmative duty to "take reasonable action to protect from violence persons exercising their constitutional rights."[306]

The alternative theory proposed by left-wing and anti-White critics of the rally, that violence was caused by a "conspiracy" to commit violence, is unsustainable given that police were expected to protect the event and unprovoked assaults on counter-protesters would have led to arrests if police had participated instead of standing down. About the fact that UTR organizers made serious and sustained attempts to induce police protection of the event there can be no doubt. Recall that in the legal deposition of former Charlottesville City Manager Maurice Jones he testified under oath that I had expressed concern about counter-protesters blocking streets surrounding Lee Park and attacking protesters outside the venue. He also testified that I expressed fear about a police stand down like what happened in Berkeley and that I had been promised a substantial police presence to keep the peace, which never materialized.

In this situation where violence is known, and expected, to be the outcome of police nonintervention, it is nonsensical for rally critics to proffer platitudes about how "the First Amendment doesn't protect violence." Of course it doesn't, but the violence would not have occurred if the police had separated the sides as they had agreed to, as police had done in Skokie in 1978. The violence which transpired was the intended consequence of government policy towards the free speech demonstration.

In the aftermath of the rally, Police Chief Thomas and City Manager Jones both wiped their text messages concerning the rally, in violation of Virginia State law. According to Mike Signer, in his Charlottesville memoir *Cry Havoc*, text messages between the three men on their private cellphones was a central mode of communication

---

[306] opn.ca6.uscourts.gov/opinions.pdf/15a0258p-06.pdf

Pyromaniac Corey Long torches a stolen Confederate flag while Don Gathers of Charlottesville Black Lives Matter grins approvingly behind him

during the rally.[307] In one directly relevant text exchange, then-Mayor Signer confronted Jones: "Why were people allowed to beat each other in the streets?" The full answer to that question has been denied to history by the destruction of Jones' text communications.

The post-rally legal rulings were a flagrant reversal of judicial precedent and a repudiation of *National Socialist Party of America v. Village of Skokie*. In the heckler's veto lawsuit concerning the police stand down, *Kessler v. City of Charlottesville* (not to be confused with the ACLU case), Judge Moon ruled law enforcement had no legal obligation to prevent violence by counter-demonstrators against the

---

[307] dailyprogress.com/news/local/crime-and-courts/city-ordered-to-pay-court-costs-following-kessler-foia-lawsuit/article_aef98af0-336b-11eb-b62a-bbf089269115.htmly

permitted rally. For all practical purposes, the implication of this is the death of American free speech. If the most controversial issues of the day can be silenced by a violent, government-sanctioned mob, the time for debate is over, and all that is left is violence in the streets.

In his judicial order Moon wrote: "[T]here was no constitutional right to state protection from a private party's heckler's veto, nor the consequences that flowed from the unprevented violence between the protesters and the counterprotesters—that is, the declaration of an unlawful assembly."[308] Though Moon claimed the *Bible Believers* precedent did not require affirmative police protection of protesters, the Sixth Circuit *en banc* decision couldn't have been more clear: "If the officers allow a hostile audience to silence a speaker, the officers themselves effectively silence a speaker and effectuate a heckler's veto." I appealed to the U.S. Court of Appeals for the Fourth Circuit, full of left-wing Obama appointed judges. They didn't even bother to offer a legal rationale before rejecting it. They just concurred with Moon, sidestepping and refusing to address our legal arguments about the heckler's veto.

The government cover-up of the rally sabotage was naked, transparent, and above the law. After it was revealed Jones and Thomas had destroyed rally communications like text messages related to their conduct, I filed a lawsuit under the Virginia Freedom of Information Act and Public Records Act, which presumably make such conduct illegal. It was nevertheless impossible to hold them accountable because the Charlottesville Circuit Court ruled no one but the Library of Virginia had standing to initiate legal proceedings for the destruction of public documents.[309] Needless to say, the State of Virginia has been less than enthusiastic about turning over that can of worms. Better to let sleeping dogs lie in a bed of our tattered constitutional rights.

---

[308] dailyprogress.com/news/12-aug/judge-dismisses-kessler-lawsuit-over-unite-the-right-dispute/article_5d496348-bd99-5521-b618-7f8118d65147.html
[309] opengovva.org/kessler-v-charlottesville-cir-ct

Epilogue

Since I got involved in the bizarre world of White Nationalism, I learned that the most dogged defenders of free speech often come with scary labels like racist, Nazi, and Holocaust denier. Which makes sense when you think about it. Free speech laws are there to protect controversial speech, not stuff everyone agrees with. In European countries with weaker legal protections for speech, dissidents are rounded up by police and prosecuted for questioning the historicity of the Holocaust, using political symbols of the Third Reich, or even opposing the torrents of Third World immigration making Europeans a dwindling population in their historic homelands.

If you have mainstream political views you might ask: "Why do I care if the government protects someone's right to be racist or question the Holocaust?" Try to see yourself outside the present context. Right now, it's "racists" who are despised dissidents. Maybe if you were born several centuries ago you might ask: "Why should I care if the king throws republicans in jail?" because you were a monarchist and the republicans were the most despised. Or maybe you were a loyal Communist Party member in the Soviet Union asking: "Why should I care if Comrade Stalin sends some capitalists to the GULAG? I hate capitalists." Now imagine being the dissident in all these circumstances. Imagine being silenced, threatened, jailed, tortured, and murdered, while the majority turns its back on you in cold indifference. Not a pretty picture.

The highest purpose of free speech is in the citizen's ability to criticize the powerful. Much of the Western world has enshrined this value as a human and civil right so that all taxpaying, law-abiding citizens have a chance to peacefully redress their grievances and a hope that one day they might improve the world, as they see it, through the power of their voice. Our societies have fallen short of that promise by giving censorship authority to many of the most powerful tyrants on the planet, opportunistically portraying themselves as victims when, in truth, they're wolves in sheep's clothing. Accusations of "racism" and "antisemitism" grant billionaire oligarchs and their government cronies pretext to exercise frightening state power in the abuse and oppression of their critics.

An apropos quote on free expression, often attributed to Voltaire, actually comes from White Nationalist Kevin Alfred Strom: "To learn who rules over you, simply find out who you are not allowed to criticize." In this context he was talking about Jewish power. You can argue such a thing doesn't exist, but what you can't say, truthfully, is that there isn't a legal regime across much of the West which incarcerates those who criticize this supposedly non-existent ethnic power bloc. Nor can you say that there aren't billionaire oligarchs funding media, politicians, and NGOs to harass and intimidate the critics of this alleged non-existent power into silence. As stand-up comedian Dave Chapelle joked on *Saturday Night Live* in 2022: "If (a group is) Black, then it's a gang. If they're Italian, it's a mob, but if they're Jewish, it's a coincidence and you should never speak about it."[310]

Although controversial speech in public venues has been chilled post-Charlottesville, the issue of free speech continues to be a much-discussed topic, predominantly in regards to online freedoms. In 2023, this concern for digital freedoms led the world's richest man, Elon Musk, to purchase the social media site Twitter and attempt to change its culture to be more tolerant of conservative and right-wing political expression. Perhaps as an old-school tech geek, Musk decided to recalibrate social media towards the freewheeling libertarian culture of the old Internet he grew up with in his youth. The jury is still out on whether Musk will succeed or eventually be subverted by pressure groups like the ADL, who lead the drumbeat for censorship.

---

[310] facebook.com/watch/?v=425611973120604

However, it is safe to say that speech in meatspace, or the real world, has been curbed after Charlottesville.

White Nationalist groups like Patriot Front continue to wave the flag of free speech, sometimes literally, for those who refuse to abdicate their rights to march and speak as they see fit. However, they face the same vindictive legal challenges from powerfully funded Jewish groups that I faced after Charlottesville. Florida activist and comedian Handsome Truth has likewise run afoul of the law on multiple occasions for distributing flyers critical of Jewish power. He was then jailed under novel theories of the "littering" statute. New laws are being invented all the time to curb free expression and old laws are being radically manipulated and reinterpreted for the same purpose.

In the tumultuous years between 2015 and 2023, I went from being a liberal, to briefly a MAGA Republican, and then a White Nationalist. Part of what radicalized me was seeing how true Strom's words were. I came to understand that the greatest threat to free expression around the world today is the influence of the Jewish lobby and their totalitarian attempts to censor and prosecute criticism leveled from rival ethnic groups.

The deluge of attacks by anti-speech extremists destroyed what little I had in my life. My already rocky relationship with my father ended in the fallout from the rally. Until I moved out of Charlottesville in the summer of 2018, I'd been rendered unable to do even the sporadic handyman gigs I worked before becoming infamous. No longer able to go out in public without being harassed, my health declined, I stopped exercising, and became substantially overweight.

Putting my life back on track started with a new rally in Washington, D.C. on August 12, 2018: the one-year anniversary of the original. I was washed out but I refused to give up. Even as the other UTR "leaders" deserted me, and prosecutors from both Charlottesville and Albemarle County used trumped up, politically motivated charges unrelated to the rally, to try and lock me up, I was determined to march and speak to prove a point, come hell or high water.

To accomplish this, I slept on an air mattress in the living room of my friend George and his girlfriend in Old Town Alexandria just outside of D.C. When the day of the march finally came, the police once again tried to sabotage the rally by forcing me and a few of my supporters to leave from the Vienna Metro towards Foggy Bottom station 45 minutes ahead of schedule. Many supporters who had traveled from across the country to participate were left behind. Nevertheless, the Metro PD upheld their end of the bargain, forming a phalanx around myself and the UTR 2 marchers against thousands of angry, belligerent counter-protesters.

With the D.C. rally behind me, I started taking any rough work I could off of Craigslist. I knew I would never have a chance of normal employment again. Over time, I learned a trade, started a business, got back in the gym, lost the weight, and healed myself. Despite being under attack by multi-million-dollar lawsuits funded by powerful Jewish groups, I worked harder than ever and restored my broken life back better than ever before.

I rarely communicate with the other speakers from UTR. Despite the shitty treatment from most of the other UTR leaders, I have persevered and managed to make some good friends and reliable allies in radical politics. There is still a great deal of bitterness and hostility amongst many of the speakers who attended Unite the Right. These days, I mostly just try to ignore those seeking conflict and focus on the positive relationships I have built with friends and allies. I consistently have warm and engaging conversations with the brave common folks who attended the rally, not for some petty ego boost, but out of legitimate concern for their people and history. "Fine people," indeed.

In retrospect, it was obvious that in order to implement a demographic winter across the West, the White Western man would have to be separated, by force, from his most idealistic achievement: free expression. As the West enters a new, more desperate phase of its struggle for survival, I hope we will not forget the idealism of our forefathers and that somehow, somewhere, on the other side of a coming victory, free speech will one day live again.

QR Codes

The numbers below correspond to the footnotes in the preceding pages that contain hyperlinks. The article headline is preceded by the QR Code, which can be accessed using a smartphone.

1. Weapons of the Charlottesville Protest

2. Black Supremacist at Unite the Right

3. BLM Leader: "They wanted us to fight" in Charlottesville

6. Thomas Jefferson statue removed from New York City Hall after complaints that it honored an enslaver

7. Who was Leopold II, why did Belgium's Antwerp remove his statue?

8. Christopher Columbus Statues Beheaded, Pulled Down Across America

9. Protesters toss statue of explorer James Cook into Victoria harbour; totem pole later burned

10. Kelvingrove statue of Thomas Carlyle vandalised with anti-police graffiti

11. Wisconsin crowd pulls down statue of abolitionist who died fighting slavery

12. Maintained in Very Good Condition or Virtually Rebuilt? Destruction of Cultural Property and Narration of Violent Histories

13. Dear Racist White People, Your Time is Up

14. Why we topple statues

15. Rethinking Revolutionary Vandalism

17. The 1619 Project and the Long Battle Over U.S. History

18. How racial groups rate each other

19. Criminal Victimization, 2018

20. What we know about the increase in U.S. murders in 2020

21. ISIS Smashes Priceless, Ancient Statues in Iraq

22. The Strategy Behind the Islamic State's Destruction of Ancient Sites

23. Iconoclasm and strategic thought: Islamic State and cultural heritage in Iraq and Syria

24. Dozens of birds, including ones named after white supremacists, are being renamed

25. Doctor Who upsets conservatives as Isaac Newton played by person of colour

26. Ritualistic Humiliation: Black-Run City of Richmond, Virginia Digs Up Remains of Confederate General A.P. Hill After Tearing Down His Statue

27. Joe Biden Fantasizes About Making White Americans an 'Absolute Minority' Through 'Non-Stop' Immigration

29. A record number of Confederate monuments fell in 2020, but hundreds still stand. Here's where.

30. Independent Review of the 2017 Protest Events in Charlottesville, Virginia

31. The disturbing timeline of Jesse Matthew's sexual violence and murders

32. Protest over police custody death becomes violent

33. 'Hail Trump!': Richard Spencer Speech Excerpts

35. Szakos decries response to statue comments

36. Change the name of Lee Park and Remove the Statue

37. Charlottesville Statues

39. Free-speech panelists say college campuses need dialogue

40. 2016 Jefferson Symposium: Free Speech on Campus - Session 1; Kessler at 2016 UVA Free Speech Symposium in Charlottesville

41. Virginia Board of Education member resigns after vulgar tweets surface

42. Road to Charlottesville: May 20th Harassment by SURJ

43. Jon Bair killed a neo-Nazi 28 years ago, and he has a message for Portland

44. Richard Spencer, president of the white nationalist National Policy Institute, punched during ABC interview in Washington

45. A Free Speech Battle at the Birthplace of a Movement at Berkeley

46. 21 arrested as hundreds of Trump supporters and counter-protesters clash at Berkeley rally

47. Against its wishes, Auburn hosts white nationalist Richard Spencer

48. Am I White Enough: Mike Enoch at Auburn

QR CODES

49. Clash with Antifa Scum at Confederate Monument in New Orleans

52. Richard Spencer Leads White Nationalist Demonstration in Front of Virginia Robert E. Lee Monument

53. Finding the helpers: Locals offer addiction support

54. Richard Spencer yells 'Sieg Heil!' and gives Nazi salute in Charlottesville

55. Baked Alaska struck a deal with the feds

56. Judge: Jackie Coakley not covered by patient-counselor privilege in 'Rolling Stone' defamation suit

57. Far-right influencer convicted in voter suppression scheme

58. The facial-recognition app Clearview sees a spike in use after Capitol attack.

59. White Student Union (documentary)

60. The Little Führer

61. 'Crying Nazi' Christopher Cantwell found guilty of extortion in rape threat case

62. SPLC on Christopher Cantwell

63. UTR permit application

64. Operation Unite the Right Charlottesville 2.0

65. Rally Against Political Violence

66. The Alt-Light is a collection of outright liars

67. KKK leader seeking Charlottesville rally has history as FBI informant

69. In letters to city and McAuliffe, ACLU, others question police tactics at Klan rally

71. Emails from CPD whistleblower

72. Kessler discusses KKK, Unite the Right rallies and his political beliefs

74. As Portland Police Stand By, Alt-Right and Antifa Protesters Beat Each Other Bloody

76. Wendy Lewis text

79. Leaked memo: Poor communication contributed to chaos in Charlottesville

80. Michelle Christian email

81. Maurice Jones notes from meeting with Jason Kessler

82. Deposition of Maurice Jones (June 15, 2018)

83. Denial of permit letter

85. Festival of Cultures attendance article

86. Charlottesville prepares for a white nationalist rally on Saturday

87. Kessler/ACLU Twitter message

88. ACLU of Virginia and Rutherford Institute Challenge Charlottesville's Decision to Move Planned "Unite the Right" Demonstration

91. So-called alt-right lieutenant caught lying over and over again about 'killing Muslims for fun' in Iraq

92. How Our Reporter Uncovered a Lie That Propelled an Alt-Right Extremist's Rise

93. Richard Spencer discovery documents

94. 'Gonna See Blood on These White Polos': Far-Right Leader Discussed Raising an Army and Killing Jewish People

95. Jason Kessler DNA results

96. Coup chat

98. Kessler is a kike

99. Kessler doesn't like Azzmador

100. Neo-Nazi 'Tyrone' exposed as US marine

101. Mosley & Monoxide mock Kessler

103. Head EMT at Charlottesville Rally Discusses Expectation of Left-Wing Violence

104. Far left militia group, Redneck Revolt, offers training manual on "kidnapping", "executions", and "terrorism"

105. Redneck Revolt Twitter post (September 18, 2016)

106. Redneck Revolt Target Practice on Alt-Right

107. Redneck Revolt Charlottesville Call to Arms

108. DHS reports show overwhelming focus on violence from left, downplaying threat from white supremacists

109. Army Records on Antifa

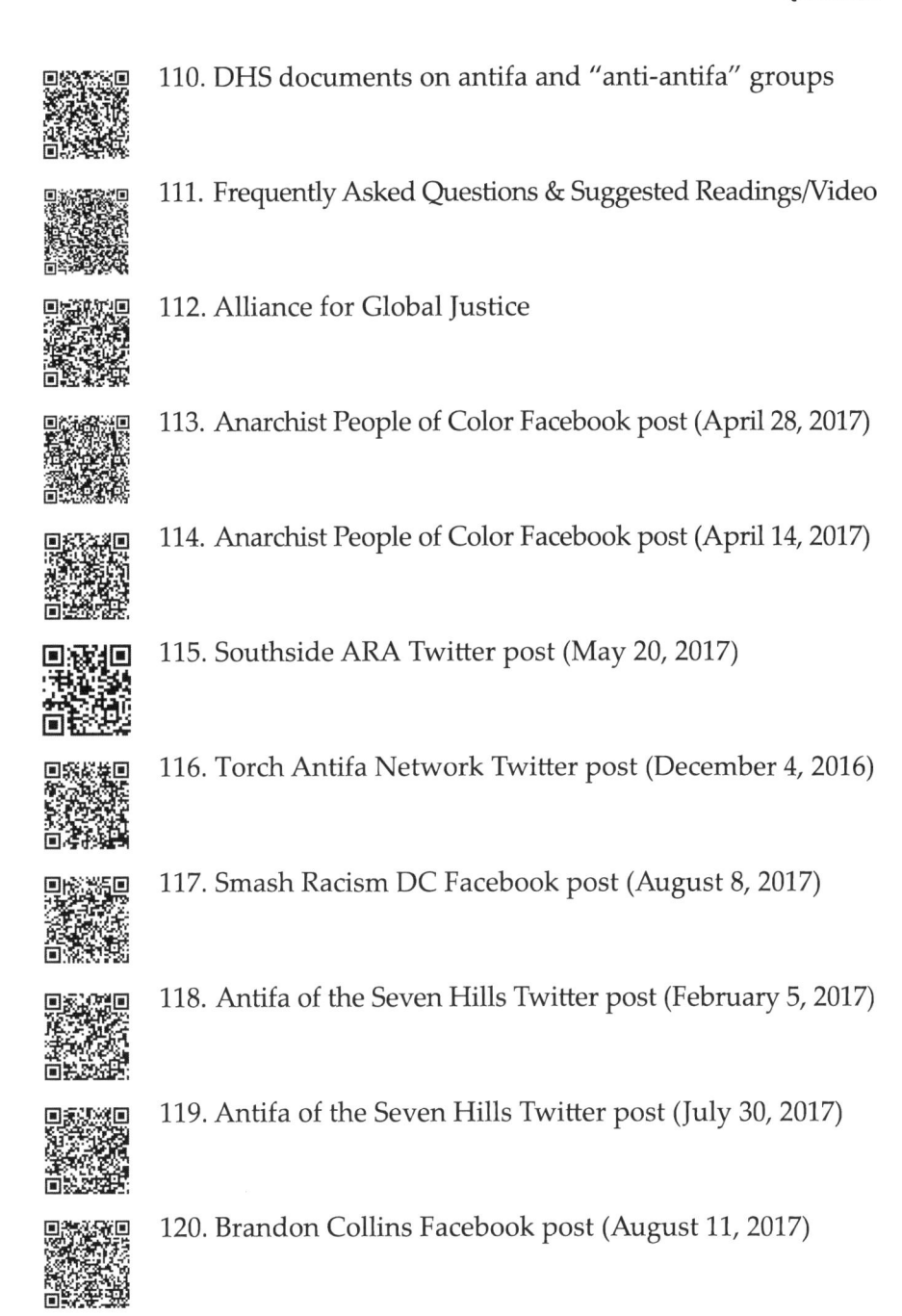

110. DHS documents on antifa and "anti-antifa" groups

111. Frequently Asked Questions & Suggested Readings/Video

112. Alliance for Global Justice

113. Anarchist People of Color Facebook post (April 28, 2017)

114. Anarchist People of Color Facebook post (April 14, 2017)

115. Southside ARA Twitter post (May 20, 2017)

116. Torch Antifa Network Twitter post (December 4, 2016)

117. Smash Racism DC Facebook post (August 8, 2017)

118. Antifa of the Seven Hills Twitter post (February 5, 2017)

119. Antifa of the Seven Hills Twitter post (July 30, 2017)

120. Brandon Collins Facebook post (August 11, 2017)

121. Joe Starsia Facebook post (July 8, 2017)

122. Know a Nazi, see a Nazi, punch a Nazi

123. Antifa of the Seven Hills Twitter post (August 10, 2017)

124. Emily Gorcenski Twitter post (August 8, 2017)

125. Emily Gorcenski Twitter post (August 17, 2017)

126. Emily Gorcenski Twitter post (removed) (June 23, 2020)

127. Charlottesville, VA: Unite The Right Plans On Friday Surprise Torchlit Rally at UVA

128. #NoNewKKK: Mobilize to Defend Charlottesville, VA

129. Fiber Optic Cable Sabotage Continues into California

130. Olympia, WA: Train Tracks Sabotaged To Stop Fracking Equipment

131. Seattle, WA: Juvie Contractor Truck Burned in Solidarity with Baltimore Rebellion

132. How Antifascists Won the Battles of Berkeley

133. Send the UN swat team and gun them all down! Display their carcasses and skulls on stakes!

QR CODES

134. It should be legal to shoot the nazies and the kkk

135. If Nazis are carrying torches, douse them in gasoline

136. I think I'd rather see the badass Nazis turned back by an aerosol-hairspray-wielding phalanx of drag queens.

137. Final Operational Order

138. Neo-Nazi 'Tyrone' Who Asked if It Was Legal to Run Over Protesters Outed as U.S. Marine

139. "Tyrone" did not attend UTR

140. *Sines v. Kessler* deposition of Steven Young July 15, 2020

141. Here's A Reel of Cars Plowing Through Protesters Trying to Block the Road

142. "Tyrone" removed from Discord

143. ACLU complaint

145. Bristow letter (July 23, 2017)

146. Vice Media stops publishing on website and cuts hundreds of jobs

147. *Charlottesville: Race and Terror*

150. Chapman memo

151. EKRE torch parade on Independence Day

152. The Up Helly Aa Viking Fire Festival

153. The Torchlight Parade

154. Carl Sandburg interview (1956)

155. This Was the Alt-Right's Favorite Chat App. Then Came Charlottesville.

156. Emily Gorcenski Twitter post (July 20, 2017)

157. My FBI Records from Charlottesville and Beyond

158. Unite the Right Meeting Before Torch March August 11, 2017

159. Angela Tabler affidavit

160. August 11 call logs

QR CODES

161. Kessler asks for police protection

162. UVA chief in contact with Kessler

163. *Kessler v. City of Charlottesville*

165. See the Sparks That Set Off Violence in Charlottesville

166. Cornel West: Antifa Came to Fight and Get Arrested in Charlottesville

167. Charlottesville Mass Prayer Service

169. Cornel West: Clergy in Charlottesville Trapped by Torch-Wielding Nazis

170. Interview: Jason Kessler on UVA Torch Rally

171. Charlottesville Torch Vigil on August 11, 2017

172. Antifa Comms Director Luis Oyola on Charlottesville Conspiracy

173. The story of two Louisville antifa in Charlottesville

174. Two innocent marines attacked with mace, kicked in the ribs and stomped on by Antifa

175. Man sentenced for role in death of skinhead

176. Sentencing for NATO 3 Set for April 25

177. 'NATO 3' plead not guilty in alleged firebomb plot

178. Big Tech gives private data to FBI

179. Emily Gorcenski Twitter post (October 4, 2017)

180. Emily Gorcenski Twitter post (September 10, 2017)

181. Emily Gorcenski Twitter post (May 28, 2018)

182. Don't criticize Black Lives Matter for provoking violence. The civil rights movement did, too.

183. Torch Antifa Network Twitter post (August 12, 2017)

184. Antifa Tom Massey Instigating Violence at Peaceful Torch March

185. News2Share Facebook video (August 11, 2017, 41:40)

186. Sam Corum Facebook post (September 10, 2017, 8-9 seconds in)

187. Fuentes Disavows David Duke

188. Nick Fuentes Guns Down Hasidic Jew in Grand Theft Auto

189. Nick Fuentes on J6: "Overturn the Barricades, Ignore the Police!"

190. David Duke: Charlottesville Rally Part of Effort to 'Take Country Back'

193. Richard Spencer Head of Security Discusses Police Escort for Speakers

194. Man Attacks Van with Stick at Unite the Right

197. Jones' cell phone wiped

200. Wade Douthit LinkedIn repost

201. FBI Got Warrants for 'Unite the Right' Organizer Jason Kessler, Antifa Activists

202. Insane New Footage from Charlottesville!!! (4:50)

203. Charlottesville August 12 Jackson Park Vicious Attack by Philly ARA and Kristopher Goad

204. ACLU of Virginia Twitter video (August 12, 2017)

206. Refuse Fascism—Mob Beatdown with Picket Signs

207. Don Gathers attacking protesters at the UTR

208. Yes, What About the "Alt-Left"?

209. Seth Wispelwey Twitter post (December 8, 2018)

210. Diversity of tactics or unity in action?

211. Frozen Coke

212. Sean Liter Dual Stick Attack on Charlottesville Protesters

213. James Neil Ritchie Sneak Attack

214. Brent Betterly mugshot

215. Antifa Terrorist Brent Betterly Pipe Attack

216. Corey Lemley Twitter post (September 23, 2017)

217. Corey Lemley Twitter post (May 27, 2016)

QR CODES

218. Katie Couric describes moment her National Geographic producers were 'doused with human urine and mud' during Charlottesville protest

219. Taylor Lorenz Gets Head Rocked by Antifa Radical

220. Corey Lemley Baseball Bat Attack

221. Chris Cantwell's Charlottesville August 12 Macer revealed as Mikey J Longo Jr. of Philly

222. Chemical Attack on Baked Alaska

223. Ike Baker Speech

226. Antifa Barricading Street Outside Lee Park & Punching Charlottesville Marchers

227. Michael Hill Fights off Attack from Nic Smith of People's Power Network

228. UTR permit application

230. KKK member gets 4 years in prison for gunshot at rally

231. Too risky: Blakney accepts plea deal to avoid incarceration

232. Rachel Myles Assaults Protesters

233. Rachel Myles search warrant

234. Man Attacked in Charlottesville Charged with Assault in Unexpected Turn

235. Richard Spencer Charlottesville Rant

238. 10 Wanted Suspects attack Trump supporter in Charlottesville on August 12, in HD!

239. Day 7: 'She's the enemy,' Fields told his mother by phone

240. Prosecutors use Hitler image texted to mother in James Alex Fields murder trial

241. Judge: Car crash meme admissible in Charlottesville murder trial

242. James Fields Was Chased with a Semi-Automatic Rifle Before Crash

243. Dwayne Dixon admits he waved a rifle at James Fields just prior to the accident

244. Nelson man sentenced to five years in armed robbery

245. Emily Gorcenski Twitter post (September 10, 2017)

246. Day 8: Fields drove at 28 mph before hitting crowd, police say

QR CODES

247. James Fields' Challenger Hit At Least Twice Before Crashing into the Crowd

249. Charlottesville: Making a Murderer part 3 of 3

250. Heather Heyer autopsy report

251. Charlottesville survivor Marcus Martin still healing after deadly rally

254. James Alex Fields shows remorse, scorn after fatal Charlottesville car crash

255. Taylor Lorenz Twitter

256. Final report: Lack of training likely cause in copter crash during 2017 "Unite the Right" rally in Charlottesville

257. Neo-Nazi James Fields Gets 2nd Life Sentence for Charlottesville Attack

258. Unequal Justice in Fields Charlottesville Trial—And, Increasingly, Throughout the Left's America

259. Remembering Waukesha: Monday marks one-year anniversary of Waukesha Parade tragedy

260. Prosecutors Decline to Charge Black Lives Matter Militant Who Ran Over Proud Boy in Washington

261. Man gets 5 years in prison for running over and killing teen after street dance in North Dakota

262. BLM activist from Long Beach no longer facing attempted murder for Yorba Linda collision

263. Driver who killed BLM protester on I-5 in Seattle sentenced to over 6 years

264. Ambien Addiction—Treatment, Signs and Risk

265. *Sines v. Kessler* deposition of Steven Young (July 15, 2020)

266. Chief Thomas press conference

267. Wendy Lewis email

268. Wendy Lewis email

270. Industrial Workers of the World

271. Dwayne Dixon—You Don't Stand By and Let People Get Hurt: Antifascism after Charlottesville

272. Roberta Kaplan Takes White Supremacy to Court

273. Search Charities Database for Integrity First for America, Inc.

274. LinkedIn founder Reid Hoffman apologizes for his role in rehabbing Jeffrey Epstein's public image in 2015

275. How 13 Weinstein Scandal Figures Come Out in Jodi Kantor and Megan Twohey's New Book 'She Said'

276. Harvey Weinstein hired Black Cube to block New York Times article, jury hears

277. Tech Billionaire Who Bankrolled Numerous Disinformation Projects Linked To $620,000 Donation To Fusion GPS's Legal Fund

278. Judge slashes millions owed by hate groups for 2017 Charlottesville rally

279. At least 25 Americans were killed during protests and political unrest in 2020

280. Exclusive: $1 billion-plus riot damage is most expensive in insurance history

281. Charlottesville's Lee statue meets its end, in a 2,250-degree furnace

282. Elon Musk Twitter post (October 27, 2023)

283. The Ritualized Defacement of Robert E. Lee

284. Confederate monument melted down to create new, more inclusive public art

285. The Most Controversial Statue in America Surrenders to the Furnace

286. Elizabeth Sines Calls Out to Judge Moon's Law Clerk

287. Staff Writing Legal Opinions for Charlottesville Judge Norman Moon Hold Egregious Conflicts of Interest

288. Dascher Pasco Facebook post (August 12, 2017)

289. Dascher Pasco Facebook post (August 22, 2019)

290. Motions filed for Recusal of Charlottesville Rally Clerks

291. Kathryn Laughon post (July 25, 2022)

292. Kathryn Laughon post (October 3, 2019)

293. My Whole World Shifted podcast

294. The Night the Lights Went Out in Charlottesville: Judicial Prejudice in a Southern Town

295. The Surprising Story Behind This Shocking Photo of Martin Luther King Jr. Under Attack

296. The Nazis' Neighborhood

297. 72 Seized at Rally of Nazis in Chicago

298. 2 arrests made during Unite the Right rally; no injuries reported

QR CODES

299. Threat of Violence Loomed Over Skokie Nazi March

300. 'Swastika war': When the neo-Nazis fought in court to march in Skokie

301. 2017 Berkeley protests

302. A Free Speech Battle at the Birthplace of a Movement at Berkeley

303. 21 arrested as hundreds of Trump supporters and counter-protesters clash at Berkeley rally

305. Independent Review of the 2017 Protest Events in Charlottesville, Virginia

306. *Bible Believers v. Wayne County*

307. City ordered to pay court costs following Kessler FOIA lawsuit

308. Judge dismisses Kessler lawsuit over Unite the Right dispute

309. *Kessler v. Charlottesville*

310. Dave Chappelle's Monologue

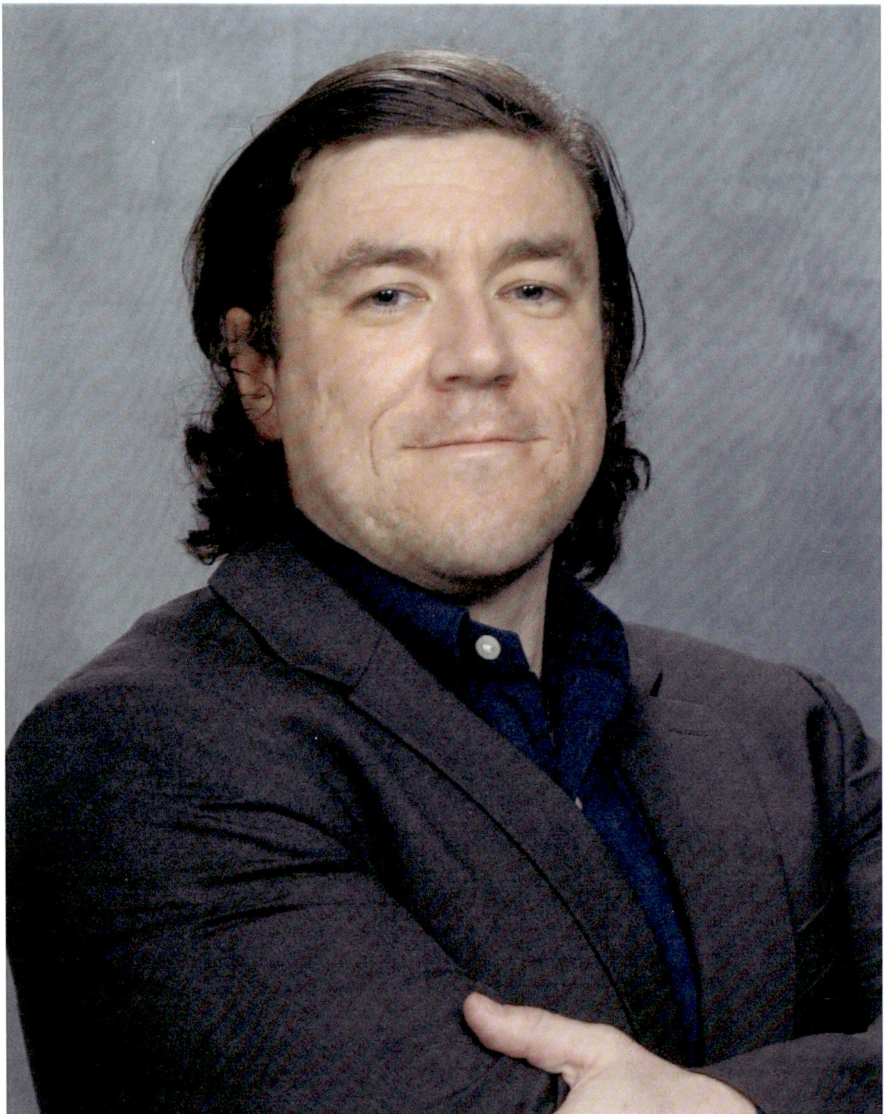

About the Author

JASON KESSLER is an author, activist, and journalist with bylines in *The Daily Caller*, VDARE, and "Counter-Currents." As one of the most famous living American political dissidents, he has been covered by outlets around the world, including *OANN*, *The Washington Post*, *The New York Times*, BBC, CNN, *DailyMail*, and Fox News. His journalism has explored topics ranging from race, immigration, free speech, and left-wing extremism.

He was born in Charlottesville, Virginia, in 1983 and graduated from the University of Virginia, his hometown university, in 2009 with a B.A. in psychology.

In 2024, he published his first nonfiction book, *Charlottesville and the Death of Free Speech*, from Dissident Press.

JasonKessler.us
twitter.com/TheMadDimension
twitter.com/DissidentPress
gab.com/JasonKessler
t.me/TheMadDimension